On the Edge of Insanity

By Emily Watson

Front Cover Artwork done by Howard David Johnson
Back Cover Photo done by Teresa Sacks
Copyright © 2013 By Emily Watson
All rights reserved.
ISBN: 1479365300
ISBN 13: 9781479365302

For my Dad who stood by me and never stopped believing in me.

TABLE OF CONTENTS

INTRODUCTION xi

PART I: WHAT ARE ANXIETY, OCD,
          AND DEPRESSION 1
    Chapter One: What is Anxiety? 3
    Chapter Two: What is OCD? 9
    Chapter Three: What is Depression? 17

PART II: FALLING INTO CHAOS 21
    Chapter Four: The Catalyst 23
    Chapter Five: Undergraduate School 27
    Chapter Six: Graduate School 37

PART III: ENTRANCE TO HELL 47
    Chapter Seven: Falling from Grace 49
    Chapter Eight: Living in Fear 55
    Chapter Nine: Someone Call a Priest 59
    Chapter Ten: Everything is Contaminated 65
    Chapter Eleven: Perfect Symmetry 71
    Chapter Twelve: The Danger of Lights 73
    Chapter Thirteen: Impulse Control 75
    Chapter Fourteen: Caught in a Loop 77
    Chapter Fifteen: How OCD Killed Fashion 79
    Chapter Sixteen: Momma is a Hoarder 83
    Chapter Seventeen: Narcotics 89
    Chapter Eighteen: The Dark Hours 93

PART IV: GETTING HELP 97
    Chapter Nineteen: Therapists 99

PART V: UNCOMMON HELP 103
    Chapter Twenty: Musings with a Medium 105
    Chapter Twenty-One: Meditation 109

Chapter Twenty-Two: Alternate Healing 113
Chapter Twenty-Three: Medications 117

PART VI: LOOKING TO THE FUTURE 121
    Chapter Twenty-Four: OCD in the Media 123
    Chapter Twenty-Five: Conclusion 127

PART VII: A NEW HELL 131
    Chapter Twenty-Six: The Dawn of Bipolar 133
    Chapter Twenty-Seven: What are the Two Poles? 137
    Chapter Twenty-Eight: A Bipolar Life 145
    Chapter Twenty-Nine: Manic Minds:
    Thinking and Talking at the Speed of Light 151
    Chapter Thirty: Manic Shopping: A Further
    Blow to Fashion 153
    Chapter Thirty-One: Little Pills of Happiness 155
    Chapter Thirty-Two: Chords of Depression 159
    Chapter Thirty-Three: Trying Times 165

PART VIII: RETURN OF MY OCD 177
    Chapter Thirty-Four: New Battles of OCD 179
    Chapter Thirty-Five: My Bathroom, the Enemy 189
    Chapter Thirty-Six: Revenge of the Bladder 197
    Chapter Thirty-Seven: Boys Have Cooties 203
    Chapter Thirty-Eight: Living with Animals 207
    Chapter Thirty-Nine: Control Issues 211
    Chapter Forty: Growing Up 215
    Chapter Forty-One: Mourning the Loss 219
    Chapter Forty-Two: Shooting for the Stars 223

PART IX: THE CRUEL MIRROR 229
    Chapter Forty-Three: My Expanding Waistline 231
    Chapter Forty-Four: The Fall of Hygiene 239
    Chapter Forty-Five: A Distorted Body 243
    Chapter Forty-Six: Chronic Stress 245

PART X: THE DARK AGES 249
- Chapter Forty-Seven: A Lifetime Ago 251
- Chapter Forty-Eight: A Life of Fear 257
- Chapter Forty-Nine: An Unclean Environment 269
- Chapter Fifty: Showering 277
- Chapter Fifty-One: Recluse 279
- Chapter Fifty-Two: January Nightshades 285
- Chapter Fifty-Three: An Unfortunate Collision 289
- Chapter Fifty-Four: Continued Bladder Problems 291
- Chapter Fifty-Five: Juries of the World 295
- Chapter Fifty-Six: Heightened Anxiety 297
- Chapter Fifty-Seven: Panic Attacks 305
- Chapter Fifty-Eight: Descent into Madness 307
- Chapter Fifty-Nine: Deliberations on Death 315

PART XI: A NEW HOPE 323
- Chapter Sixty: March Snowdrops 325
- Chapter Sixty-One: Meeting with Dorothea 329
- Chapter Sixty-Two: A Tale of Two Hospitals 335
- Chapter Sixty-Three: Support System 339

PART XII: UNWRITTEN FATE 345
- Chapter Sixty-Four: The Future 347
- Chapter Sixty-Five: Conclusions 355

APPENDIX 359
- Appendix A: Common Questions Friends and Family Have About OCD, Bipolar Disorder, etc. 359
- Appendix B: Dictionary of Medical Conditions 364
- Appendix C: How to Cope With Your OCD Symptoms 366
- Appendix D: Dictionary of Potential Treatments for OCD, Depression, and Anxiety 369
- Appendix E: Summary of Medications 371
- Appendix F: Contact Information 375

I can feel it sometimes…when the sadness drifts too deep, when the anxiety robs me of all my breath, when the darkness fills behind my eyes…I can feel it. A hidden knowing. A gentle tug. A pulsating fear. I don't know where it is, but I can feel it. I wander into the rolling meadow. The dew droplets on the early morning grass are cool beneath my feet. A gentle mist bathes me in morning's lustrous glow. But the darkness lingers. I can feel its closeness. The ground before me falls away crashing into the turbulent ocean down below. The skies burst open upon me, raining lighting down on the wave crests, illuminating the ocean in gruesome light. The clouds violently collide sending sound waves across the tranquil land. I can feel it growing closer, throbbing just before me. My foot slips, just over the edge. Air rushes up my leg, winding up my body until it reaches my head. Terrifying wails pierce my mind. How could I have not heard them before? They are too loud to bear. Demented, tortuous screams flooding every cell in my body. I can't think. I can't breathe. The world is spinning, everything spinning. Spinning. Screaming. Tugging. Pulling me downward, but to where I do not know. To the sea. To the murky cliffs. To the darkness. To the absence. Always spinning. To the emptiness. I thrust my body backward, falling hard upon the nascent grass. But I can still feel it; the echo of it is still near. The boundary has been breached. The boundary between real and unreal, between light and dark, between sanity and insanity. It has been breached. I scramble to my feet. My legs tremble. I stand alone, transfixed, teetering on the edge of insanity.

INTRODUCTION

"'But I don't want to go among mad people,' Alice remarked. 'Oh, you can't help that,' said the Cat: 'We're all mad here. I'm mad. You're mad.'"
Lewis Carroll, Alice in Wonderland

I began suffering from OCD when I was eighteen years old. A few years later, I developed bipolar disorder. Fighting these disorders has been the greatest battle of my life. I decided to document my struggles in order to help people better understand these oft misunderstood disorders. I wanted to help those who suffer from them by sharing my own experiences. I wanted to help friends and family of those who suffer better understand what their loved ones are going through. I wanted to challenge the long-held stigma that mental disorders are merely a sign of mental weakness. So I put pen to paper. This book was written at two different times in my life. Parts I through V were written when I was twenty-six years old during a manic phase in my bipolar cycle and at a time when I thought my OCD was cured. Parts VI through X were written when I was twenty-nine years old during the worst of my OCD and bipolar symptoms.

Falling Off the Wagon and Being Dragged Four Miles

"The mass of men lead lives of quiet desperation."
Henry David Thoreau

I'm tired of hiding. I'm tired of lying to those around me about what is really going on. I'm tired of pretending to be fine when I am anything but. If people are going to know me, then they are going to need to know all of me, even the flaws. My name is Emily M. Watson. I am a thirty-two-year-old aspiring author, makeup artist, and photographer, and I have been suffering from severe obsessive-compulsive disorder and bipolar disorder for the past ten years.

I was once a normal girl. I led a small but meaningful life. I grew up in small-town America, second star to the right and straight on past Cracker Barrel. My dad had his own business as a computer programmer, and my mother was a historical reenactor. Me, well, I was the shy girl in school, clever but socially awkward. I graduated fourth in my high school class and went on to receive a BS in physics. But, I fancied myself a jack-of-all-trades, conversant in all major fields of study. I had a large group of friends that regularly met for nights on the town… dinner, movie, and shopping—lots of shopping. And I had a promising future to look forward to with an infinite number of doors open to me. I was poised to enter adulthood, ready to set off on my own and follow my dreams, but all that changed in a week…in a day…in an hour…in a minute, and I would never be the same again.

In 2001, I began showing visible signs of a mental illness, though I wouldn't be diagnosed with Obsessive-Compulsive Disorder (OCD) until 2004. With the exception of my parents, I kept my disorders from everyone, only recently revealing that there was a problem. I'm ashamed to say that I didn't believe in bipolar disorder, OCD, and other mental disorders. I thought they were imaginary illnesses, and those who claimed to have them were merely weak-minded. I don't know whether my belief came from television, movies, or perhaps the fact that I had never been really sick in my life. My brain had always functioned perfectly. In my thinking, if you're sad, get over it. There are people out there with far worse problems than you. If you're anxious, just calm yourself down or do something relaxing, like listening to music or getting a massage. If you have OCD…well, that is just absurd. How can anyone helplessly feel compelled to engage in such senseless habits as washing your hands for fifteen minutes or repetitively turning a light on and off? We are each in control of our own actions; we don't have to do anything we don't want to. Even after the doctors explained to me that these disorders were real medical problems resulting from miscommunications in the brain, I still felt hesitant to tell others. However much we may have learned about these conditions in the past few years, there is still a stigma attached to their names—the stigma that they are not real illnesses. With all the new research coming in, people who suffer from these disorders should be able to come out from the shadows to faces filled with understanding and compassion. However, society as a whole is not that enlightened. After all, we have celebrities gracing every medium from the newspapers to the Internet, preaching that these disorders should not be treated with medication as any genuine or proper illness would be, but rather treated using meditation, diet, and faith in religion. These are all good things to help the mind and soul, but there comes a point with real medical illnesses when your symptoms are so severe that modern medicine is needed.

By 2006, after having suffered from OCD for five years, I was a mere shadow of my former self. The spark of light that exists in all humans had faded from me. I may have been alive, but I wasn't living. OCD had become my life, consuming every part of me. Obsessive, anxious, and paranoid thoughts flooded my mind every second of every day. I couldn't work. I couldn't think. I couldn't breathe. I was locked in a mental prison from which I couldn't escape. I was on the edge of insanity, and if someone didn't help me soon, I was bound to fall into its dark, bottomless depths. What do I do when everything that I liked about myself is gone? I was often told what great potential I had. Everyone who knew me expected me to do great things. What a disappointment I must be. I am nothing now, just a broken machine. Worthless. I wanted to die.

When 2008 rolled around, I was delivered another severe blow. Not only did I suffer from OCD, but it turns out I also suffered from bipolar disorder, an unsettling revelation made apparent only after I started on an SSRI, a class of drugs for treating OCD. Up to that point, my alternating periods of anxiety and depression were seen merely as a reaction to my OCD. But after my breakdown one dark Thanksgiving, it was evident I was suffering from a severe bipolar disorder. How could I not have seen it before? How could it have taken this long to be diagnosed? By the dawn of 2010, there was little left of my former self; years of OCD and bipolar disorder had stripped away at my body and soul. I was nothing now, just a waste of space unable to contribute to society, unable to lead a normal life.

The horrible thing about fighting these disorders is no one can see it. To the outside world, I am normal. Even in the performance of my absurd rituals, no one can see any wounds. No one truly knows the battle that is waged within me every minute. Every day I am withstanding a brutal attack on my mind. Inside I am bleeding and broken, crawling through land mines to find my way out, out of the hell I am in and back home. But no one can see that, so no one knows how gut-wrenching these disorders are. But those who live it know.

It is scary to openly reveal one's flaws when it is common nature to conceal them. But I have decided to write my experiences down, however embarrassing that they may be, with the hopes that it will comfort those who suffer and educate those who do not understand. I figured I could write this book one of two ways. I could tell the cleaned-up version, the one where I withhold some of the darkest details and keep myself looking good, or I could tell the truth, the true horror of it all, where you get to see what the disorders are really like, but where I come off not looking so good. I chose the latter. If I am going to do this, then I am going to do this all the way. I won't do anyone any good by telling the cleaned-up version. Now, I am not a medical doctor or a psychiatrist. I have not spent years studying mental disorders or counseling the troubled. However, I have spent the past ten years suffering from severe OCD and bipolar disorder, and in my opinion that makes me more than qualified to write this book.

PART I: WHAT ARE ANXIETY, OCD, AND DEPRESSION?

"I can't eat, I can't sleep, I can't write, I can't read, I can't talk to people. The worst thing is that I feel it will never end."
Marian Keyes

CHAPTER ONE
What is Anxiety?

"Don't tell me that worry doesn't do any good. I know better. The things I worry about don't happen."
Anonymous

    I have always been a worrywart, constantly stressing over even the simplest trials and tribulations in life. It is not my most endearing trait, nor is it a terrible flaw. In measured doses, anxiety is very helpful. Stress over getting bad grades forced me to work harder in school. Stress over social interactions taught me to think before I speak. And innate fears kept me on guard in potentially dangerous situations. Of course it also made me slightly neurotic at times, particularly in the arena of public speaking, where I am hardly at home. The mere thought of every pair of eyes in the room judgingly fixed upon me sent my heart racing. And all those lovely tricks that experts suggest, such as picturing everyone in their underwear, offered no relief. Shockingly, I don't want to see most of my classmates or professors, for that matter, in their skivvies. Yet, regardless of the overwhelming terror I felt at such potential public humiliation, I always managed to nervously fumble my way through the speech. The anxious feelings that flooded through my veins never crippled me. I was in control.

    Anxiety aside, I was thrilled to start college in the spring of 2000. The opportunity to take the classes I wanted, at the hours I wanted, on the days I wanted was a godsend, considering I am fiercely opposed to getting up before noon. My schedule would have been perfect except for that darned literature class that began at eight a.m. The gall of the professor! Not to mention there was a whole campus full of handsome and intelligent young men who had no idea that I was a shy, brainy geek in high school.

    My freshman year went much as I anticipated. Initially judged harshly by my fellow classmates for my stunning beauty and flippant personality, I eventually excelled beyond my own expectations, gaining the respect of my fellow classmates and winning the legal case. OK, so that is *Legally Blonde*. My first year was far less eventful, marked only by the staggering amount of homework assigned in my major. I still recall the tiresome mechanics problem that took the professor eleven pages of work to solve. It was closer to twenty for me. A single problem taking twenty pages of math to solve—unbelievable! On the positive side, I enjoyed the new freedoms of college life: no curfew, optional class attendance, off-campus lunch, and a stimulating major of my choosing. No wild parties or drinking binges for me. I was far too much of a geek to let such things take away from my study time. But sadly, before I had any real chance to experience the joys of college, I was struck down by the smallest of foes. An excruciatingly painful kidney stone catalyzed me into the battle that I would spend the next fourteen years fighting. Little more than the size of a grain of sand, it became the Gavrillo Princip to my oncoming mental war. What followed would be a dizzying array of medical problems ending with me diagnosed with an anxiety disorder, bipolar disorder, recurrent UTIs and kidney stones, and interstitial cystitis (IC, also known as painful bladder syndrome).

The anxiety disorder seemed to come on rather suddenly. It felt as if I was fine one day and then the next I wasn't. I wanted an explanation. It turns out many mental disorders tend to surface in one's adolescence or early adulthood, but they often require a trigger to catalyze them into motion (WebMD 2012). Two major events happened to me at the very end of 1999; I graduated from high school and passed my first kidney stone. Major life changes and medical problems are two such events. But it was far into 2000 before I started showing signs of the repercussions of those events—a mental imbalance—so I didn't immediately notice the connection. To say that I was less than thrilled to be diagnosed with an anxiety disorder is a gross understatement. Though, I was surprised and relieved to discover that anxiety disorders are actually real medical conditions, quite contrary to my mother's assertion that they are merely a characteristic of a type A personality. They are serious mental disorders that afflict millions of Americans. People who suffer from these disorders suffer more than just the normal amount of anxiety that every human feels. They are regularly filled with such constant and overwhelming fear and worry that they have difficulty leading a normal life. They are crippled by these emotions.

The cause behind anxiety disorders is still unknown. Research, however, indicates it may be the result of a chemical imbalance in the brain. Anxiety disorders have also been shown to run in families (Webmd 2012).

By Emily Watson

WebMD describes the following anxiety disorders.

<u>Anxiety Disorder Fact Sheet</u>

Specific types of anxiety disorders:

<u>Obsessive-compulsive disorder (OCD)</u> – It is a condition in which a person becomes trapped in a continuous cycle of recurring thoughts and behaviors. Obsessive ideas, thoughts, or images, generally based in fear or worry, continually play through the person's mind. In order to make these relentless thoughts dissipate, they perform certain routines (compulsions).

<u>Panic disorder</u> – It is a condition in which the person suffers from sudden and repeated panic attacks that cause sweating, chest pain, palpitations, choking sensations, and an overwhelming feeling of terror. I have these quite often, and they make me feel as if I am having a heart attack.

<u>Post traumatic stress disorder</u> – It is a condition developed following a traumatic event in which the sufferer experiences continual frightening and stressful flashbacks of the event. It is also marked by emotional numbness.

<u>Social anxiety disorder</u> – It is a condition in which a person feels intense fear involving normal social activities. The person is extremely worried and self-conscious about how they are perceived by others. They are afraid of being judged or doing something wrong.

<u>Specific phobias</u> – It is a condition marked by an intense fear of specific things, such as flying and snakes. The person may be so fearful that they avoid any situations involving them, like traveling by plane or hiking through the forest.

<u>Generalized anxiety disorder</u> – It is a condition marked by general and unwarranted stress, fear, and worry.

(Webmd 2012)

I mainly suffer from OCD, but I am also prone to panic attacks and intense phobias. It is hard to forget my first panic attack as it landed me in the ER utterly convinced I was having a heart attack. Imagine my embarrassment after all the fuss (EKG meter, heart monitor, etc.) that I was merely overcome with anxiety.

General symptoms of anxiety disorders:

- Muscle tension
- Nausea
- Feelings of fear, uneasiness, and panic
- Obsessive, uncontrollable thoughts
- Nightmares
- Palpitations
- Inability to be calm and still
- Ritualistic behaviors
- Shortness of breath
- Dry mouth
- Cold or sweaty hands
- Repeated thoughts or flashbacks of traumas
- Problems sleeping
- Numbness or tingling in the extremities

To me, severe anxiety feels like every cell in my body is vibrating at a frequency that I can't handle. Over the past ten years, I have experienced all the symptoms at one time or another. In fact, everyone has experienced one of the above at least some point in their life. Fear and doubt are ingrained in man's very nature. It is only when these thoughts become excessive and constant that you are diagnosed with an anxiety disorder.

<u>Emily's Helpful Information</u>
<u>Quick Facts about Anxiety Disorders</u>

- Approximately nineteen million American adults suffer from an anxiety disorder.
- They occur more often in women than men.

- They occur in equal frequency among Caucasians, Hispanics, and Blacks.
- They are generally treated using medication, psychotherapy, and/or cognitive behavior therapy, though I generally prefer New York cheesecake.

(Webmd 2012)

CHAPTER TWO
What is OCD?

"Insanity: doing the same thing over and over again and expecting different results."
Albert Einstein

Ode to OCD: Ah, OCD, my suffocating foe and occasional friend. Curse you for turning me into a broken robot forced to perform the same tasks over and over. Curse you for turning me into a broken robot forced to perform the same tasks over and over. Damn. Yet, if it wasn't for you, I wouldn't be so adept at solving television show crimes.

I knew very little of OCD until I actually experienced it for myself. OCD is a condition in which a person becomes trapped in a continuous cycle of recurring thoughts (obsessions) and behaviors (compulsions). Obsessive ideas, thoughts, or images, generally based in fear or worry, continually play through the person's mind. In order to stop those obsessive thoughts, the person usually enacts certain compulsions (Webmd 2012). It is NOT a mental weakness. It is NOT bad behavior. It is an illness, like any other physical illness, that the person cannot control. For the majority of the time I suffered from OCD, I didn't even know what I had. Granted, I knew many of my behaviors were strange in comparison with others, but in all honesty, I gave it little thought. To me everything I was doing was perfectly normal for anyone who valued cleanliness and order. So I liked to organize my room regularly. There is nothing wrong with that. I'm merely a neat person. So I wash my hands for five minutes at a time. I'm just concerned with catching any illnesses—a perfectly normal worry. So I check the lock on the door ten times to make sure it is locked. It's natural to be concerned with one's safety. These are all seemingly normal behaviors. My eventual flash of insight was actually revealed by a television show called *Monk*, which featured a lead character who suffered from OCD. As my parents robustly laughed at the many absurd actions of Mr. Monk, I watched in befuddlement as he performed many of the rituals that marked my own daily life. Was I too that neurotic? His actions seemed completely logical to me: using a wipe after shaking hands, fear of germs, and a desire for neatness. Did I too suffer from OCD? Of course once I came to this unsettling realization, I fell deep into denial. I refused to be labeled as one of the mentally weak or be stigmatized in any way. I fought tooth and nail with any doctor who dared diagnose me with such an unsavory condition. I didn't look up any information about the disorder, nor did I try to contact support groups. Any such behavior would acknowledge the problem, and I was quite keen to pretend it wasn't there. After all, OCD, like many other mental disorders, isn't exactly viewed in the most favorable of lights. Undoubtedly, this is the reason why only ten percent of sufferers ever seek any professional help (Health Central 2011). Frankly, I blame a Catholic clergyman who lived during the fourteen hundreds. In the fifteenth century, the blood soaked Malleus Maleficarum (aka The Hammer of Witches) charged those plagued with obsessive thoughts as witches and righteously burned them at the stake. If I were lucky, I would merely be charged with demonic possession and sentenced to a torturous exorcism, which only occasionally produced success. Fortunately, we have come a long way from Plato's shadowy cave, acquiring great knowledge and insight into the vast medical conditions that afflict mankind. Surprising in the light of such advances, we still hold many antiquated and negative views about mental disorders.

Five centuries have passed since the first documented case of OCD, yet the condition is still shrouded in mystery. Though views of demonic possession have been left to the past, its cause remains elusive. Current research points to a miscommunication in the brain and low serotonin levels. It is lovely to know that my brain is all mucked up. Why that happens is unclear, but genetics could play a part as early studies indicate a possible connection – a theory I tend to agree with since my mother also has OCD (Webmd 2012). She is a compulsive hoarder, but don't mention it to her as she is still in denial. Though a person may be genetically predisposed to developing OCD, usually an environmental stress is needed to trigger it. Common stresses are abuse, illness, death of someone close, relationship problems, work/school problems, and big life changes (Health Guide Info 2010). My kidney stone and my graduation were my triggers, though I didn't realize it at the time. These triggers may also worsen any preexisting symptoms of OCD. Regardless of the precise cause of OCD, the main point to remember is that it is a real medical condition like bipolar disorder or schizophrenia. It is not a mental weakness or a failing of the sufferer, a fact which I have to remind others of and myself, as I am prone to a bit of self-deprecation.

OCD is composed of two parts: obsessions and compulsions. Not all people diagnosed with OCD experience both. But many sufferers, like me, have the great misfortune of dealing with both. Obsessions are ideas, thoughts, or impulses that relentlessly cycle through your mind.

The most common obsessions are:

- Contamination
    - fear of contamination from dirt and germs
    - fear of contamination from environmental contaminants and body fluids
- Religious obsessions
    - fear of offending God
    - excessive moral or religious doubt
- Unwanted sexual thoughts
    - evil, sinful, or forbidden thoughts
- Obsessions related to perfectionism
    - need to have things in a specific order (symmetrical)
    - fear of throwing something important out
    - fear of losing things
    - inability to decide whether or not to keep or discard something
- Losing control
    - fear of harming oneself
    - fear of harming someone else
    - fear of saying curse words or insults
    - fear of horrific and violent images in one's mind
    - fear of stealing things
- Other obsessions
    - fear of making a mistake
    - superstitious ideas
    - fear of being embarrassed
- need to ask or confess things

(The International OCD Foundation 2006)

My most prominent obsession is the fear of being contaminated by germs, dirt, and smells. If it was fashionable to walk around in a biohazard suit, I would be the first in line to buy one. Let's face it; the world is not a clean place. Microscopic germs are everywhere infecting everything I eat and everything I touch. Anywhere I go I am bound to come across an unpleasant smell as the world is terribly odorous. I am really fearful of smelling bad. I don't know why. I was never the smelly kid in class nor do I recall ever being labeled as smelly. Yet these obsessive thoughts regularly pass through my mind. But it doesn't stop there. I am obsessed with everything on that list. Fear is a big part of OCD, from the fear of being contaminated to the fear of making a mistake. Obsessive fears drown out all other rational voices in my head. I fear making a mistake—not only on the big choices in life, like my career path, but the little choices, as well, like what I am going to wear today. I am so afraid I will make the wrong decision or that I will make a mistake that I become paralyzed by fear and cease to make any decision at all. I fear being embarrassed. I am afraid to stand in front of a group of people and give a presentation for fear I will do something embarrassing like forget what I am going to say or say something completely wrong. I fear harming others. I fear harming those I love. I don't know why. I could never knowingly hurt any living soul. And yet I fear it. I fear what I will do when I am unconscious, when I am asleep, when I am not in control of my actions. What will I do when my conscience isn't awake to stop me? Unwanted obsessive thoughts run through my mind. Evil or sinful thoughts take hold of me and drive me into darkness. Thoughts of demons and hell haunt me in the quiet moments of my day. I try to force them out of my mind, but like a broken record, they keep playing over and over. They lead to excessive religious and moral doubt. I dwell endlessly on my own sins. I dwell on my own struggle with God, my own search for truth amidst the darkness. From the destination of my immortal soul to the germs on the kitchen table, I obsess over it all. Furthermore I had to have everything from groceries to my living room furniture in symmetrical order or in even numbers. That means buying two of things at the grocery store so there would be an even number. Kind of an expensive symptom. Sadly, I suffered from everything on that list.

By Emily Watson

I shook someone's hand. The germs, oh the germs! I must wash my hands. Did I wash my hands good enough? Micronesia. If I didn't, then I will contaminate anything I come into contact with. The whole house could become contaminated. Did I wash my hands long enough? They need to be washed for at least five minutes to make sure that they are clean. My hands are dirty. I touched the counter, the counter where a roll of dirty toilet paper used to sit; now my hands are dirty. I have to wash my hands. I have to wash them for five minutes if I hope to get the germs off. Micronesia. I am afraid I might harm someone or some animal. What if I hit someone over the head with a hammer? What if I stab someone? I know I wouldn't do that while I am awake, but what if I do something like that while I am asleep? I don't want to hurt any people or any animals. But what if I do? I can't decide what to wear. The shirts are nearly identical, why can't I choose? What if I chose the wrong one? I can't decide. I can't choose. I can't make a mistake. What career do I chose? Micronesia. There are too many choices. What if I choose the wrong one? I could spend the rest of my life toiling away in unhappiness. What am I destined to do? I can't pick. I can't make a mistake. I can't fail. There are too many religions to choose from. What if I pick the wrong one? I'll go to hell! I am a terrible sinner. I'll probably go there anyways. The apocalypse is coming. The world is going to end. And I am going to hell.

Obsessive thoughts like these and random words and phrases continually pass through my mind. When my OCD is mild, these incessant voices only take up a small percentage of my waking mind like a television show on low volume in the background. However, when the symptoms are severe, it is like being in the front row at a rock concert. The voices are so loud and consuming that it is virtually impossible to think of anything else. When my symptoms became this severe, I ceased to function as a normal human being.

Compulsions are the result of obsessions. They are the actions sufferers perform over and over in an attempt to silence the obsessive thoughts. Common compulsions are excessive:

- Washing and Cleaning
    - bathing
    - washing hands

- brushing teeth
- cleaning
- Checking
  - checking that you did not/will not harm others or yourself
  - checking that nothing terrible happened
  - checking that you did not make a mistake
  - checking to make sure you turned appliances off, doors locked
- Repeating
  - rereading or rewriting
  - repeating (words, phrases, prayers)
  - repeating routine activities
  - repeating body movements (ex. touching, tapping, blinking)
  - repeating activities in multiples (ex. doing a task three times because it is "right" or a "good" number)
- Mental Compulsions
  - counting while performing tasks to end on a "good" or "safe" number
  - praying to prevent harm to oneself and others
- Other Compulsions
  - telling, asking, or confessing to get reassurance
  - hoarding (keeping/collecting unimportant items)
- arranging things in specific orders (symmetry)

(The International OCD Foundation 2006)

    My life was filled with rituals. If I didn't perform them, either the obsessive thoughts wouldn't go away, or I feared something bad would happen and it would be all my fault. In my most dire times, I was nothing more than a broken robot stuck performing the same tasks over and over. These actions, like their counterpart thoughts, are very time-consuming, taking up more than an hour each day depending on the severity. Washing is my fatal flaw, taking up hours of my day. Checking is a far second. Fearful of smelling or looking dirty, I spent an average of four hours a day on washing activities: two hours for showering and two total hours of handwashing. Fearful I would burn the house down, I repeatedly checked appliances when leaving the house to make sure they were in the off position. I usually had to look at the knobs at least five times to make sure they were in the off position and my mind wasn't just playing tricks on me. Why I didn't get the idea the first four times eludes me. I repeatedly checked to see if the front door was locked because I was afraid of intruders coming in, or I checked to see if my razor was unplugged because I feared setting the house ablaze. I checked the refrigerator regularly to make sure there wasn't a cat trapped in there. Decision making was terrible. Fearful of making a wrong choice, I spent about five minutes per decision, even ones so simple as deciding between two identical shirts. Even after I made a decision, I had to ask others if I made the right one, as I needed constant reassurance on everything I did. At times I felt the unbearable strong need to repeat a word or sentence over and over, occasionally even needing another person to repeat what they said over and over. This was completely and unquestionably illogical, but the impulse to do so was too strong to resist. Performing any of these actions over and over every day is extremely tiring. OCD thoughts and actions are so draining. I often felt as if I was running in a marathon, breathless and weak.

Did I lock the door? I thought I checked, but maybe I didn't look closely enough. Did I lock the door? I can't remember; I will have to check again. Did I lock the door? I know I just checked it. Agriculture. Why can't I remember it? If I don't check, I will keep obsessing about it. Did I turn all electrical appliances off? What if I didn't? There could be a spark or a short, and the whole house could catch fire. I have to check or these thoughts won't stop. The furniture in the room is all wrong. It needs to be symmetrical. Everything should be in parallel rows back from the television. My hands are dirty. They need to be washed. They need to be washed for five minutes counting in intervals of thirty. Agriculture. If I don't wash my hands properly, I'll keep obsessing about them being dirty.

You are probably asking yourself why I don't just stop performing these rituals if I know they are absurd, not to mention how tiring they are to perform. I suppose if you are thinking in terms of whether or not I can control my actions, unlike a reflex, then yes I can. But I cannot control the obsessive thoughts. Imagine if you had an annoying friend who was with you at all times, constantly talking in your ear. You can't stop this friend from talking, and because she talks so loud, you can barely hear your own thoughts. It is maddening. The only way for an OCD person to stop this annoying little friend is to perform whatever repetitive action the friend is urging. If we don't, then the voice just gets louder and louder. I can control my actions, but I cannot control the voices. So, I have to perform the action the voices say to in order to stop the voices.

I want to take issue with the analysis that OCD actions are completely baseless or senseless. While a number of compulsions like repetitively turning a light on and off are indeed illogical, many are actually based in sense and logic just taken to the extreme. Washing my hands when they are dirty is logical. Washing them for ten minutes is not. Checking to make sure the front door is locked is logical. Checking five times is not. Being slightly fearful of certain things is logical. Being so afraid to fall asleep that I take caffeine pills is not. See, all logical things just taken to the extreme.

Emily's Helpful Information
Quick Facts about Obsessive-Compulsive Disorder

- It afflicts approximately one million kids and 3.3 million adults in the United States.
- It occurs with equal frequency in women and men.
- It usually first appears in childhood or early adulthood.
- Stress and illness can make symptoms of OCD much worse.
- It is found in every race, in every culture, and in every country all over the world.
- It is generally treated using medication and cognitive behavior therapy.

(Webmd 2012)

CHAPTER THREE
What is Depression?

"That's the thing about depression: A human being can survive almost anything, as long as she sees the end in sight. But depression is so insidious, and it compounds daily, that it's impossible to ever see the end. The fog is like a cage without a key."
Elizabeth Wurtzel

I remember walking on the beach once, my feet softly leaving footprints in the newly set sand. Many other footprints surrounded my single line, undoubtedly left by playful beachgoers rushing into the surf. But as I continued my leisurely stroll, I noticed all other footprints aside from my own fading in the distance. Only my footprints remained imprinted upon a now empty beach. It was only then I realized that all the beachgoers and the entire weight of the world were resting comfortably upon the shoulders of my petite five-foot-one frame. Is it any wonder I sank into that sea of depression?

Depression touches all of us at one time or another. Sadness is a common emotion that grips us during loss or heartache. But for most it lessens, eventually passing altogether, a mere blip on our radar. For some, like me, it does not go away. The sadness that infects me comes from no tragic event. It arrives without provocation, slowly growing in intensity until it completely consumes me. This is called major depression, and I have been suffering from it for many years. I wish I could give a precise date when it started, but it grew so slowly that when I finally realized it, it seemed like it came out of nowhere. The worst of it began in early 2005 when I relocated to Washington, DC.

Depression is not simply sadness. It is not a simple emotion. It is a state of mind. It affects how I see and feel and how I perceive the world. Imagine it like a pair of rose-colored glasses, only with more of a black-tinted sheen. The glasses alter how I see the world. They cause me to see everything in the world not as bright and cheery but as dark and disturbing, thunderstorms eclipsing the scene. Once exciting and vibrant, the world is now terrifying and nauseating, frightening me to my very core...now a cold, clammy, absence. Depression feels like a heavy weight upon my shoulders. It causes an unhealthy introspection, as I am always looking down on myself. Every sadness that I see in the world further increases the depths of my sorrow. Commercials about depression depress me. I have no idea why. They just do. I usually mute them when they come on.

Depression and anxiety disorders often walk hand in hand as the lack of control in one's life inherent to anxiety leads to depression. Before I developed OCD, I was a smart, driven young woman actively engaged in the world. I knew who I was and what I wanted. After I developed OCD, I was a neurotic hermit trapped in a mental prison from which I could not escape. Everything I was, was gone. Such a complete loss of self is devastating. I fell into a deep depression.

Now, for any guys reading this book, I suggest you skip this paragraph as it deals with feminine stuff. As many girls probably already know, we are prone to mood changes just before and during our monthly cycle. For most women this isn't too much of an issue, but for anyone dealing with serotonin-related disorders, it is more important. During our cycle our serotonin levels drop, as disorders like depression are due to already low levels of serotonin, and we can get much more depressed. Even though I am on medications, I still have problems a few days every month (Webmd 2012).

Depression Fact Sheet

Some Types of Depression

<u>Major Depression</u> – It is a type of depression that results in a deep and lasting sense of sadness, hopelessness, and despair.

<u>Chronic Depression</u> – A less severe form of depression that leaves a person feeling continually unhappy but still able function in the world. It lasts for long periods of time, maybe years.

<u>Seasonal Depression</u> (aka seasonal affective disorder) – It is a type of depression that occurs around the same time each year, usually beginning in the fall or winter and ending in the spring or early summer.

Postpartum Depression – It is a period of depression that occurs after giving birth. It results from the social, chemical, and psychological changes that come with having a baby.

(Webmd 2012)

As my experiences are only with major depression that is the type I will be referring to for the rest of the book.

Common symptoms of major depression:

- Slow speech or movements
- Loss of interest in activities you once enjoyed
- Sleeping too much or not sleeping at all
- Changes in weight
- Headache
- Stomach and digestive problems
- Anxiety, irritability, and agitation
- Worsening of an already existing chronic disease
- Difficulty focusing and memory problems
- Persistent sadness with a negative outlook on life
- Feelings of worthlessness, helplessness, and hopelessness
- Lack of energy and constant fatigue
- Thoughts of suicide and death

(Webmd 2012)

I often experience all of these on a daily basis. They just all roll into one big ball of sadness paralyzing me from life.

Emily's Helpful Information
Quick Facts about Depression

- Approximately 14.8 million people over the age of eighteen in the United States suffer from major depression.
- Suicide is the third major cause of death for people between the ages of ten and twenty-four.

- It may be a symptom of other mental illnesses like schizophrenia, substance abuse, anxiety disorders, or eating disorders. Or it may simply occur in parallel with them.
- It is generally treated with medications and therapy.

(Webmd 2012)

PART II: FALLING INTO CHAOS

"A single event can awaken within us a stranger totally unknown to us."
Antoine de Saint-Exupery

CHAPTER FOUR
The Catalyst

"Sometimes I lie awake at night, and I ask, 'Where have I gone wrong?' Then a voice says to me, 'This is going to take more than one night.'."
Charlie Brown.

I was born and raised in northeast Florida. My childhood was typical of Middle America, a Norman Rockwell painting as idealistic and sentimental as baseball during its heyday. I had two loving parents, a large extended family, a group of close-knit friends, and a houseful of kooky pets. I was an adventurous tomboy climbing trees, tubing down country rivers, and camping in state parks during Florida's intensely humid summers. During the summers, I travelled the country escaping on such grand adventures as digging for dinosaurs in Wyoming and swimming with dolphins in the Florida Keys. Come fall, I was a dedicated student with a straight-A average and a spot on the yearbook staff. I graduated fourth in my high school class. Standing there on that stage, looking out at my graduating class with my diploma firmly in hand, my future looked undeniably bright. I had no idea everything was about to change.

I remember it clearly—the moment, the second everything changed… for the worse. It was the winter of 1999; though, considering I live in Florida, you could hardly call it winter. I was casually driving across the Buckman Bridge, a mere fifteen minutes from my home, after spending a few days visiting my old high school pals at Florida State University (FSU) when a piercing pain shot into my lower back. I grabbed my side in an attempt to massage the pain away as I thought perhaps it was a spasm from my four-hour drive. But it did not help. The pain was too deep to reach. As it radiated through my body, I was gripped by an overwhelming sense of fear that touched every cell in my body. It was a fear I had never before felt—a deep unsettling realization that something had gone horribly wrong. Gripped by this maddening fear, I recklessly sped home and curled up on my bedroom floor. I flailed about on the carpet for a few minutes before realizing I needed to go to the hospital. What happened next is a psychedelic blur of sights and sounds as I continually fell in and out of consciousness. Hours later, drugged with pain killers, it was discovered that I had a kidney stone attack—my first of many ahead. It was the catalyst of ills to come.

I began suffering from OCD in 2001, though I wouldn't be diagnosed until four years later. At least that was the first time I became aware that some of my behaviors might be a little odd. I was on vacation with my best friend, Christine, in Europe when another group member commented that I needn't wash my hands so much. Did I wash my hands too long? I had no idea I spent more time washing my hands than other people. This was the first time I had roomed with other girls since my trips in high school, and back then my behavior seemed perfectly normal. As we continued our travel through Europe, though, I became aware of my abnormal behavior in other aspects. Not only did I wash my hands longer, but I spent more time in the bathroom and took showers twice as long as my roommates. Something was clearly wrong. I have tried to recall earlier memories of OCD-like behavior, but nothing significant comes to mind. To me it felt like a sudden change. One day I was fine, and the next I wasn't. It was as if someone had turned off a switch in my brain, shutting down all logic and reason. My doctor informed me that it was common to begin experiencing symptoms in my early twenties, but that answer didn't satisfy me. It was completely illogical. How could my brain be working properly one moment and then malfunction the next without any external trigger or traumatic event? I later discovered that even if a person is genetically predisposed to OCD, generally it needs a trigger to activate it—in my case a stubborn little kidney stone and my graduation from high school a few months earlier, an equally momentous day.

Prior to that fateful day of the kidney stone attack, I never suffered from any major medical problems. In fact I was rarely ever sick, a slightly annoying fact, as I had no excuse not to go to school every day. I usually only visited the doctor for regular checkups, with the exception of the string of ear infections I had in elementary school. But in the fall of 1999, everything changed. I began suffering from recurrent urinary tract infections (UTI), multiple kidney stones, and interstitial cystitis (IC). These problems aren't gravely serious, but they can be very disabling, as I suffer every day in discomfort and experience days of excruciating pain in the case of the kidney stones. But, in all honesty,

I probably could have handled them and led a normal life if it wasn't for the simultaneous development of OCD, major depression, and severe anxiety. Strange that something so small could set off a string of events that left me an infirm hermit straddling the line between sanity and madness.

Emily's Helpful Information
What is Interstitial Cystitis (IC)?

> It is a chronic bladder disorder characterized by an inflamed/irritated bladder that can lead to stiffening and scarring of the bladder, decreased bladder capacity, and pinpoint bleeding. It is often referred to as painful bladder syndrome. Its symptoms are frequent urination and feelings of pain/pressure/tenderness around the bladder area. Sadly, the cause of this disorder still remains a mystery. To me it feels like a very severe UTI. I feel as if my bladder is constantly spasming, making me urgently feel like I have to go the bathroom and often going to the bathroom in my pants. It feels like there is a weight on my bladder, causing discomfort and pain. Unfortunately since this disorder is not well-understood, neither is a cure. The main solution lies in controlling my diet to avoid foods that are irritants to the condition, like tomatoes and peanuts. Managing my diet can be very effective in managing the symptoms of the disorder.
>
> (Urology Care Foundation 2013)

Emily's Helpful Tips
How to Deal with a Contaminated World

I struggled daily with living and interacting in a contaminated world. It can be a very fearful place for someone with OCD. But I picked up a few helpful tips along the way.

1. Always carry hand wipes! It is a dirty world, my friends.
2. When approaching someone who is sneezing or coughing, run in the opposite direction.
3. Avoid small children. They put their hands in everything.

4. If you don't have time to wash your hands. What? Are you mad? For the love of God, make the time. So what if you miss your flight. That happens to me all the time.
5. When opening public doors, pull your shirt sleeve over your hand and then open the door. Or, if you are wearing short sleeves, grab the door handle from the bottom; fewer people open the door that way. If you are lucky, a nice gentleman will come along and open the door for you.
6. Cover your car seats with garbage bags so you won't contaminate them after sitting in public chairs.
7. The inside handle on a bathroom door is covered in germs. It is not even safe to touch the underside of the handle. You must open the door with a paper towel. If there are no paper towels, you must wait patiently for someone to come along and open the door.

CHAPTER FIVE
Undergraduate School

*"There's a fine line between genius and insanity.
I have erased this line."*
Oscar Levant

    Though the first major symptoms appeared in 2001, OCD didn't begin to noticeably affect my life until the end of my sophomore year in college in 2002 while studying for a bachelor's degree in physics. School had always come easy to me. I was greatly lacking in any athletic or artistic ability, but I was good at school. So, it was very troubling when I noticed that schoolwork was becoming increasingly more difficult. At the time I attributed it to the natural rise in the complex materials upperclassmen are given, along with the fact that I was missing a handful of classes due to doctor's appointments for my kidneys. Though these problems were undoubtedly a factor, I now realize that the majority of my troubles were a result of the triangle of evil that had corrupted my mind. OCD affected my memory and concentration. Depression affected my mood and drive. And anxiety made me worried and nervous about everything.

    Out of the three, OCD had, by far, the most detrimental effect on my college time. Since I was young, I have been blessed with a great memory, slightly photographic in nature. Whenever I had a test in history class, for example, I would carefully read the chapters two nights before and then for the next few days I could visualize key words, photographs, and sometimes entire passages in my mind, allowing me to ace the test. My mind worked like this through most of my college stay, and then slowly it began to change, or so I thought. I began having difficulty remembering material. The photographs in my mind became faded and incomplete. What was happening to my memory?

    The last two years of college were a nightmare for me, and in retrospection I have no idea how I got through them. My mind was failing me. I was having great difficulty focusing on and learning the material. Reading a brief chapter in my physics books would take at least an hour as my mind kept wandering away from the pages. Intrusive and increasingly obsessive thoughts kept entering my mind. *Did I lock the door? Did I turn off the stove? Did I turn off the lights? Did I wash my hands good enough? Is he/she sick? Is he/she contagious? Am I going to be contaminated by his/her germs? There is a foul odor in this room. Am I going to be contaminated by it? I loaned this pencil to a friend; what if her hands were dirty when she used it? Am I going to be contaminated by the dirt?* When I did manage to read a passage without breaking focus, I immediately forgot what I read, requiring me to read it over and over until some small piece of information managed to take hold in my mind. It was intensely frustrating, causing me to decrease my social activities as I now had to devote even more of my time to my studies. Like a major in physics wasn't already time-consuming enough.

I didn't understand. Why was I having so much trouble? Was I not smart enough to handle this major? Was I losing my memory? After all it wasn't just happening in classes. I was having trouble keeping track of papers, assignments, even dates. I lost my keys continually, the last time resulting in their complete disappearance, as now three years later I still don't know where they are. My absentmindedness was encroaching on every aspect of my life and leading my mother to comment that that is what happens when you get old. Just to clarify, I was twenty-three at the time.

It wouldn't be until 2005 that I actually discovered what had happened. In one word: OCD…the evil foe that steals your mind. My memory was, in fact, perfectly fine. It was just completely filled up with OCD-related thoughts. My mind had become a virtual encyclopedia of cleanliness, logged with detailed accounts of how everything I considered contaminated in my house and other frequented locales had gotten dirty. Furthermore, I had a constant stream of obsessive thoughts running through my mind at all hours. My memory was full, and my conscious mind was entirely preoccupied with these relentless thoughts.

Did I turn off the stove? I thought I checked, but maybe I didn't look closely enough. I'll have to check again. Did I turn the stove off? I just looked, but I can't remember; I'll have to check again. Did I turn the stove off? All right, I know I just looked; please don't look again. But if I don't look I will keep obsessively worrying about it. Did I check to make sure the door is locked? I'm sure I did, but I have to check again or I will obsess over it. Did I wash my hands good enough? If I didn't then everything I touch will become dirty. I could contaminate the entire house. My hands are dirty. I touched the counter, the counter where a roll of dirty toilet paper used to sit, so my hands are dirty. I have to wash my hands. I have to wash them for five minutes if I hope to get the germs off. There are germs everywhere. I am afraid of getting infected with them. I must wash my hands constantly. I must wash surfaces of things constantly. I can't shake hands with others. I can't be around those who are sick. I fear bad odors. I fear becoming contaminated with them. I fear smelling bad. I fear being infected with the smell. I must avoid bad odors. I shook someone's hand. What type of dirt or germs did they have on it? I need a hand wipe. That would be rude wiping my hands right in front of them. Oh, who cares? I need to get the germs off. Darn, I am out of wipes. I need to go to the bathroom to wash my hands. Where is the nearest one? Is he still talking to me? I have no idea what he is saying; all I can think about is the bathroom. Quick, I see a bathroom, excuse myself. I must wash my hands. I must wash them for a good five minutes to get all the dirt and germs off. I'm trying to pay attention in class, but the girl next to me is sniffing. She must be sick. She is oozing out germs. I must get away from her, but I can't; class has already started. She is sniffing and sneezing and spreading germs all around her. They are going to attach themselves to me. I can't think. I can't pay attention in class. All I can think about is her nasty little germs invading my body. Get them off of me. Get them away from me. Someone spray her down with disinfectant.

Thoughts like these ran through my mind constantly. Every minute of every day I was under siege from them. Every seemingly inane thought I had would be mutated by my OCD into a long string of "What-ifs."

Did I turn the light off? What if I didn't? The whole house could catch fire. Did I lock the door? What if I didn't? Some bad person could rob us or even kill us. What if I got shot but didn't die? What if I got hit in the leg? It might have to be amputated. Oh God, what if I only have one leg? Well, I could get a prosthetic. I would still be able to walk, maybe even dance. But what if I got shot in the spine?

I could become paralyzed. What if I became paraplegic? Or worse, what if I became quadriplegic? Oh God, what would I do? I just walked through a foul odor. What if it attaches itself to me? What if it sticks to my clothes and my purse? What if it then transfers to my car and then my house? What if it contaminates everything I own? What if a shower won't wash away the smell? What if the smell is stuck on me? I will become the smelly girl. No one will want to be around me. No guy will want to date me. I will be disgusted by my own stench.

My obsessive thoughts were a constant voice in my mind, making it difficult to focus on anything school-related. These thoughts consumed my conscious mind, making it difficult to focus on anything, let alone the complicated major of physics. Furthermore, I couldn't learn anything new as my memory was full of OCD-related facts. My brain contained a running list of the contamination level of everything in my house and frequent locales. I could literally tell you when and how items had gotten dirty. I was like an encyclopedia of cleanliness. My memory was nearly full, and my conscious mind was under siege from OCD-related thoughts.

Studying itself was difficult, but test-taking was practically impossible. Always a cause for stress growing up since I settled for nothing less than an A, tests now caused a panic worthy of Godzilla. Unlike homework, which I had a week or more to do in the quiet of my own home, tests were timed and taken with the whole class—two big problems for me due to my burgeoning OCD. By my junior year in college, focusing on anything was very difficult with my mind consumed by obsessive thoughts. Adding a time limit only further stressed me out. The day of the test I would walk into the classroom visibly shaking with anxiety. I would choose a desk as far away from my classmates as possible so I would not be distracted. But as the classrooms were rather small, it didn't really help. As soon as start was called, my attention was drawn to the incessant sound of pencils fervently pounding on each desk. Why were people writing so loudly? Were they trying to distract me from the test? The noise is unbearable! How can I concentrate? As if that weren't bad enough, the intermittent sneezing and sniffing of usually at least one kid in the class would force me to become aware of my own breathing pattern, as I did not want to catch any germs. I would go through a cycle of holding and releasing my breaths, emphasis on the holding. The idea of small germs floating through the air sent my OCD into overdrive. Is that just allergies or does he/she have a cold? Is it a cold or the flu? Is he/she contagious? If he/she is he/she shouldn't have come into school today; he/she could infect us all! I can see it now, little germs floating through the air laying siege on my body. I need a disinfectant. Quick, someone get me a hazmat suit. Still not having started on my first problem and in a complete tizzy over germs, I attempted to focus on the test only to discover, as my eyes briefly left the page, a small spider strolling right by my desk. Did I mention my unwarranted fear of spiders? Of course now I had to take the time to put my book bag on top of the next desk and arrange my feet Indian style so that the spider wouldn't be able to climb on me or my belongings. However, now for the rest of the test, I would be preoccupied by the spider's movement, constantly checking to make sure it didn't come too close. Eventually I would manage to focus on the test but only after wasting ten minutes on senseless things. But by then I would be on the verge of a complete panic attack as I had now wasted important test-taking time. How I managed to take all those tests in such a condition still surprises me. My only explanation is that I am very competitive. I always wanted to have the highest grade in the class. My obsessive need for perfection probably momentarily trumped my other issues.

But my stress over tests was nothing compared to the terror I felt every time I walked into my chemistry lab. Obsessive fears of contamination by dirt, germs, smells, and hazardous chemicals had begun encroaching upon my daily life. I became desperately frightened of chemistry lab, no doubt, in part, stemming from the fact that I blew up a test tube in my very first lab in high school. No, I'm not kidding. I blew up a test tube. Every other kid in the room was doing a nice job on the lab. Of course, I had to be the one to screw things up. There it was standing well and perfect above the Bunsen burner and then wam! Shards of glass flew all over the room and even struck some poor kid. Don't worry, he was fine. Oh, the humiliation! Though I thoroughly enjoyed the lecture portion of the class, its corresponding lab was a nagging pain in my side. Let's consider the obvious for a moment. The university is basically letting students play with dangerous chemicals under limited supervision. We are talking about twenty-year-old kids, who have no proper training in the handling of toxic materials, attempting to perform an experiment after merely skimming the lab sheet, probably preoccupied with their party plans for the weekend. Really, am I the only one slightly frightened by this? Performing each lab was like navigating a minefield. First and foremost I had to make sure that I never came in any physical contact with the chemicals. I was really scared of burning my skin with acid or getting harmful solutions in my eyes. I wouldn't even touch a beaker that held them. Fortunately my lab partners were happy to handle the materials as long as I told them exactly what to do and performed the mathematical calculations necessary. Being a geek came in handy. But that was the easy part. Constantly making sure that I didn't touch anything that came in contact with the beaker that contained the chemicals, now that was hard. I couldn't even touch the work counter; who knows when they were last washed. Surely they cleaned it daily but unlikely between every lab. There was probably some residue of a dangerous chemical still clinging to the table. And if it got on my folder, then it would get in my backpack and eventually end up in my house, thereby contaminating the entire apartment with toxic chemicals. Furthermore, I was constantly worried about everyone else in the class. I knew my lab was being conducted with excellent precision, but what was everyone else doing? What if someone messed up and caused an explosion, thereby leaking toxic chemicals into the classroom? What if someone tripped and splashed chemicals in my face? I could go blind! A never-ending array of fears flooded my mind as I was trying to concentrate on my lab. Fortunately I only had to take two chemistry labs. Physics labs, of which I had many, were far tamer, never containing anything potentially hazardous. One lab did contain a radioactive isotope, but the professor assured us that it was not emitting high levels of radiation and was contained within a shielded casing. That's nice, but I still used the lab station on the other side of the room.

    More than these specific moments of OCD behavior, my nature, my very character, was slowly degrading from the weight of the disorder and my growing depression. Depression didn't affect me greatly during my undergraduate study. Usually in good spirits, I only sensed an undercurrent of unhappiness in moments of solitude. I began losing interest in things I once enjoyed. My interest in my major greatly dwindled as

By Emily Watson

I was angry at the amount of time it took to complete my work in order to compensate for my inability to properly focus. I should have known something was wrong when I was more interested in organizing folders and cleaning the lab than doing actual physics work. In fact I became excited at the mere prospect of coming home and doing some early spring cleaning. But the persistent noise in my mind and my continuous bladder pain made me very irritable. I was constantly cranky, becoming annoyed by the smallest things, such as the sound of someone chewing.

I was also growing increasingly obsessed with cleanliness. I have always been a bit of a clean freak, liking everything to be thoroughly cleaned and neatly organized, but it had begun to take on a bit of an extremist element. My bathroom times started to increase. Once able to make it in and out on a classroom break, I now required more than five minutes to be in there. I was spending more time in there than any of my friends, and most of that time was spent washing my hands. I didn't think much of it at the time. I just figured I was a little more careful about cleanliness than they were. No big deal. But by the end of my undergraduate studies, I spent a good fifteen minutes in the bathroom every time I went—a drastic increase from the five minutes that the average person spends. I spent eight of those minutes just washing my hands, which I was convinced were filthy. But it was more than that; I was becoming increasingly agitated with my environment at home. I had six cats and lately the lack of cleanliness inherent with having pets was weighing on me. I was becoming obsessed with trying to keep a clean environment when it was clearly impossible to do so. Cat fur everywhere! Litter boxes overflowing with pee and poo; it was disgusting. It used to not bother me, yet now it was all I could think about.

I spent most of my undergraduate years in a state of constant anxiety. My major in physics was making me miserable. I so thought I would love physics when I was in high school. I expected to breeze through college work quite easily. But I learned pretty early on that I didn't like that as a major. Of course, in retrospection, I don't know how much of that was OCD-related and how much was my true feelings. I did enjoy the lab work I did with Dr. Pekarek (I started doing lab work with Dr. Pekarek my sophomore year of college. The work was more interesting than the classes. The work I did actually got published in a physics journal. My name is listed on it under authors.). But overall I was very unhappy. I stayed with physics partly because I didn't know what else to choose and partly because I had wanted it for so long that I wasn't ready to give up on it. But it took up so much of my time. Physics is arguably the hardest major out there and so requires a great deal of study all by itself, but you factor in OCD and the study time nearly doubles. I had little to no social life. I wasn't allowing myself any free time to relax and rest. I was making myself miserable, and this was only making my OCD worse. My whole goal in life was to make good grades, and the stress I put on myself to do so was greatly worsening my OCD. It was a vicious cycle.

In spite of the growing instability in my mind, I managed to complete my BS in physics and began planning my entrance to graduate school. But by the winter of 2004, my OCD, depression, and anxiety were noticeably worsening. I should have slowed down and focused on my health, but that wasn't my mode of operation. I have always been driven to excel. I work hard and get good grades. That is who I am. If I wasn't doing that, then who was I? I decided to go to graduate school to study national security affairs, as I had become fascinated with a career in government, particularly something in the intelligence sector. I usually always had the news on in the background of my house to stay on top of the current events. Twenty-four-hour news channels, what a brilliant idea. I always feel connected to the world. It was quite a switch from my physics roots, but I was very interested in the topic. I soon discovered, however, that once I passed the threshold into severe depression, OCD, and anxiety, my mind no longer worked the same way as others, and without any help, my condition would quickly deteriorate.

<u>Emily's Helpful Tips</u>
<u>Common Ways to Avoid Handshaking</u>

It seems like everywhere we go we have to shake hands with someone. It is a universal sign of greeting. But it is also the number one way to spread germs. How then do we avoid doing it without seeming like a social deviant? Here are a few tips I picked up along the way.

1. Live somewhere cold so you can wear gloves all the time.
2. Always have something in your hands like books or a bag.

3. Say you have some skin problem like eczema or flesh-eating bacteria. The latter is more effective.
4. Pull your shirtsleeve over your hand and then shake. Obviously this only works if you are wearing long sleeves.
5. Just be honest and say you suffer from OCD. Some people are very understanding.

CHAPTER SIX
Graduate School

"Not to have control over the senses is like sailing in a rudderless ship, bound to break to pieces on coming in contact with the very first rock."
Mahatma Gandhi

My move to DC, in 2005, initially seemed quite promising. I was out on my own for the very first time. I lived at home during my undergraduate degree. Since school was only twenty minutes away, there was really no need for me to move out. Plus it was financially cheaper. But now I was out on my own, and I was loving it. I had my own apartment. My own apartment! It was a cozy little nook five blocks shy of the White House. The last time I moved into a new place was before kindergarten and I have no memory of it, so I had no idea what a new apartment was like. The moment I stepped into it, I knew it was my apartment. It welcomed me through its doors and bathed me in the warmth that only home could offer. Amidst a cold and unforgiving city, it was my little haven. It was beautiful, fresh, and clean—an OCD person's dream. The walls were washed in subtle white paint, bare yet decorative. Softly woven sandy carpets stretched the length of the apartment, save the bathroom and kitchen, which were paved in tile. I loved walking barefoot on the carpet, the smooth fibers stroking the bottoms of my feet. No shoes were allowed. All the counters were covered in smooth green granite, a touch of color to an otherwise neutral palette. There were two closets. One I stored my coats in; the other was a walk in closet. It was magnificent. I don't know if I mentioned this already, but I love clothes. Many a happy day was spent shopping at the mall. Now I had a large closet to store all my treasures. The closet, however, was nothing compared to the bathroom. It was three times the size of mine back home. Three times the size! It had a beautiful vanity with a huge mirror. It was brilliant! The apartment was a one-bedroom, though, in retrospect, I could have done with a studio, as I spent most of my nights asleep on the couch. An OCD trait—I don't like small, dark places. There was only one small window and no lights in the bedroom. The living room, on the other hand, was brilliant. A huge floor-to-ceiling window graced the back wall, opening out onto Embassy Row. Light bathed the room in an angelic glow. But it wasn't just the living quarters that were promising; I also was accepted at a noted university, the Institute of World Politics, where I was to study national security affairs, with plenty of connections to government jobs. I was also accepted to Georgetown University but I turned them down for the smaller, more intimate Institute. But perhaps the coolest thing, I was living in the seat of power for the entire country.

I loved DC. Well, not during the winter. I hated it then. It was far too cold. Even under layers of clothing, it was still miserable to walk out in the snow. Granted it was beautiful. I remember staying up late one night studying in front of the fireplace and watching newly fallen snow waft down from the heavens. So peaceful. So serene. But walking out in it…oh, the horror. I found myself stranded one day in January by the Jefferson Memorial. Apparently cabs are hard to come by that time of year. I walked in the freezing cold for over an hour before I finally found myself a cab. The wind was like ice, and it blew through my three layers of clothing. Even my monstrous coat was not enough to save me from Jack Frost's hand. On the plus side, I look really cute in winter coats. Too bad there aren't many chances to wear them here in Florida. My favorite is this long navy cape that my mom used for Civil War reenacting. Whenever I wore it, I felt like a wizard or an elf from *Lord of the Rings*. But, cold weather aside, I really did love DC. I remember the start of spring…the Cherry Blossom Festival. The city was awash in pale pink blossoms. They lined the streets all the way up to the Jefferson Memorial, like a watercolor painting dipped in pastels. Enchanting. Standing there under the trees, pink petals in my hands, I felt like a fairy-tale princess. I strolled around the Cherry Blossom Festival with a friend. Good food, unique mementos; it was a carnival of sights and sounds. The festival aside, I loved walking around the city, popping from monument to monument, from museum to museum. The wealth of history of the city is boundless. I dreamily danced across the streets with all the world at my feet. Magic was in the air. I think I liked the Lincoln Memorial and the adjacent reflecting pond the best. Sitting there on those majestic steps, I could see out onto the city straight up to the National Monument. Beautiful. Oh, but I did love hanging around the White House, never knowing if something exciting was going to happen. I walked by a number of times, hoping to see the president walk out, but had no such luck. Although I did get one male tourist ask if he could take a picture with me. I don't know why. I did look particularly cute that day, so maybe that was it. Funny really. I loved the Smithsonian Air and Space Museum too. (I have been obsessed with NASA ever since I was a child. I always thought I would be working there one day. Sadly, things didn't work out that way. I didn't love physics enough to pursue a career in it or astronomy, or rather physics didn't love me. I just couldn't handle it. It was too hard. But still I love what could have been.) Oh and the shops! How could I forget the shops? The shopping district around Georgetown was wonderful. I only got around to visiting there twice but what an experience—all the big name stores in fashion. I bought a pair of stilettos there. Not that I would ever wear them because I can't, for the life of me, balance on a tiny heel, but it is good to know that they are there. I took the Metro to and from the shopping district. It was my first time and my only time ever taking it, and thank goodness I had a friend with me who had been on it before, or I would have been completely lost. I was too scared to try going on it on my own, so I never went on it again. I stuck with taking taxis. More expensive, but fortunately I didn't have to take too many because I liked walking most places.

Part of what I liked about DC was the school, the Institute of World Politics. It was only five minutes from my apartment so I usually walked there, except during winter when I took a cab. It was housed in a historic old building. The craftsmanship was beautiful. The interiors were all dark-stained wood, except for the stairs which were carpeted. The school was very sophisticated and employed many distinguished professors who were frequent guests on the news networks. I learned a lot in just one semester. I took two classes: Ideas and Values in International Politics and Twentieth Century Politics. Fortunately both classes were at night, so I got to sleep late which is good for me because I am a night owl. Twentieth Century Politics was my favorite because we learned about all the major events of this century and how they have impacted the world. It was very eye opening.

It was all very exciting! But my problems, which I had so greatly tried to hide and ignore, were ready to rear their ugly heads. Depression hit first. I initially denied it when I was diagnosed with depression shortly before leaving. Deep down I knew I was, but I was ashamed to admit it. After all, I had nothing to be depressed about. I had a stable, loving home life with parents who were still married after three decades together. I had a solid network of good friends. I was at the top of my class in school with many *doors* open to me regarding my future. And in all my life, I never had anything truly bad happen to me. I was never abused; in fact, my parents were opposed to spanking. I was never wanting. I was never tortured. I was never raped or beaten. I didn't suffer from famine. I didn't live in a country where free will was repressed or genocide was accepted. I had a wonderful life. I couldn't be depressed. I shouldn't be depressed. So I denied it. I tried to ignore it, tried to make it go away. But I couldn't. Unlike at home where I had a stable support system to stop me from spiraling out of control, here in DC I was alone. I had one good friend attending school with me, Naomi, an old pal from high school, but between school, work, and church she was very busy. So I was alone. With no one to distract me from my own thoughts and with a lighter workload than I was used to in physics, the feelings that I tried to ignore poured into my mind like a deluge. One upsetting thought would set me off on a downward spiral, ending in me feeling completely hopeless and worthless.

> *Did you see that look of surprise the teacher had on his face when I correctly answered the question? He probably doesn't think I'm smart. None of the students think I'm smart. Why did they even let me into this school? I'm not smart. I don't know anything about world affairs. I was silly to think I could handle this. I'm so stupid. Already twenty-five and I haven't done anything with my life. I'm almost thirty years old, and I have no job and no husband. I am a failure. Completely worthless. No one will ever love me. I'm never going to do anything worthwhile with my life. I want to die.*
> (Thoughts while sitting in class)

In the course of one minute, I could go from the peak of contentment to the depths of despair. I would follow this downward spiral at least once a day.

By Emily Watson

The boy I liked just kissed me on the cheek. A kiss on the cheek! The universal body language for "I just want to be friends." I thought he liked me. I must have done something wrong. I always do something wrong. I am such a loser. No guy will ever want to date me. I'm not pretty enough. I'm not smart enough. I'm not funny enough. I am worthless. No guy will ever want me to marry him. I'll be alone for the rest of my life.

The more depressed I got, the more frequently these downward spirals would occur, leaving me drowning in a sea of depression.

OCD was the next to hit. Intrusive and disturbing obsessive thoughts plagued me every day. Worries and fears over everything took up my time—time I needed for school. I obsessed over the bathroom. When was I going to go? How long would it take me? How long would I need to wash my hands? I washed my hands repetitively. They were never clean enough. I was finicky about what I would and wouldn't touch. I wouldn't shake hands with others—a minor problem as people at this school were big on handshaking. I cleaned the house with obsessive precision. I wouldn't allow people to use shoes on the carpet, and anyone who sat on the couch must sit on top of a sheet. I repetitively turned lights on and off. I don't know why. I just did. I felt compelled to do so. I worried over everything, even the smallest of things like what was I going to have for dinner that night. I worried over getting a good grade at school. I worried over dying. I worried over the end of the world. These weren't things that I thought about occasionally. I obsessed over them night and day. All this took up time. My OCD always left me behind on schoolwork. I continually had to ask for extensions on papers—something I never used to do. I felt like such a slacker. My OCD affected my time at school as well. I had class only two days a week, but I was there for many hours at a time and therefore preoccupied with the bathroom. I usually avoided using public restrooms, but since classes were hours at a time, I had no choice. Staying there so long, my OCD mind inevitably became obsessed with the bathroom. Public restrooms are beyond stressful for me. They are a teeming cesspool of germs and unpleasant odors. How often are they even cleaned? They certainly aren't checked by staff regularly, as I constantly come across bathrooms without soap or toilet paper. Fortunately I carry around a pack of hand wipes and a full change of clothes everywhere I go, but I refuse to carry toilet paper. That is just crazy. To my distress, there was only one single-stall bathroom near my classroom, and all the students lined up there during the break. If I used that restroom, everyone would know that I spent fifteen minutes in the bathroom, eight of which I spent washing my hands. It was a rather old building so the walls were painfully thin. Verging on a panic attack at such a disastrous situation, I luckily came across a second single-stall bathroom. One floor down, ten feet to the right and twenty feet to the left, I found my salvation. On the downside, I was always a bit nervous going down there as it was usually deserted at night. Not that I minded deserted places, but if you will recall, this was a very old building—the ideal haunt for some restless ghost. FYI, I had recently developed an obsessive fear of ghosts. Yet, I pressed on. As my bathroom ritual lasted fifteen minutes and our breaks were only ten minutes, I was always at least five minutes late to class, which was quite evident to the approximately ten students whose eyes turned my direction as my platform heels echoed on the wood-paneled floor. The entire first half of my classes was spent planning my bathroom strategy that would attract as little attention as possible. The second half of my classes were spent absorbed in another series of obsessive thoughts, usually involving my paranoia that the other students thought I was stupid. Completely preoccupied by my continual flow of obsessive thoughts, I usually only comprehended fifteen minutes of the three-hour lectures. This may very well have started during my undergraduate years, but since my major was physics, the discussions centered on complex mathematical equations, which were always written on the board. All I had to do was write down what it said without even thinking. No such luck with international security affairs, which is heavy in discussion and debate. I saw a chalkboard only once.

    Paranoid my mental instability was written on my face, I rarely hung out with others, especially avoiding group outings. No matter how large of a group I was in, I felt completely naked and exposed even though I was bundled in layers of warm clothing (usually four or five as I am from Florida where sixty degrees is considered winter). I was sure everyone could see how disturbed I was. How could they not? I no longer had complete control over my obsessive behavior. Contamination and control obsessions ruled my mind. I was obsessed with maintaining my own cleanliness and the cleanliness of the things around me. I feared dirt and germs and, worst of all, foul odors. I had an innate need to be in control of everything. I feared if I wasn't that something bad would happen. My conversations were blatantly obsessive in nature; anyone who spoke to me more than once was well aware of that. I would speak on the same tired subject for hours on end, unable to talk about anything else, to the chagrin of my family and friends. Many of the conversations revolved around this boy I liked as I obsessed over whether he liked me back. I would analyze every detail of our encounters, trying to find the smallest possibility that he might like me back. It was crazy. I was crazy. Futhermore, I couldn't hide my compulsive behaviors. I spent fifteen minutes in the bathroom every time I went out, eight minutes of which I spent rigorously scrubbing my hands to the shock and awe of anyone around. I looked like a doctor scrubbing in for surgery. I avoided shaking hands with anyone, even if that meant appearing rude. Furthermore, my physical appearance was suffering. My acne was rampant due to my excessive stress, and my hands and legs were covered in scaly, red eczema. I was paranoid with how I looked. I have always been slightly concerned about others' opinions of me but never to such an unhealthy extent. In retrospection, that was very narcissistic of me. Most people simply don't think that much about other people; they are too consumed with their own lives.

Sadly, avoiding hanging out with others also meant avoiding dating. Shame, as Washington, DC, seemed to have the patent on handsome, intelligent young men. I was especially interested in this one boy. I obsessed hours on end about whether or not he liked me back. All I wanted was for him to ask me out on a date. But, despite my desire to have a meaningful connection with someone else, I simply couldn't bring myself to date. My realm of what I considered contaminated had spread to all people. They were no longer people; they were giant contaminants. Once content to just avoid handshaking, I now avoided any physical contact with others. The mere thought of kissing made me sick. We often take for granted the fact that the smallest touch connects us to others, reminding us that we are not alone. Forcible separation from such a connection cut a deep slash in my heart. Most days all I wanted was a hug from my mom or dad, the subtle note only parents can play in assuring us that everything will be all right. But I couldn't. I was trapped. Not by any barrier the eye could see, but by a mental prison in which such things were not allowed.

My free time instead was spent on the growing number of rituals spawned by my OCD. My primary obsession was my need for cleanliness. I showered for an hour every day and washed my hands an uncountable number of times, each time lasting about eight minutes. Above all else, I needed to be clean, free of any dirt, germs, and most especially bad odors. I feared smelling. But I was also obsessed with keeping my new apartment as clean as when I first walked in. I continually cleaned countertops, carpets, desks, etc., to make sure everything looked tidy and new. Having guests over was troublesome as I knew they would not understand my rules of cleanliness. Don't use shoes on the carpet! Always use a towel or sheet to cover the couch before you sit on it! If I could have Saran-wrapped the entire apartment, believe me, I would have. Keeping my apartment as clean as an operating room was very tiresome. I could see my friends growing irritated by my irrational rules, but I couldn't help myself; the apartment needed to remain clean. That was more important than that comfort of my friends.

Beyond my primary obsession for cleanliness, I became obsessed with everything else at one point or another. If something happened to upset me, like a bad test grade or a perceived affront by a boy I liked, it became all I could think about. My only way to silence the relentless chatter in my mind was to talk to others about it. I could sense friends and family growing tired of my obsessive ranting, but I couldn't stop. They would continually try to change the subject, but my mind couldn't focus on anything else. I had tunnel vision. Only another all-consuming obsessive thought could divert my attention. I felt detached from myself, hearing my obsessive thoughts and watching myself act out compulsions, fully aware of their absurdity but completely unable to control them. It was as if an outside force had taken over my body.

Ironically, the only thing I wasn't obsessed about was my safety. Shocking considering I was warned by everyone about the high crime rates for the city. I was actually quite comfortable strolling about during the daytime, passing national monuments and hanging out by the White House, hoping something exciting would happen. So many cops and secret service agents were stationed along most city blocks that I always felt protected. Of course the secret service agents weren't there to protect me, but surely no one would commit a crime right in front of them. I'm not foolhardy though; I certainly wouldn't go around by myself at night. A young woman walking by herself at night down a dimly lit alley-way littered with parked cars engulfed in the steam rising up from the potholes…I think I saw that movie of the week.

This vibrant city lay at my feet, yet I was too consumed by my problems to enjoy it. On my good days, of which there were too few, the city was a carnival of sights and sounds that I roamed through with the wistful flair of a nonpromiscuous Carrie Bradshaw. On my bad days, the city was a cold, unfeeling wasteland in which I was stranded. Surrounded by thousands of souls, yet completely alone. That's the thing about all mental disorders; they are very isolating. The battle that I face is entirely within me—within my own mind. I always feel alone.

My last few weeks in DC I barely left the apartment. I didn't even go out for groceries, opting instead to get delivery pizza, which thanks to the marvelous microwave, stretched to three or four meals. I spent most of my time sprawled out on the couch watching hours of senseless television. My only contacts to the outside world were my cell phone and the living room window overlooking Fifteenth Street. The crying baby next door and the relentless noise of the city—nuisances to most—provided me with comfort as the apartment didn't seem so quiet and uninhabited. I was often plagued by bouts of insomnia, staying up for forty-eight hours at a time with only twelve hours of sleep in between. I wanted to cry all the time, but the strange sadness that afflicted me seemed too deep for tears.

By the end of my first semester in DC, my condition had drastically deteriorated from when I first arrived. All this promise lay before me, and I was uncontrollably destroying it. This time I knew I needed to get help, and I needed to be back at home. It was the first time I had given up on school, and, though I knew I needed to focus on my health, it still made me feel like a failure.

<u>Emily's Helpful Information</u>
<u>What is Eczema?</u>

> It is a hypersensitivity, like an allergy, in the skin. It leads to long-term inflammation, which causes the skin to be very itchy and covered in scales. Long-term scratching and irritation causes the skin to thicken and look like leather. Though eczema is most likely genetic, certain

condition can make it worse, such as dryness, environmental irritants, water, stress, and changes in temperature. Winter always makes my eczema worse; fortunately, I live in a temperate location and have warm sunny weather most of the year. The best thing to help an outbreak of the rash is to take an oral dose of a common steroid, like prednisone. I swear, if that pill isn't pure magic, as the day I start taking it, my rash virtually disappears. If your doctor is opposed to oral steroids, then a steroidal hand cream is your next safest bet. The only downfall is thinning of the skin from constant use. So, the creams should be used sparingly and only when absolutely needed. For daily use, I recommend Kinerase hand cream. Though expensive, it is the only hand lotion I have found that soothes the dry skin of eczema without causing any further irritation. Unfortunately, I have no solutions for hiding the embarrassing patches. Embarrassed by the large swath on my legs, I refused to wear shorts, condemning myself to wearing tight, heavy, cumbersome jeans in Florida's blisteringly hot and humid summers. Beauty is pain.

(Webmd 2013)

<u>Emily's Helpful Tips</u>
<u>Common Lies to Use When my Friends Wonder</u>
<u>Why I Spent So Long in the Bathroom</u>

Inevitably at some point, you are going to have to use the bathroom—the dreaded public restroom—when you go out. Your friends and colleagues are going to wonder why you are in there so long. Here are a few helpful lies to get you out of a tight spot. The truth is always best, but I often didn't want to discuss my disorders with others because I thought they wouldn't understand.

1. There was a line.
2. I got a call on my cell phone.
3. I ran into someone I knew, and we started chatting.
4. I got lost. (Obviously only helpful if you haven't been there before.)
5. Ummm… (You're taking too long! Quick! Change the subject!)

PART III: ENTRANCE TO HELL

"Thy fate is the common fate of all, into each life some rain must fall, some days must be dark and dreary."
Henry Wadsworth Longfellow

CHAPTER SEVEN
Falling from Grace

"The ultimate measure of a man is not where he stands in moments of comfort and convenience, but where he stands at times of challenge and controversy."
Martin Luther King, Jr.

"Everyone is a moon and has a dark side which he never shows to anybody."
Mark Twain

    Upon my return from DC in the summer of 2005, I was but a shadow of my former self. In the beginning when my OCD wasn't really bad, I could talk myself out of my OCD behavior. Whenever an obsessive thought entered my mind, I took a moment to recognize it and then used reason to stop myself from enacting the resultant compulsive behavior. It sounds simple, actually rather silly to anyone whose brain is wired correctly. But to me, it was nothing short of an all-out battle, as every atom in my body and thought in my head was pushing me toward that action. Now it never stopped the obsessive thoughts from entering my mind, but it did stop me from acting on them. As my OCD worsened, all reasonable thought went out the window, along with the idea of living a normal life. I could no longer dismiss my obsessive thoughts. What was once a few annoying voices chanting in my head was now a stadium full of screams that drowned out all rational thought. My mind, which was once able to solve highly complex mathematical equations as if they were basic algebra, now could not even do a simple crossword puzzle in the *TV Guide*. Logic, reason, and intelligence had been replaced by utter chaos. Forced to the realization that I needed help, I began seeing a therapist and trying various medications. Sadly, at first, neither would work.

    I was slipping into chaos. Hundreds of obsessive voices lay siege on my mind. *Did I lock the door? Did I turn off the stove? Did I turn off the lights? Did I wash my hands good enough? Is he/she sick? Is he/she contagious? Am I going to be contaminated by his/her germs? There is a foul odor in this room. Am I going to be contaminated by it?* I was forced to perform a series of rituals in order to make the voices go away. But they never did. They were always with me. Bidding me. Haunting me. Consuming me. My biggest obsession was cleanliness. I had to be clean and everything around me had to be clean. That led to my most time-consuming compulsions. Now every time I went to the bathroom I spent thirty minutes in there. What was I doing in there? It used to take me only five minutes. Clearly I was overly wiping myself, making sure there wasn't even the smallest trace of urine left on my bottom. That took about fifteen minutes. Then I spent another fifteen minutes washing my hands according to a precise handwashing ritual that I had devised. I left that bathroom cleaner than anyone else. I could have gone into surgery with hands as pristine as mine. Needless to say, I stopped using public restrooms, as my rituals garnered too many stares. But it wasn't just cleanliness obsessions that were beating me down. Religious, control, perfectionist, and other contamination obsessions were attacking my mind. There were hundreds of voices spiraling in my head. I couldn't think. I couldn't breathe. I tried to fight them off by performing the stupid little compulsions, but it was not enough; there were too many. I was paralyzed.

Once a vibrant young woman on the verge of an exciting future, I was now a hermit confined to a small apartment from which I was too ill to escape. I had become the fragile glass doll that my fair skin and rosy cheeks had always resembled. The slightest trouble and I would break. If something happened to affect my delicate balance, like a cat peeing out of the litter box, I would completely shut down. It was like a system overload to my broken robot. Though a college graduate, I felt like I was once again a small child. As I got sicker, I became ever more dependent on my family—far more so than I ever was growing up. I couldn't drive anymore, partially because the medications I was on were sedating and partially because I was no longer in complete control of my actions. One of the last times I drove I became so frightened by a small spider crawling in my car that I lost all focus on the road. My conscious mind had become completely obsessed with the spider's movement, fearful that it would crawl on me. Fortunately I was driving on a road I had been on hundreds of times before, so my subconscious managed to get me safely home. But I knew that would not always be the case. Now, if I wanted to go out, I needed someone to drive me. Not a problem for my family but an understandable inconvenience to most of my friends. My best friend, Christine, was the only one unaffected by the burden.

In the end, it didn't really matter that I couldn't drive, as I rarely ventured out. While I was still at college, things weren't too bad, so I was able to pretend I felt OK and hide any prominent symptoms. But that was no longer an option. Even if I found some way to hide the numerous OCD rituals that now governed my daily life, I simply didn't have the energy to pretend like everything was OK. My heart was too sad to act happy. More than that, I was just tired of lying to everyone to cover up what was really going on in my life. It would have been better to simply tell the truth, but I was afraid of what people would think. I was afraid how they would view me. I was afraid they would think that I was weak.

Anger, once a distant relative, now visited me daily. The weight of my disorders produced such frustration that I verbally lashed out at any family member within five feet. I have never been an angry person. The consummate Melly, I was usually the picture of sweetness and grace, choosing to look at all the good in life. But as I was dragged deeper into my mental prison, I became a woman on the edge. The constant pain from my bladder problems and the growing chaos in my mind placed me in such a precarious state that the slightest irritant would send me into a stress-filled rage that Miss Scarlett would envy. I despised myself for being so filled with anger. I wasn't angry at anyone in particular. I was angry at the situation I was in and the lack of control I had over it.

A very irritating fact of OCD, or any mental disorders for that matter, is that it is inescapable. Unlike troubles at school or work, which can be left behind on the weekends and during seasonal vacations, OCD is always with me. No matter where I go or what I do, the flood of obsessive voices always follows me. In contrast to most people, vacations were far more stressful to me than any day at home. For starters, I absolutely would not fly, so any vacation had to be within driving distance—surprising since I used to fly all the time. I logged enough frequent flier miles to fly to Hawaii and back for free. Furthermore, we had to rent a car. Under no circumstances was I going to ride in my mother's car. I knew what she put in there: a cat-sprayed spare tire, cat-sprayed luggage, mildewed tidbits, and an antique toilet—utterly disgusting, not to mention completely unsanitary. Were that only the most stressful part. Packing was beyond tiresome, as it was a carefully ritualized process, taking a least an hour or two. However, if the trip was with my mother, I had to be extra careful the entire time so as not to let any of my things touch hers. Being a hoarder she didn't take good care of any of her things, haphazardly stacking luggage and clean clothes openly for animals to lie on or worse.

As if my mental deterioration wasn't devastating enough, my physical appearance began mirroring my inner turmoil. To add insult to my growing list of injuries, I discovered that long-term anxiety affects you physically as well as mentally. It is one thing to be sick, but I hated actually looking sick. It is far more difficult to hide my problems. My bushy head of hair had begun thinning at an alarming rate. My skin, plagued by eczema, was made all the more obvious by my pale complexion. And my weight kept dropping. Granted, that may not seem like a horrible thing amidst our country's current obsession with all things skinny, but as I am already petite and slender, further weight loss just qualified me for the science room skeleton. Forgive me for falling prey to vanity, but I am still a young woman and it really bothered me. Walking around looking like a pale skeleton with thin, mousy hair and skin covered in red, flaky bumps didn't strike me as the best way to get a date. I remember going to the hospital once, one of many times for my kidney stones, and the nurse commented that she could tell I was very ill because of how pale I looked to which my mother causally responded, "Oh no, that is how she normally looks." Thanks, Mom. I get it; I have fair skin. I can't help it if I actually reflect the sun.

Worst of all, I suffered alone. I was trapped in a mind that was no longer my own. I desperately cried out for help from my parents as if somehow they could save me from the growing insanity that the doctors and their pills had failed to cure. But they couldn't help me. No one could. I did not have a band of brothers to help me in my fight. I stood alone on a battlefield that was entirely within my own mind.

<u>Emily's Helpful Tips</u>
<u>The OCD Handwashing Ritual</u>

Over time I developed a standard handwashing ritual to make sure I properly cleaned my hands the exact same way every time. It is long and

By Emily Watson

tedious and I dearly wish I didn't have to do this, but I had no choice. If I wanted to make sure I had clean hands, I had to follow every inane step.

1. Turn on faucet. Faucets are covered in bathroom germs, but it is OK to use hands because I am about to clean them.
2. Use the warmest water skin can stand, as it kills germs better than cold water. If only cold water is available, I should probably use a hand wipe after I have completed the entire ritual just to be safe.
3. Use foaming liquid soap because it is the best at producing lather. If I have to use bar soap, I use Dove because it is best for sensitive skin. Powder soaps are the absolute worst at producing lather so if I come across a bathroom with it, I must find another bathroom, or I will never get my hands properly clean.
4. Begin by lathering up the front and back of hands for a total of thirty seconds. Only count out twenty of the seconds, though, as thirty is a bad number. If I count to thirty, bad things may happen.
5. Lather up each arm up to the elbow. Each arm must be washed for thirty seconds each, but only count out twenty as before.
6. Lather up the front and back of hands again for thirty seconds. Count out twenty.
7. Now it is time to rinse. Rinse the top and bottom of right arm for thirty seconds per side. Count out twenty.
8. Rinse the top of the right hand three times and then the palm three times.
9. Repeat steps 7 and 8 for the left hand and arm.
10. Go back to right hand and rinse it until I feel it is clean enough, generally one or two minutes.
11. Repeat step 10 for left hand.
12. Never touch anything during this whole process, if I do, I have to start over at step 4.
13. Use a paper towel to turn off the faucet as I don't want to touch it because my hands are clean now. Use another paper towel to dry hands. Use another paper towel to open the bathroom door.
14. No new steps. I just can't stop at number thirteen because it is an evil number.

CHAPTER EIGHT
Living in Fear

"The only thing to fear is fear itself"
President Franklin D. Roosevelt (FDR)

Fear, a major characteristic of OCD, was taking me over. My OCD had advanced so much that I was fearful of everything. Being so uncontrollably afraid was new to me. I have had my share of fears growing up just like everyone else, but they were never paralyzing. I could usually overcome them or do things in spite of them. I have a fear of public speaking, but I still gave oral reports in school. I have a fear of sharks like anyone from the *Jaws* generation, but I still went to the beach and played in the surf. I have a fear of flying, but I still got on many planes to travel everywhere from Oahu to Rome. But when my OCD became severe, everything I once did now scared me beyond words. My fear controlled me now, and I was paralyzed.

One fear I had was that any time the smallest of things was wrong, I would become consumed by the fear that it was much worse. A small irritation in my eye would require an immediate visit to my doctor, as I was petrified I would go blind. A patch of redness on my skin, a sure sign of dryness to anyone else, was flesh-eating bacteria to me. Every time the news brought up any stories about illnesses, I became flooded with fears of pandemics and epidemics. Every problem I had in the world was a breath away from becoming an epic fear. I couldn't control it.

Another one of my fears was that I was horribly afraid to touch anyone, as I was convinced everyone but me was contaminated. That was probably the worst of all my obsessions. I already felt so alone and isolated from everyone that no longer being able to touch others was devastating. I felt so alone and sad that all I wanted was a hug from my mother or dad but I couldn't. My cats would stare at me with their longing little eyes, but I couldn't touch them either. All it did was make me sadder. Even in a crowded room I felt so alone. I was heartbroken.

One of my greatest fears was making the wrong decision. I am a perfectionist. In school I couldn't turn in any work, like science projects and essays, unless they were absolutely perfect. Getting an A wasn't good enough; I had to get an A+. I had to be the top grade in the class. I had a work ethic that my friends envied and my teachers loved. But what was once an advantage became a disadvantage with the onset of OCD. I was so obsessed with being perfect that I ceased to be able to make any decision, fearing I would make the wrong one. Even the simplest decisions were fraught with peril, like picking between two identical shirts, fearing I would choose the wrong one and, in effect, paralyzing me from moving forward with just about anything. *What if I picked the wrong outfit and went out looking like a fool? What if I pick the wrong selection for dinner and ended up with a stomach ache? What if I turn left instead of right and get into a car accident? What if I chose the wrong career? My life will be ruined. I can't make a mistake; I can't choose the wrong thing; my whole future depends on this one decision.*

Above all else I feared contamination from dirt, germs, smells, and anything that would alter the pristine state of my body. I desperately feared being smelly. I don't know why. I never had a problem with being smelly. I was always clean and fresh, so why this sudden preoccupation with odors is beyond me. Smells became a potent virus that I could contract merely by being in the presence of them. I avoided cigarette smoke, ducking out of places to avoid the toxic cloud. I feared perfumes, buying deodorants and shampoos that were odorless. I washed my hands incessantly to make sure no lingering smell from foods stained them. But it wasn't just smells; it was germs. I was afraid I was going to catch every illness imaginable, even the rare ones. Going out to public places was like walking through a minefield, but instead of metal explosives, it was germs. Anyone was a possible carrier; anyone could penetrate my personal space. The goal: get from point A to point B without making contact with anyone or risk catching some illness. But the substance I feared contamination from the most was urine. I was desperately afraid of getting any urine on me. That was why going to the bathroom was so troublesome and why it took so long. I had to wipe myself over and over to make sure no urine was left on me. Then I had to wash my hands vigorously to clean off any trace of urine. Unfortunately, that wasn't the only time I would have to deal with urine. My cats, nine to be exact, would constantly spray and pee all over the house. Urine would get on the floor and on my things. It was horrible. I couldn't deal with it.

By Emily Watson

I would freak out and start crying. It probably would have been easier on me to not have animals, but I couldn't bear giving them up. I love animals, especially my animals. I couldn't abandon them. It's not their fault I'm sick.

CHAPTER NINE
Someone Call a Priest

"Nothing in life is to be feared. It is only to be understood."
Marie Curie

By the beginning of 2006, I understood why the Church thought people who suffered from OCD were possessed by demons. Not that I thought I was actually possessed by a demon, mind you, but I was quite sure evil forces were always lurking in the shadows around me. Unwanted dark and disturbingly evil thoughts would frequently pop into my mind. I was afraid that simply the appearance of those thoughts would somehow cause them to become real. I avoided most horror movies or television shows, as I did not want to put anymore thoughts and fears into my head. But they came from somewhere, from the disorder. Evil thoughts are a common symptom of OCD, along with religious and moral doubt. How very odd—a disorder that makes me fear evil. That is so nonsensical; I do not understand how that can be so, how a mental illness can completely change how my mind works. I guess I have to look at it like I would a disease on any other organ. Heart disease affects how the heart functions. Hypothyroidism affects how the thyroid works. OCD just affects the mind, thereby making me obsessively fearful of evil.

All things relating to the devil scared me immensely. I was frightened by the numbers thirteen and 666. I never liked saying them even while counting, which was hard to avoid when my undergraduate major was rich in math. I always got nervous passing the thirteenth floor while riding on an elevator. I didn't think much of it at first. Some people are just superstitious. I remember viewing an apartment on the thirteenth floor while scouting for lodgings in DC. I politely asked if they had rooms on any other floors, as I did not like the idea of living on the thirteenth floor. I considered it an evil number and thought it would be dangerous to stay on that floor. The shocked look on the realtor's face let me know I was the only person she had come across who was troubled by that. It wasn't just numbers that frightened me; I was terrified of anything evil, especially demons and ghosts. I thought they along with vampires, werewolves, and zombies were all lurking in the darkness around me waiting for the right moment to attack. They haunted my waking hours and terrorized me in my sleep. My parents tried to tell me that such things aren't real, but I didn't believe them. I know they are real. I can feel it. They're out there quietly killing innocents and waiting, biding their time to attack. They are everywhere battling good just outside our field of vision. Fearful something evil was living inside my closet, I slept out on the living room couch. I even feared going in my room at all, especially at night. (I, also, slept on the living room couch because I was claustrophobic and I didn't like sleeping in my room with the door shut. I had to have the door shut because I didn't allow the cats in my room. I had to have one room in my house that was clean and cat free.) I was constantly afraid I was being shadowed by demonic beasts and that at any moment they would appear before me. They're out there—evil creatures—causing the chaos and the darkness in the world. They're out there and they're coming. Others don't see it, but I do. In my most disturbed moments, I was actually more afraid of being attacked by a demon than a real live person.

Fears revolving around religious and moral doubt consumed me. Sure that I was a terrible sinner, I fretted endlessly about going to hell. Evil thoughts ran through my mind in the silence of the day, visions of committing crimes and horrendous acts. *Was I evil? Was I a murderer waiting to kill? Was I one on/off switch away from turning into the evil souls I saw on the news?* Fearful of what I might do and in an effort to cleanse my soul, I decided to attend a Bible group at school, once in high school and once in college. Holding the little Bible my Grandma Maude gave me, I sat in a circle with the rest of the group. Fully prepared to have the word of God wash over me and dispel any evil inside of me, I quietly listened as the group's chairman began: "We begin today with the book of Revelation and the coming apocalypse." *Crap!* "Judgment Day is believed to be coming soon. All those who have accepted our savior, Jesus Christ, into their hearts will be saved and taken to heaven. Those who have not will be faced with the Four Horsemen." *Double Crap! Have I accepted Jesus into my heart? I thought so. I mean, I was baptized when I was young, and I think I have led a pretty good life. But what if I haven't? Oh my gosh, I'm going to hell! Will it be in the next ten years? The next five? Next year? Why is nobody else completely freaked out? The end is coming! The end is coming!* On the verge of having a complete panic attack, I decided it was best not to return. I truly left with the fear of God in me. Not exactly what I was going for. What is the likelihood that I would run into that topic both times? I could pass it off as coincidence, but my OCD mind was convinced that I was being sent some form of message, specifically that the apocalypse is coming soon, and I am meant to go to hell.

Driven senseless by my fears, I was spurred to enact superstitious rituals to ensure my safety. I slept with salt by my bed, kept positive crystals near me, and wore a Christian cross and medal around my neck at all times that I got in Vatican City that was blessed by a bishop. When the necklace wasn't on, I felt completely unprotected. To get rid of any dark thoughts, I would repetitively sing the same song over and over, usually some Christmas carol, as I was convinced only those songs would drive evil away. Praying was an incredibly tedious endeavor, as I felt that in order to assure the safety of myself and my family, I needed to ask protection from just about everything. I was so afraid I was a terrible sinner. But I couldn't just say "everything"—no that would be far too easy. I would actually have to list every possible thing I feared happening. If praying is like a phone call to God, then he had a lot of people on call waiting while he listened to my senseless chatter.

Even in sleep I wasn't spared the ghastly thoughts that haunted my waking mind. Terrifying nightmares of death and destruction only Stephen King could imagine regularly convulsed me out of a deep sleep. I became so disturbed by these nightly visions that I was scared to go to sleep. Being afraid to go to sleep is just horrible because it can't be avoided. At some point I must go to sleep. It's really rather strange that visions of demons, ghouls, and the evil beast himself weighed so heavily upon my mind, as I strictly avoided all horror movies. Adventure, fantasy, mystery, and romance are all great. I am especially fond of science fiction, always making time to watch *Doctor Who* and the *Stargates* (*SG1* and *Atlantis* to all non-sci-fi geeks). But horror movies? Absolutely not! Yet, if these disturbing visions weren't coming from things I saw on TV, then where? From a disorder, from OCD, from a miscommunication in my brain?

I was deeply worried I would harm others. I have never physically hurt any people or animals in my life. OK, so I did kick a boy in that special region when I was in middle school, but in my defense he wouldn't stop teasing me. And I did shove a boy in eighth grade, but that's because he stole my books. Perhaps I was just a little too anxious to use my newly found fighting skills from Taekwondo. Both those lapses in judgments aside, in truth, I could never hurt anyone—not really. I could never even hurt an animal. In fact I actually rescue abandoned animals and genuinely feel bad whenever I accidentally kill a bug. So why were there graphic images in my mind of doing such terrible things? I tried to block them out, but they flashed through my mind in my quietest of moments. Maybe I would never consciously do horrible things, but what about my unconscious—the part of my brain that is in charge when I'm asleep. I'm not aware of what's going on then, so what if I do something bad? As if I didn't fear sleep enough already, now I had to worry about what my subconscious was doing. I could never hurt any living thing nor would I want to. So why did I constantly fear doing so? My only answer is that it is a result of the disorder. I have no logic to explain it.

Evil thoughts aside, I was desperately afraid of dying. Every possible way of dying flashed through my head daily: drowning, burning in a fire, electrocution, poisoning, car accident, murder. All excruciatingly painful ends that I wished would never come to me. I couldn't stop from imagining them in my mind. The cold water piercing my body as I convulsed beneath the surface desperate for air. The searing flames tearing through my body burning every ounce of flesh as I am contorted in agony. The meaty hands of some unknown man wrapped around my petite neck stealing the air from me. I could see it all happening. I feared death so much I stopped doing things with any risk to them. I stopped going out by myself, afraid that some guy would grab me and murder me. You hear about those stories all the time on the news. I stopped flying because I was afraid the plane would crash. A mechanical problem with the plane sends it into a stomach-turning dive, which I absolutely hate and which is why I don't go on roller coasters. The plane then crash lands on the land, smashing the people to pieces and burning them alive, or lands in the ocean where the people drown. Neither choice is very pleasant. And that's ignoring the threat of terrorists. Factor them in and the plane could explode in midair. Who on earth will willingly get on these death traps? That left me with a big problem. I have always wanted to go to Great Britain and walk along the misty moors. But how could I do that when I am so afraid of flying. Well, perhaps I could take a ship. No, that wouldn't work either as I am afraid of rogue waves. I am worried some huge rogue wave will come and tip the ship completely over like it did in *Poseidon* and everyone will drown. So basically I am stuck on this continent until I can get over my fears. Furthermore, I fear what will happen to me after I die. I'm also fearful of people thinking I'm dead when I am actually alive and then being buried or cremated alive. What if I am buried alive and wake up trapped in a coffin unable to breathe…a small, dark place with no air? I would be terrified. But what's the alternative—cremation. What if I wake up in the middle of the oven being burnt to ashes? I figure there is only one option: burial at sea. They just toss my body overboard. That way if I am not dead and I wake up, all I have to do is swim to the surface. And I should be buried with a waterproof cell phone, that way I can call for a boat to come pick me up.

Frankly, I thought I was completely mad. Normal people don't go around being afraid of paranormal evil forces. Then I discovered that the fear of evil thoughts is actually a common OCD obsession. What an unbelievably strange characteristic to be listed as a common symptom for a disorder. Nonetheless, it was quite a relief that my fears were the result of a brain malfunction and not in fact some psychic awareness that I was being stalked by forces of evil bent upon my complete and utter destruction—or perhaps something less narcissistic.

Emily's Helpful Tips
How to Deal with Evil Thoughts

Evil thoughts constantly run through my mind. I feel insane being flooded with such demented thoughts. What normal person is fearfully obsessed with the paranormal? I couldn't stop myself from thinking these demented thoughts, but I could try to fight them off. Here are a few weapons I came up with.

1. Repeat a helpful mantra when you are afraid. It really does help. I like to use a line from the movie *Children of Dune*: "Fear is the mind killer. I will face my fears. I will let them pass through me."

2. Avoid all horror television shows and movies! Trust me, all they do is put more fearful thoughts into your head. Despite my own advice, I would watch the television show *Supernatural,* because the two lead male characters were unbelievably handsome. I mean seriously, wow. But it would always freak me out, like really freak me out to the point where I am afraid to live my life.
3. Remember, you are more likely to die in a car accident than be killed by a demon or ghost.
4. No matter how you feel, I assure you, you are not possessed by a demon.
5. Though just to be safe, avoid Salem and Catholic Priests.

CHAPTER TEN
Everything is Contaminated

"Cleanliness is next to Godliness."
Ancient Proverb

Other obsessions and compulsions aside, above all else I was obsessed with cleanliness. "Contaminated" had become my new favorite word, and I used it frequently. My need to be clean and surrounded by cleanliness was my dominant compulsion, as I was perpetually worried about being dirty and smelling bad. What on earth had happened to me? Where was that girl who went camping, who climbed in trees, who lay in the morning's moist dirt for hours digging for dinosaur bones? The person who stood before me now in my slightly askew mirror resembled nothing of the girl I once knew. I was a robot now—a robot whose sole purpose was to root out all that was contaminated and cleanse it.

My daily life was now nothing more than a series of rituals designed to foster cleanliness. Every time I went to the bathroom, I stayed in there for at least thirty minutes compelled to wash my hands all the way to my elbows, until they were cracking from dryness. My hands were washed according to a precise ritual ensuring they were washed the exact same way for the exact same time, approximately fifteen minutes. Whenever I touched anything in my house from food, to a cat, to the remote control, I had to immediately use a wipe or wash my hands, as I considered everything to be contaminated. Surely you are wondering why I did it, as were the many strangers who openly gaped at me when I used public restrooms…hardly a confidence booster! But you must remember whenever these incredulous thoughts enter your head that your brain is working properly whereas mine was clearly malfunctioning.

Showers were by far the worst. The longest and most grueling ritual, they lasted for a whopping three hours and had to be done every day. Usually I showered immediately when I got home, afraid to contaminate my room with any outside dirt and germs. However, as time went on, I became extremely worn down by the amount of energy it took to perform my rituals along with the continued bladder/kidney problems that were raging in my body. Unable to reduce the length of time my rituals took, I tried to find ways to simply avoid them altogether. I began lengthening the time between showers. I went from every other day, to every few days, to once a week, to once every two weeks, to once every three weeks and finally to once a month. Yes I showered, on average, once a month. Ah, curse my obsessive need to confess! Now you know my most embarrassing secret. I'm never going to get a date now. Surprisingly, even showering that little, I still felt cleaner than anyone else in my house, since I constantly washed my hands and changed clothes and bedding daily. Even brushing my teeth was a ritual, as I was so afraid that if I didn't brush them just right I would get a cavity. Brushing took approximately ten minutes.

Fear of smelling bad was one of my big OCD fears. I used to feel the need to sniff every new item coming into my house to make sure it didn't have an offensive odor, as I was horribly afraid of having a bad odor attached to me or my things. I was so afraid to get contaminated by some nasty smell that I would have a panic attack if I came into contact with one. On vacations, I often had to switch hotel rooms, convinced the first room had an odor. Granted, I have an excellent sense of smell, but in those circumstances, I am quite sure it was my imagination. Though, I have read that people with IC have an increased sense of smell. My very own superpower! Frankly, I would have preferred telekinesis.

In spite of my obsession with cleanliness, I have nine cats, no doubt a surprising fact based on everything I have written so far. My family and I are big animal lovers. We rescue stray cats and dogs. All were strays that we took in. As you can imagine, having cats isn't the easiest thing for an OCD clean freak like me. Fur is constantly left on furniture. Cat dander floats through the air. They don't wipe themselves after they go to the bathroom. When they are sick or just in a bad mood, they will pretty much urinate or spray anywhere they please, which is hardly conducive to cleanliness. My friends often asked me why I didn't just get rid of them, as they are likely making my OCD worse. But honestly I never even considered it. I had my cats long before I got sick, and it wasn't their fault I was having so much trouble. I was just as bad when I had a nice, clean, cat-free apartment in DC. Getting rid of them wouldn't cure me; I would simply become obsessed with something else. Besides, they were a part of my family, and I don't just kick family members out because they are unclean. I mean, really, with her crazy hoarding, my mother was far less sanitary than the cats. What would you have me do then, get rid of her as well? The most ideal solution, of course, would just have been to get my own apartment, but unfortunately that was not feasible. My decision to go to graduate school was costly, as my school did not offer a full scholarship and living anywhere near DC basically involves breaking the bank. So when I returned home, we just didn't have the funds to get me my own place, and since I was so sick, I couldn't work to bring in money. It was probably for the best, though; I was having so many problems that I really needed to stay at home so my family could help me.

 Cleanliness was one of the most important things to me. I found myself enthralled by commercials touting cleaning products. My mind tingled with what precise cleaning I could do with the magical little devices. A day of scrubbing and washing had become my new idea of fun. Cleaning cleared my mind. It calmed me down and made me feel centered. The messier the house, the more chaotic my mind. The cleaner the house, the clearer my mind.

 My obsessions and compulsions had a detrimental effect on my social life. I basically stopped all social activities going out on the average only once a month. I feared germs so much that leaving the house at all was a very stressful venture. I was governed by so many rules that it was impossible to act normal. I absolutely would not shake hands with people, making up excuses if I had to. If I was cornered into that action, as when I met the president of my college, I made sure I washed my hands soon after or used one of my trusty hand wipes—a lifesaver in a very dirty world. I couldn't open doors either. I used paper towels at home, but it would be too conspicuous to use them outside. Fortunately, being a young lady, there are often gentlemen nearby who kindly open the door. If I found myself alone, I used whatever article of clothing I had on that could be stretched for the task, like a long sleeve. Knowing that my thirty-minute bathroom visits would put a dent in plans with friends along with garnering some rather rude stares when I washed my hands, I always made sure to go before I went out and not drink much while I was gone—a stressful situation when I would be out later than I planned. Day-long trips were virtually out of the question, unless I wanted to get dehydrated, but on special occasions, like the Fourth of July, I would make the effort to go out, though not without an entire change of clothes and plenty of wipes in case I got dirty or engulfed by an unpleasant odor. If only that were the end of it, but alas my list of rules continued on. Any contact with others was forbidden: touching, hugging, and kissing. That one really put a dent in any dating plans. When faced with a handsome young man, all I could think about was the last time he washed his hands and if he cleaned himself well enough in the shower. Real romantic thoughts. Needless to say, I did not date for a period of time. So, let's summarize, in my early to midtwenties, I didn't date, I rarely went out with friends, and I got a bachelor's degree in physics. Ah, the wild, carefree days of my twenties!

Emily's Helpful Tips
The Thought Process of an OCD Clean Freak vs. a Normal Person

In order to understand just how different the brain of an OCD sufferer is as opposed to a normal person, I have provided an example of the thought process I would go through after finding that Kitty, my oldest cat, peed outside of the litter box—an irritating incident that occurs every so often, though it is not her fault. She is going on twenty years old, and in her confusion, she sticks her head inside the litter box but pees outside.

Normal Me

- Oh no, the cat peed outside the box and left pee prints on the floor!
- Great, I have to get some Clorox wipes and clean it up.

OCD Me

- Oh no, the cat peed outside the box and left pee prints on the floor!
- Great, I have to get some Clorox wipes and clean it up.
- But wait, how far do the paw prints go? Where do they lead?
- Oh no, the chair! The cat jumped on the chair! Now I have to wash the chair cushion too!
- Wait, when did this happen? Probably within the last ten minutes. I could have walked in a paw print and not have known it!

- Oh no, I probably got some pee on my shoes!
- Great, I have to wash my shoes now. Wait, after walking in the pee, did I walk anywhere else?
- Where did I walk within the last ten minutes? Let's see, I got off the couch and walked though the hall to my room to get the scissors. The scissors? Why did I need the scissors? Oh yeah, to cut the tag off my pajama bottoms, which means I only walked a few feet into my room since the scissors are on the end of my dresser. OK, so that means I only have to wash the floor a few feet in my room, but I will have to wash the entire hall floor.
- That is a lot of washing. Are there enough Clorox wipes? Oh no, what if there aren't? What am I going to do? OK, I found them; there are plenty.
- Wait, my dad is home. Did he walk anywhere within the last ten minutes? If so, then he might have walked through some pee residue that got on the floor from my own shoes. Yes. He came out to ask me a question. Was that before or after I walked through the hall with pee on my shoes? After. Darn. Now dad's shoes have to be cleaned along with the floor in his office.
- Oh God, I tripped! Earlier I mean. In the hall. Darn. I tripped and my foot slipped out of my flip flop and onto the ground. That means I got pee on my sock too, which, since I put my foot back in the flip flop, means I also got pee on the top of my shoe now as well as the bottom!
- OK, don't panic; just throw away the sock and wash the entire shoe.
- Oh no, wait. I sat on the couch after tripping with my legs Indian style, which means I spread pee onto my pants and the couch. OK, breathe. It's OK, I can fix this. Just calm down.
- What do I need to do? Make a list. Wipe up pee puddle, wipe up pee prints in living room, wash chair cushion, wash the floor in the hall, wash the entryway into my room, wash the floor in my dad's office, take off my socks/shoes/PJs, wash my shoes, put on new pair of socks and pants, put on shoes, wash my dad's shoes, wash the couch…

- I feel dizzy. Too many racing thoughts. I can't think straight. But wait, what if the pee soaked below the top layer of the couch. I can't clean that. We'll have to get a new couch…
- The thoughts are still going, but there are too many to hear clearly. Overwhelmed, my dad finds me squatting on the floor in the hall, rocking back and forth, crying hysterically, completely convinced that I am covered in pee and the entire house is contaminated beyond repair.
- Moral: Urine is Evil.

CHAPTER ELEVEN
Perfect Symmetry

"All of us failed to match our dreams of perfection."
William Faulkner

I like symmetry. My whole world has evolved around math, so is it any wonder I like mathematical perfection—perfect symmetry? The world looks so much better, makes so much more sense when everything is symmetrical. Makeup must be perfectly applied on both sides of the face. Any flaw must be corrected until both sides match. Books and magazines on a coffee table must be perfectly aligned and organized into comparable stacks. If I drop one pasta noodle on the ground, I must drop a second to match. When I go to the grocery store, I must buy certain items in pairs to be symmetrical. The furniture, in my house, must be properly aligned in symmetrical patterns. The world must be even; odds are not allowed.

CHAPTER TWELVE
The Danger of Lights

*"In the beginning there was nothing. God said, 'Let there be light!'
And there was light. There was still nothing, but you could
see it a whole lot better."*
Ellen DeGeneres, (attributed)

I would often turn lights on and off repeatedly. I was quite convinced that if I didn't turn the light off just right, the light would somehow malfunction and set fire to the room. Really quite logical in my screwed up way of thinking, but not to my mom, who while staying with me in a hotel in DC, asked if I was sending light signals to someone in another room. No joke there; she was actually serious. How do I possibly respond to a question like that?

Emily's Helpful Information
Bizarre Phrases that would Repeat in my Mind

A significant trait of OCD is the repetition of words and phrases both in my head and aloud. They rarely made any sense, at least for me, but rather seem to be a random compilation of words. Here are a few of my more memorable musings.

- Agricultural anomalies are occurring with greater frequency.
- Vagrant streams of incoherent data.
- Vodka martini with a twist is something that simply can't be missed.
- Agricultural anomalies are occurring in patterns of three.
- The Magna Charta is my friend and so it shall be to the very end.
- Micronesia. Micronesia. Where are you? Where are you? Where is Micronesia? Where is Micronesia? I don't know. I don't know. (To the tune of "Farah Jahka.")

CHAPTER THIRTEEN
Impulse Control

"Action is eloquence."
William Shakespeare

Inherent in OCD is the problem of controlling one's impulses. When we have an obsessive thought, we feel a very strong compulsion to act on that thought. The impulse is almost impossible to deny. Take my handwashing rituals for example. When my hands feel dirty, specifically after I use the restroom, I feel an intense impulse to wash them. The impulse is too strong to resist, and I succumb to its wishes. Often times the impulses are benign, like getting a forbidden cookie, washing my hands for an extra ten minutes, or pressing on my door an extra ten times to make sure it is locked. However, other times the impulse leads to dangerous consequences. For example, sometimes I look at the flame of a candle and feel the irresistible urge to place my hand in the flame. Why? I don't know. It is just some bizarre impulse. Yet its strength is almost too much to resist even though I know that action will burn my hand. In another example, when walking on the treadmill, I often feel the strong impulse to hop on one leg. Dangerous? Just a bit and slightly odd, but nevertheless it was unbelievably strong and I nearly acquiesced. These obsessive thoughts are voices in my head. Normally there are thousands of voices all screaming for attention. The only way to silence them is to do whatever they say, whatever the impulse is, and perform their little rituals. Of course I try hard to resist the urge if there is danger involved.

CHAPTER FOURTEEN
Caught in a Loop

"What lies in our power to do, it lies in our power not to do."
Aristotle

"Self-control is the quality that distinguishes the fittest to survive."
George Bernard Shaw

"I count him braver who overcomes his desires than him who conquers his enemies; the hardest victory is the victory over self."
Aristotle

OCD is a very time-consuming disorder. My rituals take up large chunks of my day. Showers take four hours. Bathroom trips take one to two hours. Brushing my teeth takes ten minutes. Washing my hands takes twenty minutes. All these tasks involve performing the same action over and over from washing the same arm in the shower ten times to brushing my teeth in the same pattern five times. I call these loops. To perform these rituals is to get trapped in a loop. I constantly get trapped in loops. It is the reason I am late most of the time. I am obsessively worried that my bedroom door isn't shut. If it's open, cats can get in it and ruin its status as a clean zone—my only clean zone in the house. So keeping it shut is very important. I press on the door for ten seconds to make sure it is closed. But sometimes that isn't enough. If I am particularly anxious, then I feel the compulsive need to press on it another ten seconds and then another and another. I get trapped in a loop, performing the same task over and over. When asked what took me so long to get ready, I respond, "I got stuck in a loop." This doesn't just happen at home, it happens everywhere I go. I'll be walking in a grocery store when I step on a discolored mark on the floor. I'll have to go back and look at that mark to make sure it was an old stain and not something fresh that could get on my shoes. Once I thoroughly check it, I walk away only to return a few moments later to check again. I have stumbled into another loop. I will have to go back and check that mark between five and ten times to be convinced that it was just an old stain. It's an insurmountable compulsion. When my hands are dirty, I have a specific ritual I have to follow to make sure they are clean. Depending on my stress level, I have to perform this ritual multiple times. I get caught in a loop. When I turn something off, like a light or the stove, I worry that I didn't turn it off properly and I am fearful it would start a fire. So I have to check to make sure I turned it off, over and over again. I get caught in a loop. All in all, loops take up over fifty percent of my day. The intense anxiety it causes puts a terrible strain on my mind and body. Loops are exhausting. The repetitive motion tires the body out, especially if the loop goes on for more than a few iterations. But what is most tiring is the mental strain placed on the body. I don't want to be trapped in these loops. Every fiber of my being is fighting against these compulsive actions. My mind burns in opposition.

CHAPTER FIFTEEN
How OCD Killed Fashion

"Fashions fade, style is eternal."
Yves Saint Laurent

I like clothes! I admit it. I am afflicted with the vanity of fashion. Many happy high school weekends were spent strolling through the local mall with my equally afflicted friends. The day after Thanksgiving was by far my favorite shopping day of the year—the extravagant sales, the bustling crowds, and the first breath of the jolly holiday air that infused every day in December. The memories are so potent I can taste them. But in spite of their vividness, they seemed like a lifetime ago—maybe even someone else's life.

Nothing about the mall was enjoyable now. It was not a pleasant afternoon activity. It was a composite of noise, germs, and utter contamination. It was a strange, surreal video game. The goal: traverse the dangerous terrain without becoming contaminated by refuse, germs, and foul odors. It used to be fun buying new clothes; now I only went to the mall if I absolutely had to. Of course, any busy day was now crossed off: weekends, holidays, and especially Black Friday. It was far too difficult to avoid contact with others when the walkways were packed with hundreds of bodies. The incessant noise was enough to make me fantasize about hitting anyone who walked in my space with my makeup-laden purse. As that is not the social thing to do, I felt it was best to avoid the temptation. I would like to take this opportunity to point out that people, in general, are actually pretty dirty. We emit foul odors, we carry contagious diseases, and we put our hands on everything. But ignoring all theses extras from *Outbreak*, even an empty mall was a hazardous wasteland. How was I possibly going to buy new clothes if I couldn't try anything on? However cute the outfit, I couldn't bring myself to try it on. Who knows how many other girls had already put it on their bodies. *What if they were sick and blew their nose on the outfit? What if they were afflicted with some foul body odor and left their stench upon the shirt?* Even if they weren't, surely they weren't clean enough. To be properly clean, you need to take a three-hour shower, and

I am quite sure they didn't. I won't even go into the horror of trying on a bathing suit. Fortunately that wasn't a necessity, as I am not much of a beach bunny—a good thing for sunbathers all over, as the mere sight of my pearly white skin in a tiny suit would inevitably blind anyone on the beach. No need to send thank-you letters. But returning to the horror that is the mall, trying on any clothes was clearly out of the question. I opt now for online shopping.

Laundry also fell into my circle of cleanliness. One day, like a flash of insight, I realized I had been doing my laundry all wrong. How come I didn't see this before? Yes, I had made sure I was thoroughly clean every time I stepped out of the shower, but I completely forgot to factor in the clothes I would put on afterward. Washing clothing once was simply not enough to get my clothes clean. All clothing should be washed at least three times, except for underwear and socks, which should be thrown way after one use since they are contaminated beyond repair. Thank goodness for dry cleaning, as by the theory ignorance is bliss, I could assume that anything I sent over there would be properly cleaned without the suffocating stress of doing it myself. I think for OCD sufferers, it is better to be in the dark. If I don't know something is dirty, then I can't obsess over its radius of contamination.

OCD is very devastating on one's wardrobe. Half of my clothes I tossed out because I thought they were too dirty to be saved. The other half were becoming faded and holey, as I was convinced that everything had to be washed three times in order to rid it of any contamination. A lot of good clothes died that year. I wish I could say I was aware of the insanity of my actions at the time, but sadly I felt everything I did was completely logical. I was more shocked that I didn't realize how truly dirty my clothes were sooner.

<u>Emily's Helpful Tips</u>
<u>OCD Packing Ritual</u>

If I planned on having a good trip, it was essential I packed properly. It was a very ritualized process that could take up to a couple of hours. Here are the basic guidelines I had to follow.

1. First, begin with the sniffing of the luggage. Every inch, inside and out, of each bag must be thoroughly sniffed to make sure no

foul odor has attached to it. If no odor is found, continue to step 2. If I find a bad odor, however, the luggage must be immediately thrown away.
2. Next, wash my hands in strict accordance with my handwashing ritual (see Chapter 8) to ensure they are clean enough to handle my clean clothes. It is very important that my hands only touched the clothes, as everything else, especially doorknobs, is dirty. Paper towels are used to touch anything else. If I slip up, I must start the ritual all over again.
3. Everything from clothes to deodorant must be packed in individual ziplock plastic bags and sometimes even double-bagged for extra safety.
4. Carefully pack the plastic bags in the luggage, making sure clothes are packed in the bag with clothes and toiletries are packed in the bag with toiletries.

CHAPTER SIXTEEN
Momma is a Hoarder

"Less is more."
Robert Browning

A hoarder is the eternal foe of an OCD clean freak. How the two can be categorized under the same disorder is simply unfathomable to me. If obsessive cleanliness is the child of OCD, then hoarding is its demon spawn. They are in complete opposition to one another, and two people suffering from them should never live in the same house. Yet, in an ironic twist of fate, such an absurdity happened. I am, of course, the obsessive clean freak. The compulsive hoarder with which I share a home is my mother. She, however, is buried in denial, literally. Yet she continuously berates me about my OCD flaws.

My mother has always had traits of a hoarder, keeping such unimportant items as newspapers, magazines, bags, and mail. However, it has only become severe within the last ten years. She is afraid to throw anything away because she never knows when she might need it. An understandable feeling, but as with all OCD actions, it is just taken to the extreme.

The piles of junk my mother kept (aka the pile of evil, which it shall now be called) was once only confined to her bedroom. I had tried to clean it up on a few occasions prior, but it always piled back up. If you can visualize that scene in *Star Wars* where Luke, Leia, and Han were trapped in the trash compactor, then you have a good idea what my mother's bedroom looks and smells like. I have since decided the task is just too big. At this point, I'm convinced it is a biohazard and needs government intervention. I genuinely fear an avalanche, which would bury my cats.

We have tried to prevent her hoarding from entering the communal areas, but we have yet to be successful. What began in her bedroom, as an isolated incident, has since spilled over into the kitchen, dining room, and part of the living room. I have to be vigilant to keep it from spreading any more, as if left to her own devices, she would undoubtedly fill up the entire apartment. I find it best to just avoid those areas. If I want a nice cooked meal, then I have to get take out, as it is impossible and horribly unsanitary to try to cook in that kitchen.

As unpleasant as living with a hoarder can be, I was able to handle it until 2005 when my own OCD entered its worst stage. Being an OCD clean freak and not being able to live in a clean environment was very destructive to my mental stability. I was often so overwhelmed by the mess around me that I would lock myself in the bathroom and cry. My mind was so overrun with obsessive thoughts cataloging the filth around me that I was virtually catatonic at times. My mom could see the degradation of my mental and physical health, yet she did nothing. She didn't think she had a problem, and she resented the fact that we were asking her to throw her own stuff away. She refused to clean it up and gave me and my dad the evil eye to make sure we didn't dare try on our own. No doubt, you may be wondering why I didn't just move out. It certainly would have solved the problem. But it just wasn't an option at the time. I was too ill to work, so I didn't have the money. My dad was the only earner in the family, and it would have been unfair and overly taxing on him to make him pay for two apartments. And so what was I to do? I was fighting my own physical and mental ailments, and I was trapped in an environment that was actively impeding my struggle. So I did it. I decided to clean the house. I took the opportunity to tackle my mom's three hoarding zones: the kitchen, dining room, and master bedroom while she went on a week-long trip with my Grandma Delaney. That week in 2005, I was left with no choice but to try to sort through some of her things, as the dining room had become impossible to navigate along with emitting a most unpleasant odor. Only then did I see the depths of her hoarding. Within the boxes and bags stacked to the ceiling, I discovered the most random of things. At least a hundred complimentary hotel bathroom amenities (soaps, shampoos, conditioners, etc.) were scattered amongst her things. Napkins everywhere from Disney World to the local Krispy Kreme littered every container. Old medicine bottles, used sunscreen, and unimportant scraps of paper were randomly thrown in with expensive jewelry and important paperwork. Many boxes were water damaged due to some flooding we had years earlier and were now covered in black mold. It was a toxic mess. The most horrifying of all finds, however, were the many items, such as the picnic cooler and my precious high school diploma that she had taken and hoarded away, which were drenched in cat urine and spray that she knowingly kept, unable to throw them away. A few of my cats liked to spray throughout the house. It smelled like I was living in a public restroom! Most disturbing of all is when I discovered that the couch I had been sleeping on had been sprayed. I had been sleeping in cat urine! Oh, the absolute, indescribable horror of it all! You can only imagine, the obsessive clean freak that I was, how long it took me to wash my hands after touching that. My usual ritual was nowhere near sufficient. Seeing and having to clean that disgusting mess really made me red in the face, but I reminded myself that she was suffering from an uncontrollable disorder just as I was. It wasn't her fault. Though admittedly out of the two, my OCD was more sanitary and better for the environment: trying to make the world clean one human at a time.

To my dismay it took me days to clean only 70 percent of the dining room, even though I worked more than eight hours each day. I worked hard on the kitchen, but it was a mess. To say that the kitchen was merely disgusting in no way describes the toxic mess that permeated every orifice in that room. Dishes covered in discarded food mingled freely with cat food dishes covered in uneaten food and strands of hair, which were left soaking together for days at a time, emitting an odor that was anything but appetizing and drawing out a colony of ants from who knows where. Open containers of every type of food from peanut butter to cream cheese often littered the stove. The kitchen table, long ago foregone as an eating surface, was buried in old newspapers, unopened mail, and random scraps of paper my mom deemed too important to toss away. The mere sight and smell of it disgusted me let alone the idea of actually cooking in there. My mom tries little to discipline the cats, letting them climb on every surface in the kitchen, rarely wiping any of these cooking and eating surfaces with disinfectants. I used to try to clean up after her, but as she refused to change her behavior, it just became pointless, as she would dirty it back up in less time than it took to clean it. Cleaning up after her just became a full-time job. I opted instead to eat out or buy food that didn't need to be cooked, as I found it more sanitary than trying to cook in the kitchen. I also used plasticware to avoid the inevitable pile-up of dishes in the sink. Not the most environmentally friendly thing to do, but in fairness, I only took a shower once a month. When my mom returned home, she was absolutely livid.

How dare I go through her things! How dare I throw out her personal possessions! Only after I explained what exactly I threw away did she calm down, though she was clearly nervous to leave the house for more than a day again. Eventually she went on another trip, and I decided to tackle the rest of the kitchen and bedroom. Though ordered to stay out, it had to be done, if only to create a pathway for my dad to get to the bed.

Despite my valiant effort, not long after I cleaned the dining room and the kitchen, the horror of bags and boxes returned. How could that possibly happen? I threw out at least ten full trash bags of useless junk. Where did this new pile come from? And that's when I discovered it. Hoarders don't just save stuff; they constantly try to acquire new stuff, which is probably why the disorder is usually accompanied by compulsive buying. No matter how well I organized and cleaned the room, the useless junk of the world would always pile back up. I was living in an OCD clean freak's nightmare! My mom collected, or rather hoarded, many types of things. She regularly buys yards of fabric, though she already has numerous piles of pieces that she has yet to use. Of all things she had to collect, antiques were her favorite and in my opinion the worst, as by their very nature they are dirty. Our apartment is a virtual antique store containing everything from Civil War sewing machines and rocking chairs to a portable antique toilet, which she carried in her car for a week, showing it off to everyone, including the cute boy I was smitten with. Embarrassing childhood moment—check!

Everything piled back up in my mom's room too despite all my cleaning. Her room, the seed from which her hoarding spread, is barely navigable even today. Two small trails existed, allowing my parents to reach the bed. You would be shocked to discover that I cleaned part of her room only a few months ago. At one point my dad couldn't even get to the bed. Her room was so covered in dust and mold that I became physically ill just trying to clean it. If I choose to clean it again, I will need a gas mask.

My mother was buried deep in denial. No matter how much I pleaded with her to get help for her own health and my dwindling sanity, she still refused to accept that she had a problem. I would think that as a sufferer myself I would be able to get through to her, but to my distress, I was preaching to deaf ears. I always knew I had problems. I knew I was suffering from OCD and depression, but I was too embarrassed and ashamed to admit it, as I thought they were conditions of weakness. Even after being educated on them, I was still afraid of the stigma that hung over them. But when I had to quit graduate school in 2005 and returned home to lead a secluded, paranoid half-life, I realized I needed help. More than that, I wanted help. I wanted my life back. That is the paradox of self-destruction; in the end, the person has to want to get better. And clearly my mom isn't there yet.

After what you have just read, you may not have the most favorable opinion of my mom. But you must understand that it is not her. It is her disorder. Like an improperly wired television that produces a distorted picture, the improper wiring in her brain is giving her a distorted view of the world. One thing that you must understand about a hoarder is that they will never clean up their mess. Even living in complete squalor, they don't think they have a problem. Trust me, no amount of rational discussions, blow-out quarrels, or tearful pleading will convince them otherwise. But what was most harmful was the destructive effect it had on my family. My mom's hoarding was tearing our family apart. How could she care more about her things than she did about me and my dad? What was worse was her deafening denial in which she continually asserted that she had no problems that needed fixing, and rather I was the one with the problem. She continually hurled passive-aggressive comments at me, scolding my OCD behavior. What is different about an OCD hoarder as opposed to some other types of OCD is that to the outside world they appear perfectly normal. Once they step outside of their homes, they are just like anyone else. They are able to socialize with friends and hold steady jobs whereas my OCD is carried with me outside of the home.

Emily's Helpful Tips
How to Live with a Hoarder

It is hard being a hoarder, and it is hard living with a hoarder. I don't resent my mom and her problems; she is just as sick as me. It is just hard for two polar opposites of OCD to live in the same house. Here are a few tips I picked up along the way.

1. They will never clean up, so if you want to live in a clutter-free house, you have to be the one to do the cleaning. But be

respectful. Only throw out blatant examples of trash, and attempt to organize the rest. Items you might need: trash bags, broom, cleaning wipes, vacuum, gas mask, hazmat suit, and bulldozer.
- Getting angry with them doesn't help nor, for that matter, do reasonable discussions. Advising them to seek help is the best option.
- Don't let them do the grocery shopping, as they tend to buy in bulk…seriously "I just bought a bomb shelter" bulk!

CHAPTER SEVENTEEN
Narcotics

"O God, that men should put an enemy in their mouths to steal away their brains!"
William Shakespeare, Othello

One troubling fact about having OCD is that it may lend itself to substance abuse problems. Growing up I was never tempted to use drugs or drink alcohol. I didn't want to take anything that would dull the sharpness of my mind nor did I like the idea of losing control of my actions. Ironic that I would later develop OCD, as that is the epitome of not being in control. Yet, in spite of my fervent anti-drug policy, in late 2006 and early 2007, I found myself in love with Demerol. Yes, I admit it. I love Demerol. It is a lovely, beautiful drug that I fantasize about when it is not around. It makes me very happy.

Frankly, I blame my kidney stones. After having three attacks, the first one being in 1999, the doctor gave me a prescription of Demerol to suppress the pain of the attacks so I would not have to go to the ER each time—a godsend considering how much I despise going to the ER. Prior to 2006, I only took them during my attacks, which generally occurred at least twice a year. I never had a desire to take it for any other reason. Then, while having an unbearably severe panic attack which none of my current medication could calm down, I tried a Demerol. Thus, I made my first mistake. For a few sweet hours, I was drawn out of that alternate reality of maddening fear to a place of pure, seemingly endless bliss. But sadly it wasn't endless. By the next morning, I was once again overcome by the deafening chaos of OCD and the unbearable weight of depression. Yet now that I realized a pill existed that cured all my problems, I wanted to take it all the time. Unlike all the antidepressants that I had taken up to that point, it was the only pill that gave me any relief of my symptoms. For the first time in a long time, my mind was clear and calm. But I only had a two-week supply of Demerol left, and when that ran out, hell would once again descend upon me undoubtedly with a far greater fury. All reason would suggest not taking any more, but I did not care to listen to reason. I only cared about remaining in that happy, peaceful place. I would deal with the consequences later.

When those blissful two weeks ended, I was right back to where I started. Fortunately, or rather unfortunately, my prescription was almost out-of-date, so I casually requested more from my doctor. Since prior scans still showed numerous kidney stones and I had no history of drug abuse, I got more without any hesitation. To my dismay, I was only given ten this time. Knowing I had a very limited supply, I convinced myself I would only take one in my most dire hours—a noble idea I was certain I could obey. But I couldn't stop thinking about how my salvation was in the house. Just twenty feet away lay my only deliverance from the hell I was trapped in. Why should I deny myself the normalcy and happiness that others so freely have? Why should I condemn myself to this insipid insanity? So I took it. For another blissful week, I rejoined the human race, talking to friends, going to the movies, basically living some semblance of a life. But that week ended far too soon, and, as before, my symptoms wrapped themselves around me like a large boa constrictor, cutting off my circulation and eliminating all thought. I desperately wanted more pills, but this time I had no easy way to get them.

Of course red flags began to pop up in my head. Frankly, I didn't care. I knew it was wrong to take a narcotic daily, but it was the only pill that helped me. Unlike people who use drugs to get high, I was using drugs just to feel normal. And frankly it had a heck of a lot less side effects than any of the SSRIs that had previously been stuffed down my throat. At my next doctor's visit I told her about the whole situation. I genuinely believed my powers of persuasion would convince the doctor to give me more. I calmly explained to the doctor the logic behind taking Demerol daily. She, of course, combated with their addictive tendencies. Really? Demerol's addictive tendencies! What of all those SSRIs? Every one produced a withdrawal worthy of any opiate. I had such severe vertigo after stopping Luvox that I couldn't ride in a car without taking a Phenergan to stop from vomiting. She, of course, said that was completely different. I, however, remain unconvinced. Sadly, my valiant attempts at logic were less than convincing, as were, for that matter, my heartfelt pleas to be freed from the prison I was in. Her only suggestion was to try another SSRI. What was I to do now? Regardless of the concerns she voiced, all I could think about was getting more

Demerol. I couldn't continue living on the verge of insanity! Then I remembered the original reason for which I needed the pill; the kidney stone attacks were still a problem. She hesitantly agreed to leave an emergency prescription for Demerol in my file. If I had an attack, I could come down to the office and pick it up. I lasted for a couple of weeks before I was forced to cash in that prescription. I had a kidney stone attack—seriously an actual attack, though part of me does wonder if my strong desire for Demerol actually caused it. Two did the trick, but apparently I can't take just two. As long as it was in my house, I couldn't stop thinking about it. It became another obsessive thought. When can I take another Demerol? Where did my dad hide it? Needless to say, one week later all the pills were gone again. Clearly, until I am better I cannot be within ten feet of Demerol.

With my key to Shangri La taken from me, I turned my hopes to alcohol. Television always portrays drinking alcohol as relaxing—a way to escape my daily troubles. How low I had fallen to look to television for my salvation? I had only had two sips of alcohol prior to 2007, and neither was very memorable. I wish I could say the same for the three unholy wines I ingested one very stressful night. Why on earth Jesus would turn water into such a vile liquid is beyond my comprehension. At least it quelled any future urges to have more sips—a fortunate thing, I suppose. I miss Demerol…

Basically considering I never drank or did drugs in high school, I am the last person you would expect to praise narcotics as a potential treatment for severe OCD and depression. It is not as if I am the only one who feels this way. Low-level narcotics have been used to treat people with depression in specific cases. In fact, narcotics were an approved treatment until the 1950s. Now, I am not suggesting that anyone who is depressed should run out a get a prescription for morphine. Not at all. Most people will find relief from typical antidepressants. However, for specific cases, in which standard drugs don't work, I think the medical industry should consider using low-level narcotics as a treatment. In all honesty, in my most severe moments, those drugs saved me. They brought me out of the darkness, lifted my spirits, and gave me hope that there are drugs out there that would make me feel like myself again. I maintain that small doses of certain narcotics should be used to treat OCD, depression, and anxiety in cases where the usual antidepressant medications have failed. Since I have yet to find a doctor in my area who shares that opinion, however, I am forced to continue trying the approved medications.

CHAPTER EIGHTEEN
The Dark Hours

"Hell is oneself, hell is alone, the other figures in it merely projections. There is nothing to escape from and nothing to escape to. One is always alone."
T. S. Eliot

From 2006 to early 2007 marked the hardest times I have been through so far in my life. Since I developed these mental disorders, I have become two people: the happy, healthy girl I portray to the world and the miserable, sickly girl I only reveal to my family and closest friends. Long before I was diagnosed, I knew something was wrong. My thoughts and behaviors were clearly different than those of others. But I hid the problems partially out of shame and embarrassment, partially because I didn't want to be judged or pitied, and partially because I was afraid others would not want to hang out with me. I was deeply depressed inside, but I couldn't show others. I couldn't let them know how I truly felt. So I hid my illnesses, always putting on a happy face and joking my way through conversations. But over time as my conditions worsened, my feelings and actions were harder to hide. I was tired of lying to others to cover up my strange behavior. It was too hard to act OK when every part of me was crying out in pain. I began decreasing my interactions with others, rarely going out, talking on the phone less, and brushing off attempts at communication with many of my friends. Everything I was going through was so personal and difficult that I just didn't want that many people to know. And since it was so consuming, it was really all I had to talk about. So instead of lying about how I felt, I just chose not to contact others, further isolating myself from life.

In the beginning, the obsessive thoughts were few and far between, like one or two voices talking in my head. *Did I lock the door? I thought I checked, but maybe I didn't look closely enough. Did I wash my hands good enough? If I didn't then I will contaminate the entire house. Did I turn everything off? What if I didn't? The whole house could catch fire.* But by 2006, it seemed as if hundreds of voices were screaming in my head. I could no longer distinguish any individual obsessive thoughts; it was all just chaos. Obsessive, paranoid, anxious thoughts were flooding my mind every minute. I couldn't think. I couldn't breathe. I felt like I was drowning. And the most frightening part of all was that I knew no one could save me. The only way I can describe it is imagine if you suddenly developed the ability to hear other people's thoughts and you couldn't tune them out. First you can only hear the thoughts of those nearest to you. Irritating and annoying but not too distracting. Then you start to hear the voices from the houses nearest to you as well. It is rather distracting now, and you have trouble focusing on what you doing. Finally you hear the thoughts of everyone in the neighborhood, and they are drowning out your own. You can't focus. You can't think. You can't work. All you want to do is crawl into a dark closet and sit with your hands over your ears. But you can't block out the sound because it is coming from inside your head. That is what severe OCD feels like, at least to me—a maddening flood of voices that I can't drown out. Never wavering, never sleeping, always screaming, and driving me to the edge of insanity. I can't distinguish what they are saying, but I have a good idea…*check to see if the door is locked, wash your hands, clean up the contamination.* So I continued performing my usual rituals, adding more and more in the hopes that it would quiet the noise in my head, but it didn't. I was going insane, and it frightened me to my very core. The real world fell away, leaving me in an alternate world, a disturbing, warped version of reality from which I feared I would never escape.

My world was now confined to the living room couch. I was plagued by constant fatigue, worn down by years of anxiety, my muscles too weak to move. Any small outing would drain me so fully that I would sleep for the next few days. I had such a high anxiety level all the time that the slightest problem would send me straight into a panic attack—now a daily occurrence. My pulse racing, my heart throbbing in my chest, my mind racing on a maddening track, I was losing what was a left of my mind. I tried so many ways to naturally bring down my stress level. I tried breathing deeply. I tried meditating. I tried to take my mind off it by watching a movie. Nothing worked. The anxiety would continue to rise. The OCD would spike. And the depression would grip ever tighter. It was a vicious cycle, all three disorders feeding off each other, creating a maddening Bermuda Triangle in my mind. Only unlike the real triangle, there was no way out.

By Emily Watson

These aren't conditions that come and go. They are with me all the time. Every minute of every day is a battle. There is never a moment of relief, never a moment to rest and recharge. Even in sleep I am plagued by the nightmares of the issues that haunt me during the day. Most days I long for death if only to have relief. The battle just becomes too tiring. No one can help me. No one can fight for me. Regardless of how much support I have or how many people are around me, I am in this battle alone. The battle is in my head, so only I can fight it. I had tried so many things to help me at this point and nothing was working. I needed it to stop. I needed it to stop right now. I was on the edge and if something didn't help me soon, I was going to jump.

Poetic Musings

Unseen
by Emily Watson

In the silence of the day
A presence haunts, I cannot say
Burdened by this unseen foe
I fear to stay, I fear to go

In the shadow and in the light
In the morning and in the night

Its presence never seems to fade
This darkness that I can't evade
The specter haunts my very soul
And soon this fiend will take its toll

For weary has become my day
Since fight no longer keeps at bay
That which oppresses and resides
To haunt me till the day I die.

PART IV: GETTING HELP

"Human misery must somewhere have a stop; there is no wind that always blows a storm."
Euripides

CHAPTER NINETEEN
Therapists

"Doctors are men who prescribe medicines of which they know little, to cure diseases of which they know less, in human beings of whom they know nothing."
Voltaire

    The decision to get help is a pretty hard one. I spent the majority the past six years in denial, resisting treatment. Once I realized I needed help, it was a long road before I started seeing any improvement. It got seriously bad before it ever got better. By this point, I have to admit, I was becoming disillusioned with the medical profession. Since 1999, I had spent more time in doctors' offices and hospitals than I had my first eighteen years of life, and frankly, I was disappointed with the results. It took years before I was ever properly diagnosed, my symptoms at times being considered a sign of lupus, thyroid problems, and my favorite, my imagination. For a doctor, or anyone for that matter, to suggest I was feigning an illness was beyond my comprehension. How could someone accuse me of such a thing? I was a good kid. I was a straight-A student. I had lots of friends. I had good parents. I was poised to have a wonderful future. Why would I want to destroy that? Why would I want to be sick? Just because the doctors couldn't figure out what was wrong with me, they assumed I was making it up. Needless to say I spent the first few years of my disorders trying different doctors in the hopes of finding a good one but too often being met with arrogance and apathy. A few diagnoses were made during this time, though, regarding my bladder/kidney problems. I was diagnosed with kidney stones, urinary tract infections (UTI), and interstitial cystitis (IC), but unfortunately it would take time to narrow down my food intolerances.

    In 2004, none of my mental problems had been diagnosed. My symptoms in correlation with various bladder and skin problems were seen as a single illness probably immunologic in origin. I temporarily parted ways with my primary care physician, Dr. Prince, and started seeing in internist at a hospital two hours away in Gainesville, FL. Dr. X, as she will be referred to, was cold and clinical lifted only by her comely appearance. I was not a human being; I was a meager patient with an undiagnosed illness. She initially thought I might have lupus, but that was eventually proven otherwise. So was every other major disorder until only mental illness remained. My bladder and skin problems were problems unto themselves and not related to the grocery list of symptoms that belayed my inner mind. She determined I had a severe case of OCD and a serious bout of depression. She insisted I see a psychiatrist and take a lot of pills, or else I wasn't going to get better. Her arrogance and her condescending tone were notable in every conversation I had. My years of hard work in physics were meaningless before her Harvard-lined halls of her education. What I thought and how I felt didn't matter. I acquiesced and began seeing a psychiatrist, Dr. Y, who she recommended in mid-2004. I ceased seeing Dr. X at the end of 2004, after having grown tired of her sterile condescension and cold demeanor.

I saw Dr. Y on and off for two years, during which I was prescribed a number of different antidepressant medications. In my opinion, it was a waste of the $200 I had to pay for each hour-long session. I felt patronized and belittled each time, as Dr. Y treated me like I knew nothing of medicine or my own mind. It was a feeling I didn't much like nor was used to. All my life, especially in college, when I was dedicating my life to a major in physics, I was treated with respect for my excellent work ethic and high academic achievement. Yet now I was being treated like an ignorant child. I may not have had a medical degree, but I was not stupid. Years of science classes gave me a very logical way of thinking. And even though my mind was messed up, I was still aware of the world and myself. I know myself better than anyone else. I know how I feel and what I am going through better than any doctor. Regardless of any medical degree, we are each the best judge of ourselves—a fact that many doctors seem to have forgotten.

From the minute I walked into each session, I felt judged. Every word I said was being broken down and analyzed according to the generic definitions in psychology books. If I mentioned a simple fight I had with my mother, it got turned into my mother and I have a tumultuous relationship. When I recounted that I don't date much because I generally know fairly quickly if someone is right for me, it became I was afraid to get hurt. When I said that I was unhappy in my major and wanted to switch careers, the psychiatrist told me that I hadn't given it

By Emily Watson

enough of a chance to which I assertively reminded her that I spent four years earning my degree and was involved in active research for five years. Yet she still thought I was being presumptuous. I may have felt the need to randomly turn a light on and off repeatedly, but that didn't mean I was not aware of my likes and dislikes. Many of my interests were the same as they were before my brain began having problems. The examples are endless, but needless to say, every time I left her office I felt frustrated, angry, and definitely not better. Bitter, yeah just a bit. But don't mistake my own experiences with a general disapproval of the entire profession. In fact, I have had two friends, one with ADD and the other with seasonal depression disorder, who found great relief in seeing a psychiatrist. My point is simply that seeing a psychiatrist was not the right course of action for me. Whether it was due to her failing or my own stubbornness is debatable.

At the end of 2006, I went back to Dr. Prince solely and continued my treatment with her. She was nothing like the other doctors. Amazonian in height, she bore the demeanor of an aggressive warrior and a gentle healer. Her office had the imprint of small-town doctors gone by—cozy and warm. Out of all the doctors I had seen in recent years, she was the first who I thought was really invested in me getting better. I genuinely believe that she is trying everything in her power to get me better. But more than that, she saw me for who I am: an intelligent young woman. She understood that though I was suffering from these mental disorders, I was still the same girl who got a BS in physics, the same smart girl I always was. She understood that I was the best judge of what was going on with me. Never patronizing, always understanding, she treated me like a normal young woman. She respected my opinions, and that was perhaps the best part. I know I'm sick, and I know I'm not in complete control of my mind, but a large part of my mind still works, and I still have valid opinions. And Dr. Prince always understood that. What would come next is a dizzying array of medications, as we tried to find one that would work. But first I tried an alternate path.

PART V: UNCOMMON HELP

"There is surely a piece of divinity within us, something that was before the elements and owes no homage unto the sun."
Sir Thomas Browne

CHAPTER TWENTY
Musings with a Medium

"All that we see is but a dream within a dream."
Edgar Allan Poe

    I met Dorothea Delgado in the November of 2005 when I attended her medium workshop in Key West, Florida. I was hesitant to go at first as I was afraid, irony aside, that there might be some crazy people there. After all the only people who would be attending such an event would be ones claiming to have psychic powers—a remark usually only an insane person would say. But the moment I saw her, I could tell she was a kindred spirit, a non-crazy kindred spirit. In a stark room best suited for a PowerPoint presentation, she radiated kindness and love. Though her physical appearance clearly mirrored Florida—wavy, long blond hair and sun-kissed skin—she resonated with the aura of a wizened soul. I hesitantly approached her and extended my hand. Her touch was warm and welcoming. She studied me over and said, "You're not drinking enough water." How could she possibly know that? I knew I didn't drink enough, but I didn't show any outward signs of dehydration. I even had a bottle of water with me during class. Yet somehow she knew. Of course, what else did I expect; I was at workshop for mediums.

    Comfortable that I had met a genuine medium, I proceeded to ask her about my disorders. Her answer was short and to the point: mental illnesses are due to a condition called soul-fracturing. According to her philosophy, we have each lived many previous lives—some on the earthly plane and some in higher realms. Our souls go through cycles of reincarnation, cycles of rebirth. What happens to us in those past lives is carried with each of us in into the next life. If we lived happy, healthy lives, then that positive energy flows through us to the next life. If our lives were unhappy, plagued by tragedy and traumatic experiences, then our soul would become fractured. Our past traumas would manifest in this life as such conditions as bipolar, OCD, and anxiety.

    A past life? I had a past life? The idea was wholly unfamiliar to me. Could such a thing be possible? Somehow I lived before and that life is now affecting this life? That is unimaginable. But what if it is true?

What happened to me in my past life? What century did I live in? Did I live in ancient Rome? Did I study with Plato on the steps of Greece? Did I live in England during Arthurian times? Did I live during the heyday of Egypt? Who was I? Was I a heroic warrior or a simple maiden? Was I a tragically doomed queen, or was I a lowly peasant? I had to admit, I was fascinated. If I could learn about these past life traumas, could I overcome my mental disorders? Maybe I wouldn't have to take pills anymore. The possibilities were endless.

Dorothea suggested that I see a past life regression therapist. They are medically trained psychiatrists who involve past life regression in their healing. Brian Weiss perfected the technique, but many therapists across the nation are certified in it. How come I never heard about this before? It may be outside mainstream medicine, but that doesn't make it any less true. Dorothea led me to a woman named Pamela A. Strother. She was a friend of hers and only practiced a few miles away. Despite my curiosity, I was very hesitant to sit down with her. After all, the process involved me being hypnotized. I would have to be in a hypnotic trance in order to recall my past lives, as that knowledge is stored in the subconscious. Besides, I wasn't sure I really wanted to know what my past lives were like. If they were really that traumatizing, then maybe they shouldn't be recalled. What if I remember some traumatic death that I can't deal with in the here and now? But eventually my curiosity won out.

Her office was much like my first psychiatrist's office, whitewashed walls, untidy desk, and a long white leather sofa. I don't know what I was expecting, maybe a chakra poster or a fairy wand, but it reveled in its plainness. Getting hypnotized was an arduous process, much to my surprise. There were no swinging pocket watches or mesmerizing photographs, only her voice—her soft, deliberate voice attempting to calm my restless spirit. I had to concentrate on the energy flowing through my head and out beneath my feet, my chakras aligning as my body sank deeper and deeper into complete relaxation. We had to perform this process numerous times before I could finally settle into the quiet, peaceful valley in my mind. Then there I was, wading through knee-high flowers in the meadow of my psyche. Gentle breezes kissed my face as I spun around in joyous celebration. Complete and peaceful rest. But I could not remain there, however much I wanted to. I needed to find my past lives. I thought of them, and suddenly there they were before me. Three giant TV screens set on the apex of the hill. They were images, frozen into being. I slowly scanned the screens. The far left portrayed the image of a young girl, about thirteen years old, dressed in a long grayish-blue dress with an apron and matching bonnet. Her golden hair peaked out from beneath the hat in two long braids pointing down to the water pale she carried. Before her sat an olden town—a preindustrial shipping village lined with cobbled roads beneath a stormy sky. Who was she? Was she me? I didn't know. I could only stare at the picture; I couldn't enter it. Frustrated, I turned my focus to the center picture. A young girl, perhaps sixteen or seventeen sat Indian style beneath a tree-filled expanse. Her clothing bespoke of an ancient Indian tribe from premodern times. Her long black hair flowed gently down her side, a beaded picture sewn on her leather-worn chest. But despite my valiant effort, I could not enter this picture either. I turned to the last picture, hoping I would find some answers in that. This frame had two people in it, a male and female child about six years old. They were both dressed in their finest Sunday clothes, bright white in the noonday sun. The little girl had a brilliant red kite in her hands, and the two were laughing as they frolicked outside their Edwardian palatial home. But to my great sadness, I couldn't enter this picture either. I could hear distant noises, the footsteps of horses and carriages echoing from inside each frame, but I could never press play.

    I was deeply disappointed that I couldn't explore any of my past lives. If they were causing my current problems, then how could I fix them if I can't find out what happened? Fortunately, I had a one-on-one session with Dorothea coming up. I asked her if she sensed anything about my past lives. She gazed at me, her eyes penetrating right into my soul, and said that I was severely abandoned in one of my previous lives. Abandoned? What like an infant left to die? The idea seemed somehow preposterous. Feeling no resonance to the story, I tossed it aside and continued with my session. Two days later something interesting happened. Her words struck a hidden chord inside me, revealing a deep-seated fear that rested in my subconscious. I was afraid of being abandoned; I was afraid of being alone, especially now when I was broken, when I couldn't survive on my own, when I needed someone to take care of me. Could she be right? She said it was best I didn't remember any more lives as they were too traumatic.

I don't know whether or not our souls reincarnate. Perhaps I have lived before. Perhaps I was seriously abandoned. Perhaps the traumas of my former lives have left deep scars upon my soul, fracturing it to an unhealthy degree. I don't know. For now, at least, I choose to believe that the next stop after this life is heaven, not another life. I am tired now, so very tired; the thought of another hard life is too much to bear. Everything I learned over those few weeks still remains with me. The ideas are evocative, but I have yet to come to a conclusion.

CHAPTER TWENTY-ONE
Meditation

"Men occasionally stumble over the truth, but most of them pick themselves up and hurry off as if nothing ever happened."
Sir Winston Churchill

    I have always wanted to be adept at meditation. Movies always portray meditation as the way to higher spiritual knowledge—the ancient warrior who uses it to learn martial arts, the wise man who uses it to perceive the future, the lone hero who uses it to obtain supernatural powers. To truly know yourself, you must spend hours meditating on your own being. To truly understand the world, you must sit in complete repose, pondering the unspoken word. How I envy that knowledge, that connection to some higher realm. If I could, I would sit in quiet meditation for hours on end, expanding my mind and harnessing my own inner power. Perhaps I could develop some latent supernatural power. Maybe I could become a medium, helping people connect with a lost loved one. Maybe I could become a great warrior. I have always yearned to be a great warrior, like the ancient Samurai or the modern-day monks of China's Shaolin Temple. I have longed to wield a sword with such grace and precision that passersby would be transfixed in my aura—the smooth silver blades slicing through the air in the rhythmic pattern of a master's hand. To live by one rule and one rule alone: protect the innocent, the weak, and those who cannot protect themselves. Fight for justice. Fight for truth. Fight the fight that no one else can fight. But the sword-yielding warriors of yesterday have no place in today's modern world. The sword has been replaced by guns and bombs. I tried to walk that path as best as I could. I took up fencing during my college years. The long steel blade felt at home in the palm of my hand, like it had always been there, like it had been waiting for me to find it. Every slice, every stab of the blade felt more natural than a pencil in my hand. But it wasn't meant to be; my body saw to that. Only a few lessons in, I had to acquiesce to defeat, the OCD taking all of my energy and my will to go on.
    I have been told that meditation is good in helping depression and anxiety. During my foray into alternative medicine, after having been

taught a few different ways to meditate, I did try it on numerous occasions. I calmly sat Indian style on my carpeted floor, back straight, palms up, and cleared my mind. Breathe in. Breathe out. Then the obsessive thoughts flowed in. *My room smells funny. Did I get something on my shoes? Oh no, where did I walk? Is it on my carpet?* Stop it, concentrate. Breathe out. *Did I lock the door? What if I didn't? Someone could break in and kill me!* Breathe in. *Did I wash my hands good enough? What if I didn't? I could contaminate the entire house.* These relentless thoughts kept disturbing my breathing exercises. Needless to say, OCD and meditation do not mix. The constant influx of intrusive and obsessive thoughts is not conducive to creating a quiet, serene place. I just got very frustrated.

Despite my hopes and dreams, meditation is not possible for me—at least not now. Undoubtedly, a bipolar person could sit in quiet repose, but it is impossible for someone with OCD. Believe me, I have tried. I cannot sit in absolute silence and focus on a single thought because hundreds of thoughts are flying through my mind at any minute of the day. Despite my ardent efforts to focus on anything, the obsessive thoughts push right through. Does that mean I will never find inner peace? Is it just a sign of mental weakness? I fear it so. I fear my own failings. But I have to remind myself it isn't me. It is the disorder.

Emily's Helpful Information
An OCD/Bipolar/Anxiety Person Trying to Meditate

Close your eyes. Listen to the sound of my voice.
All right, my eyes are closed, and I am listening to the sound of his voice. Listening to the sound of his voice. OK, I can do this.

Relax every part of your body beginning with your head,
All right, relax my head. Take deep breaths and relax my head. My head hurts. Did it hurt before? Just relax. I probably have a headache. I need some Advil. No, just relax. Did I lock the door? Just now, did I lock it? I can't remember. Yes, I did. No, wait, I didn't. I should go check. No, I have to relax. Relax my head. My head hurts.

<u>then your neck,</u>
Wait, I'm still on my head. I haven't relaxed my head. OK, OK, deep breaths. Relax my head then my neck. But my head still hurts. Breathe deeply. My arm hurts. What did I do to my arm? Maybe I strained it. I hope it isn't anything serious. What if it is? Just relax. The door lock. Did I lock the door? What if I didn't? What if some intruder comes in? I'm scared. I have to go check on the door. No I have to relax; I am sure I locked it. Back to my head.

<u>then your shoulders,</u>
Shoulder! No, no, no. I'm still on my head. Who can relax this fast? OK, really got to focus now, back to my head. Relax, relax, damnit.

<u>…then your knees,</u>
What? Are you kidding me? I'm still on my head. The door, the door, did I lock it? My arm pain, what is it? Relax. Relax. Relax.

<u>then your ankles. Let go of any pain. Just Relax.</u>
My ankles! My head isn't relaxed. The pain is bothering me. I can't just wish it away. My head hurts. What about the lock? Ugh, I can't remember. I can't get up and check; I have to relax. Relax. But if I don't someone could come in. Relax my head. I have a headache. I need some Advil. Just relax.

<u>Your entire body is now relaxed.</u>
What?! I am not relaxed! Stupid voice on tape!

<u>Now focus on your breathing. Breathe in deeply. One. Two. Three. Now exhale. And again.</u>
Breathing. OK, I can do this. Breathe in deeply. What's that noise? It sounds like a gentle tapping. Breathe out. Where's that noise coming from? Is someone here? Is it an animal? Breathe in. The tapping is mind-numbing. Where is it coming from?

<u>Now put your awareness a few feet above your head. Now on one side of your body. And now on the other. Be aware of any energies that are not in balance with your own body.</u>
Do what? OK, I have no idea how to do that. I'm here, I'm not there. My awareness? What? The tapping, the tapping! Oh my head hurts. Stop the tapping; it is driving me insane. Energies, what are you talking about? My energy is low, does that count? Why am I to be aware of them? What am I trying to do? I'm confused. The door isn't locked. The tapping, the infernal tapping.

CHAPTER TWENTY-TWO
Alternate Healing

"Medicine is a science of uncertainty and an art of probability."
Sir William Osler

It seemed as soon as I was diagnosed with a mental disorder, doctors and therapists began treating me as if I did not know my own mind. OCD and depression are not disorders that affect people's perceptions of reality. I always knew what was real and what wasn't. I wasn't hallucinating. My mind was still sharp and discerning. But above all else, I knew how I felt. But the doctors with which I was faced did not seem to understand or care. One went so far as to suggest that getting a boyfriend would help. It had always been my understanding, however, that if you aren't OK by yourself then you will never be OK with anyone else. That comment, absurd as it was, was the final straw. With the exception of Dr. Prince, the doctors I saw were aloof, patronizing, and ignorant. The therapist made me feel frustrated and angry. And the numerous drugs I had suffered through trying offered me no relief. It was then I washed my hands of modern medicine.

After dropping my therapist and my internist at the beginning of 2006, I was very disgruntled with modern medicine and sought out alternative treatments. My first step was to consult a medium. I always found the prospect of someone genuinely being psychic very intriguing, ironic considering I got a major in physics, which on the surface is in diametric opposition. Knowing that a lot of people out there claiming such abilities are frauds, I did some research before picking one out. As I said above, I met Dorothea Delgado in Key West. She understood me better in one session than a year with my therapist. And I genuinely felt she cared about me getting better. To my surprise, she was dead-on in her analysis of my health. She knew I was ill before I even told her—a shocking fact considering I wore a continual poker face to mask my condition and went out of my way to make sure my appearance was the picture of health. But to my surprise, she saw right though my façade, immediately zeroing in on my stress level, pointing out that even though

I was alive, I wasn't living. I was spiritually blocked. I needed to focus on getting better before I could move on with my life.

She directed me to a nutritionist, Marie Fairchild, and that, I believe, is when my healing began. Her warm spirit and genuine desire to help immediately won me over. My hour-long phone session with her every other week helped me more than any doctor and always lifted my spirits, which were desperately low. It was she who convinced me that it is not a weakness of mind to need to take medication. Coming from someone who has dedicated her life to alternate healing yet understanding that when your symptoms are severe enough medication is needed, she lifted my lingering reservations about antidepressant medication. After that I went to my general practice doctor and talked to her about giving these drugs another go. Let's just hope that the FDA doesn't discover some horrible side effect of the drugs and pull them from the market. Go ahead, laugh at my obsessive worry, but it has already happened to me once. I continued to talk to Marie biweekly and followed her nutrition guidelines to help heal my body while the pills helped to heal my mind. She always listened to how I felt without any judgment, and instead of focusing on my many flaws, she always reminded me of the good things about me, thereby teaching me to focus on the positive.

Having proper nutrition is important whether you are healthy or sick. However, if you are sick, it is particularly important because food allergies or sensitivities may be the cause of or merely a contributing factor to your problems. Marie has many examples of foods making people sick. It is a lesson I learned well when I discovered food affected my IC. Once I was diagnosed with IC, I was provided a list of potential triggers, foods and drinks, which will irritate my IC. This is no short list. After ruling out the top triggers like caffeine and tomatoes, along with a few others, I got very frustrated and stopped trying. But as fate would have it, I accidentally discovered my trigger. One day, distracted by numerous errands, I went a long time without eating. Needing a quick dose of energy, I scarfed down two peanut butter cups, my all-time favorite candy. A few hours later, before I had a chance to have a proper meal, I was overcome with my usual bladder pain. Actually, it was the first time I had pain that day. Were peanuts my trigger? That would sure explain a lot as I ate nuts and peanut butter at least once a day and everyday I was plagued by bladder pain. After testing my theory, I discovered peanuts were the culprit. Eager to stop the nagging pain, I immediately stopped eating peanuts, which was rather hard, considering I absolutely love them and they are a staple of my daily diet. Nonetheless, I did it and I haven't experienced that pain since. You have no idea the relief that comes when you are finally free from a debilitating pain. Furthermore, I discovered peanuts were not only causing my bladder pain but also my acne. Two weeks after dropping peanuts, my skin cleared right up for the first time since middle school. So if a single food can cause all of that misery, then certainly another specific food could play at least a small part in mental disorders. After all, not drinking enough water can cause depression.

 I spoke by phone to Marie for an hour every other week. She lived in San Francisco so we couldn't do an in-person session. I felt a special connection to Marie almost like we were kindred spirits. I don't know if she had that connection with all of her patients, but I like to think that our relationship was special. Those feelings aside, she helped to get my nutrition under control. Marie did a number of tests to determine if I was deficient in any vitamins and minerals, as that can play a role in mental disorders. For example, a deficiency in vitamin D can cause depression. She helped me to eat better, convincing me to lower my sugar intake and increase my protein. She taught me about nutrition and its connection to the spirit. Her calls were the highlight of my week. I so looked forward to talking to her. She understood me better than any doctor ever had. She saw right through to my soul, and she made me feel like it was beautiful. Talking to her brought some peace to my chaotic mind. She was like my guardian angel. But fate had other plans. Sadly, she passed away from cancer in 2008. I never got to say good-bye. I miss her.

CHAPTER TWENTY-THREE
Medications

"I was under medication when I made the decision not to burn the tapes."
Richard M. Nixon

Fortunately today we know much more about this oft misunderstood disorder, OCD. We know that it is a malfunction of the brain and not the result of any mental weakness, so the age-old techniques of witch burning and exorcism should no longer be prescribed by your doctor. Treatments today are far less painful, though being analyzed by a therapist for an hour made me want to stab myself in the head just to get out of there.

I have to admit, I was very hesitant to take any antidepressants. For starters, I felt I didn't need them. I was under the false impression that OCD, depression, and anxiety were mental weaknesses that could be fixed by the strength of one's own mind. I was stubborn and arrogant and had no doubt I could beat this on my own. Furthermore, I didn't like the idea of being on any drug long-term. But, begrudgingly, I eventually acquiesced—at first because the doctors were so adamant and later because I realized how much I really did need them. Since I suffer from three major medical conditions, it was very difficult to find a medication to treat all three or even just two. Not to mention I also ran into the problem that a certain pill may treat one while making the others worse. I have gone through a dizzying array of pills over the past few years.

My Medication Analysis

Medications for OCD

The OCD Foundation lists eight drugs shown to be effective in treating the symptoms of OCD: Anafranil, Effexor, and the SSRIs Lexapro, Luvox, Prozac, Zoloft, Paxil, and Celexa.

Prozac - Sadly it did not work. How wonderful it would be to get the right pill on the first try, but alas I was not so lucky. I had many more to go.

Zoloft - Ah, Zoloft, the one and only way to become a zombie without actually coming back from the dead. It completely drained me of all emotion. I found I could watch the scariest of movies without even flinching while my poor friend screamed like a banshee in the crowded theater.

Luvox - Luvox was my least favorite, and I still carry some animosity toward it. It offered little relief from my symptoms and created some rather unpleasant side effects. It dried out my body so much that my mouth was barely producing any liquid. No matter how much water I drank, I couldn't keep any moisture in my mouth. My eyes were so dry and red that eye drops offered little relief. But absolutely worst of all, my continual dry mouth caused my gums to recede. Gum recession when I was twenty-five! Really! My hair was thinning and I was covered in blotches, did I really need one more reason not to go out in public? I'm still rather miffed about that. I apologize for my moment of girly vanity.

Lexapro - Lexapro was absolutely horrible. It drastically upped my anxiety level, making me feel as if I just drank ten cups of coffee.

Effexor - How can I forget Effexor? Like the others it was simply ineffective, but the withdrawal is forever burned in my memory.

Anafranil - It didn't work.

Celexa - I never tried it.

Paxil - Unbelievably it worked. Almost all my OCD symptoms went away.

(The International OCD Foundation n.d.)

Medications for Depression

I was diagnosed with depression and anxiety before OCD, so I have also tried additional pills especially for those conditions. Webmd lists these drugs for depression.

Wellbutrin - Wellbutrin had no noticeable side effects but unfortunately nor did it have any positive effects.

Elavil - I was initially prescribed Elavil for my IC. Though Elavil is listed as a depression drug, it has an off-label use as a muscle relaxer for the bladder, in essence calming the continual bladder spasms inherent to IC. Sadly, it offered my symptoms no relief, instead producing some bladder cramping and constipation. It offered no relief for my depression, either.

Neurontin – Neurontin is actually an anticonvulsant; however, its off-label use includes the treatment of depression.

Medications for Anxiety

Webmd lists the following medications for anxiety.

Clonazepam (Klonopin) – It made me very sleepy, though not nearly as bad as Seroquel.

Xanax - I tried the anti-anxiety medication, Xanax, to use in the case of a severe panic attack. First it put me to sleep, and then it gave me sleep paralysis.

Don't get discouraged over the time it may take to find a medication that works for you. I know how frustrating it is to continually go on and off different drugs, but the relief you will feel when you find one that works is worth the wait. It is unlikely that the first drug you try will work, but considering how many are out there, you have a good chance of finding one that will. But you will get through it. Just don't be afraid to stand up for yourself. If, after an appropriate amount of time, you find the drug doesn't work or causes really unpleasant side effects, tell the doctor you want to change medications. After all the doctors I have seen over the past years, there is one thing I have learned: they are not gods. They have a vast amount of knowledge and experience, but they are not omniscient or infallible. Don't be bullied and intimidated by them. Stand up for how *you* feel and what *you* believe. In the end, you are the best judge of how you feel.

PART VI: LOOKING TO THE FUTURE

"Look not mournfully into the past. It comes not back again. Wisely improve the present. It is thine. Go forth to meet the shadowy future, without fear."
Henry Wadsworth Longfellow

CHAPTER TWENTY-FOUR
OCD in the Media

Frightened by a loose snake, Detective Adrian Monk is standing on the table in a house he is investigating.
Capt. Stottlemeyer: "I thought you were afraid of heights."

Adrian Monk: "Snakes trump heights. It goes germs, needles, milk, death, snakes, mushrooms, heights, crowds, elevators."
TV show Monk

    The television show *Monk* and the movie *Elektra* are positive representations of people suffering from OCD. *Monk* is excellent in representing those with OCD. It shows that people who suffer from this disorder are not weak idiots but often very intelligent individuals. Plus, at least for me, it helps me learn to laugh at myself. I was quite shocked to discover while watching *Elektra* that the two main heroines, Elektra and her protégée, both suffered from OCD. Though the term was never actually used in the movie, I think their actions suggest they do. We see that both of the heroines have counting rituals, a common OCD compulsion. When Elektra moves into the lake house, early in the film, we see that she needs things to be ordered or arranged in a very specific way as she places her bathroom supplies perfectly parallel to one another. Those are some examples in the media I can find of OCD.

<u>Emily's Helpful Tips</u>
<u>Top Ten Movie And Television Comedies That Lift My Mood</u>

<u>Movies</u>

1. *Galaxy Quest*
2. *Night at the Museum*
3. *Little Miss Sunshine*
4. *Blackbeard's Ghost*
5. *Three Fugitives* (Mom's favorite)

6. *Father's Day*
7. *White Christmas*
8. *Ever After*
9. *10 Things I Hate About You*
10. *She's the Man*

Television Shows

1. *The Big Bang Theory*
2. *Psych*
3. *Monk*
4. *The Nanny*
5. *Friends*
6. *Grounded for Life*
7. *Dancing with the Stars*
8. *America's Next Top Model*
9. *Wizards of Waverly Place*
10. *Restaurant Impossible*

Top Ten Dramatic/Action/Fantasy Movies and Television Shows That Lift Me Out Of Darkness And Take Me Into Another World

Movies

1. *The Lord of the Rings trilogy*
2. *The Star Wars movies*
3. *The Indiana Jones movies*
4. *The Pirates of the Caribbean movies*
5. *Harry Potter movies*
6. *Rush Hour trilogy*
7. *The Avengers*
8. *Sense and Sensibility*
9. *Field of Dreams*
10. *The Da Vinci Code*

By Emily Watson

<u>Television Shows</u>

1. *Doctor Who*
2. *Stargate SG1 and Atlantis*
3. *The West Wing*
4. *Sherlock Holmes (BBC version)*
5. *NCIS*
6. *MTV's The Challenge*
7. *Charmed*
8. *Xena: Warrior Princess*
9. *Star Trek (all)*
10. *Castle*

I also love watching bicycle races. I am a big fan of the Tour De France and the USA Pro Challenge.

CHAPTER TWENTY-FIVE
Conclusion

"What does not destroy me, makes me strong."
Friedrich Nietzsche

    I am happy to say I am doing loads better as of the end of this section of the book. I began taking Paxil in early 2007, and it has worked like absolute magic. The worst part of the OCD for me was the continuous stream of thoughts that so flooded my mind that I couldn't think. I felt like I was drowning. But about four weeks after I started the medication, the water in my mind began to part, finally giving some clarity in my mind. I could actually think again. I could write. I could do the TV crossword puzzle—not the greatest achievement, but I was ecstatic. At last I had a moment of relief. The obsessive thoughts weren't completely gone, but they had lessened by such a significant degree, and the ones that were left I had far better control of. That three-hour shower? Yeah, got that down to one hour and twenty minutes. Still quite long, but it is a huge improvement to me. My goal is forty-five minutes to one hour. I no longer wash my hands up to my elbows—a welcome relief to my dry skin. My counting is now limited only to washing my hands and taking a shower. I don't need to use a wipe every time I touch something. I am no longer angry all the time; in fact, I really don't get mad at all. I'm generally mellower. And guess what? I only have to check things once now. I do love the return of free will.

    A month ago I had my first visit to the ER in two years for a kidney stone, thus killing the hope that I no longer had any in my body. As I am not a fan of the hospital, I desperately tried to avoid going, but as my doctor was out of town and I had no Demerol, I was left with no choice. Though my OCD was much improved, I was not keen to put it to the test so early in my recovery. But the nauseating pain was hard to ignore. I knew what was coming. I had been through it many times before. There is no place more contaminated than a hospital. It is a teeming cesspool of sickness and malaise, housing every germ imaginable. No amount of cleaning solution can possibly rid it of every germ. It terrified me. The first ten minutes were tough, especially as I was forced to pee in a cup so they could test my urine to see if I was having a kidney stone attack, which, on a side note, seems really unnecessary. Was my body not contorted enough in pain to convince them? Were the previous seven or so attacks on my record not evidence enough? Or perhaps the CAT scan they did twenty minutes later showing handfuls of stones in each kidney was too confusing? Sigh. Back to the cup situation. So, flailing about in pain, not only did I have to deal with using a public restroom for the first time in years, but I had to urinate in a wee little cup. Cue suffocating panic attack! Go ahead, laugh at my deep stress, but as I am not a boy, peeing in a cup is messy. Despite my aggravation at the entire situation, I was able to calm myself down in record time. The contamination fears that had previously ruled every aspect of my life for the past six years no longer had a tight grip on me. I was able to release the fear. The dark cloud of OCD that affected my vision finally began to part so I could see things as they really were. The hospital was not a dark and dingy place. It was clean and sanitary. There was no reason to be fearful and stressed—well, aside from the kidney stone. The beds were freshly made—no sign of fecal matter or flesh-eating bacteria. This was not a place to fear but a place to heal. For the first time, I lay in a hospital and I was perfectly calm, unencumbered by the OCD voices that once haunted me, even before they shot me up with morphine.

Though I have greatly improved, I don't yet feel completely stable. Perhaps it is due to the fact that my recovery is still rather recent. After all, it was only a few months ago that insanity nearly overtook me. Such a thing is hard to forget. I am still haunted by the fear that I am one false step away from disaster. I don't know if my OCD, depression, and anxiety will ever fully go away. For now, at least, my OCD is under control. In the back of my mind, I know that I am still vulnerable to it. I try not to put myself into situations that will unduly increase my stress level. But what of the things I can't control, like heartbreak and death, or any deeply traumatic situation? Will I be able to handle it? Will the pills still keep me balanced? Or will I snap? Though I am momentarily semi-stable, periods of illness, tragedy, and intense stress can reactivate my dormant OCD behaviors. I have found that knowing my triggers helps me control my response, like at my recent visit to the ER. I am still fearful of relapsing, but I expect as I move further away from those events, that fear will subside.

By Emily Watson

<u>Emily's Helpful Information</u>
<u>What I Have Learned</u>

- OCD, depression, and anxiety are not mental weaknesses. They are real medical illnesses that can have a serious impact on your daily life.
- It is OK to admit you are sick.
- Some people aren't going to understand and are going to judge you, but you can't let that bother you.
- I shouldn't just use modern medicine or alternative healing. I need both to get better.
- Everyone is flawed or screwed up in some way. It is all just a matter of who can hide it the best.

PART VII: A NEW HELL

"It requires more courage to suffer than to die."
Napoleon

    It is significant to note that sections of this book were written at completely different times in my life. The first half of the book, all that is dealing with OCD, was written in 2007 and 2008 during a hypomanic phase shortly after I started on Paxil. At that time my OCD seemed to be virtually cured, and my bipolar had yet to emerge. The second half of the book, everything dealing with bipolar disorder and a renewed OCD, was written during the worst of the symptoms in 2009 and 2010. Every thought, every feeling, is exactly how I felt at the moment. The writing is a bit more discombobulated, but the effect is an enlightening look into the mind of a crazy person.

    You might be surprised to know that I am a fiercely private person. I don't have any Internet websites. I am not listed on Facebook or MySpace. As my name is shared by many others, including two famous actresses, you would be hard-pressed to find anything about me online. Growing up I was just as tight-lipped. My friends would often get onto me for not sharing enough information about myself. But I just didn't like everyone knowing my business. And as a few of my friends were quite the busybodies, I did not like the whole school knowing my secret crushes and deepest feelings. So why am I writing a book that reveals, in vivid detail, all of my innermost thoughts and feelings? Because I truly believe it will help people better understand mental disorders and break the long-held stigma that has been attached to them. I figured that I could write my story one of two ways: one, the edited version, where I told the cleaned-up side of the story that portrayed me in a good light and omitted the darker bits or two, the unedited version, the real truth in all its cringe-worthy and disturbing details. Am I worried about how I will be seen by others? Absolutely. Am I worried that after revealing I showered only every five months that I will never get a date again? You betcha. Am I worried people are going to pin me as crazy? Of course. But, if I didn't reveal the truth, if I only painted a watered down, rosy view of the truth, then who would I be helping? Sure, I might come off a little better, but I wouldn't help anyone else.

CHAPTER TWENTY-SIX
The Dawn of Bipolar

"Anybody remotely interesting is mad, in some way or another."
The Doctor, Doctor Who

In the spring of 2007, my general practice physician, Dr. Prince, started me on a new SSRI called Paxil. For a brief honeymoon period, life became noticeably better. My OCD was waning; the incessant voices drowned down to a dull murmur that I could almost ignore. I could control even my worst compulsions. It seemed as if Paxil had cured me. Paxil was the key to my OCD. I could finally release myself from the dank prison in which I was trapped. But what I thought was the normal world was merely a larger prison, one I had not even seen in my OCD haze, one I was too tired to fight my way out of.

It turns out that not only did I suffer from a major anxiety disorder, but I also suffered from a bipolar disorder, and things were about to get much worse. Bipolar disorder, formerly known as manic depressive disorder, is a mental illness characterized by extreme shifts in mood, specifically from mania to depression. The relief that I had been feeling was not in fact a cure but rather an extended manic phase. You see, SSRIs, like Paxil, may make the symptoms of bipolar worse. Specifically at high doses, it may increase the severity of mania. In my case, it worsened my mania drastically and may have worsened the cycling between it and depression. Sufferers have to take a mood stabilizer to compensate for that effect. However, we didn't know I was bipolar, so Paxil was left unchecked.

I had been suffering from anxiety and depression for many years prior to my start on Paxil, but it had been thought that they were merely a reaction to my OCD. However, four months after I started Paxil, things began to change. I am not sure what caused it. It may have been the Paxil. But either way, those mood swings became more intense and started cycling back and forth at a rapid pace, tossing me between pulsating mania and desperate depression. In a period of just three to four months, I cycled down from every month to every day, like a wooden roller coaster continually rising to the anxious peak of mania and falling to the desolate depths of depression. I could feel the fall in my stomach, butterflies dancing about. Every day I would cycle back and forth between mania and depression. My emotions were uncontrollably lashing out in every direction. I was strapped to the roller coaster and unable to get off. Every minute was filled with the intensity and anxiety of a weightless fall, a sensation that is meant to be fleeting and cannot be sustained. You can't cope with such a sensation for more than a few minutes. Man is simply not meant to. No one can stay on a roller coaster all day every day. The body simply can't handle it. I couldn't handle it. I couldn't cope. How could I cope when the situation was in constant change? How could I cope with being depressed when a moment later I was manic?

Depression and anxiety had haunted me since my first kidney stone attack. Two opposite ends of the emotional spectrum in which I spent most of my time. Like two ends of a magnet, two opposite polarities joined together. Two poles. Bipolar. With the introduction of Paxil, each end got worse. My depression slowly got worse, very frequent and sudden deep, deep drops of depression, nothing my doctor was giving helped. Had a kidney stone attack, went to ER, got hydrocodone. Hydro helped, got addicted to narcotic for four months...even though hydro only helped a bit...still depressed, just kept me from dropping too low. Doc said got to get off narcotic, thought I knew what it felt like to withdraw from drugs...no freaking idea...so horribly traumatic that the idea of taking another narcotic scares the hell out of me...four days of hell that felt truly like two weeks followed by six days of semi-hell. Finished withdrawal, went badly downhill...badly, doc realized I had severe rapid cycling bipolar disorder...which as bipolar disorder can be hard to diagnose, especially when combined with other disorders like OCD...she didn't realize it until the Paxil made it worse. What? Are you telling me that had I not gone on Paxil I would be fine? No. SSRIs like Paxil don't cause bipolar disorder; they can just worsen the mania unless a mood stabilizer is added. Good to know because Paxil really does reduce the OCD, and I can't go back to pre-Paxil OCD, though it has been flaring up lately due to the massive amount of anxiety my body has been under from the hydro withdrawal and the bipolar and the series of colds, UTIs, etc., I have kept running into within the last six months; but OK, bipolar, check, give me medicine before I lose it. I mean really, I can't keep going like this; I am so tired, so very, very tired...once I thought about it and researched it, I can tell I had bipolar before—my constant mood swings from anxious to depressed, how quickly they shifted; but seriously that is how I got addicted to the narcotics in the first place, because they gave me some rest. My body and mind are just so very tired; I can't believe this has been going on for eight years now. God, that is virtually my entire twenties; I've lost so much time. I can never get it back; it's gone.

By the time I was finally diagnosed with the disorder, during what would come to be known as Black Thanksgiving in Fall 2007, I was cycling every minute. Sixty seconds of maddening mania followed by sixty seconds of solemn depression. The few weeks in and around that time are nothing more than a blur to me. Much of what I know comes from my doctor and my family. It is difficult to recall a moment of such instability; the impossibility of staying cognizant in any one minute when I was shifting between the two poles so rapidly was a phenomenon my doctor could see flashing through my eyes. Windows to the soul. Windows to all the turmoil. I remember chaos, complete and frightening chaos, and the inability to cope when each minute created a different state of being and the gnawing fear that I would never be OK again.

Emily's Helpful Tips
How to Cope with Depression

Depression isn't easy. It is one of the most difficult experiences I've ever had in my life. To truly cope with it, I recommend you see your general practice doctor or a psychiatrist. However, I have listed a few minor ways that helped me take the edge off.

1. Find an old movie, television show, or book that you loved as child and re-watch or reread it. I found that it helped trigger feelings from my youth—feelings of happiness, safety, and love. Just a small remembrance of those times gave me some peace and some rest—at least for a little while.

2. Have your doctor check to see if you are deficient in any vitamins and minerals. Deficiencies in key nutrients, like vitamin D, can contribute and even cause depression.
3. Eat a little bit of dark chocolate each day; it is proven to be a mood booster.
4. Start a journal to keep all of your thoughts. I know it sounds cliché, but it really did help to write down my feelings for this book. It felt like I was spitting out poison.
5. Exercise regularly. It is proven to help depression.

CHAPTER TWENTY-SEVEN
What are the Two Poles?

"It is doubtless a vice to turn one's eyes inward too much, but I am my own comedy and tragedy."
Ralph Waldo Emerson

Before going forward it is necessary to detail exactly what bipolar disorder is. Bipolar disorder, formerly known as manic depressive disorder, is a mental illness characterized by extreme shifts in mood, specifically from mania to depression. The phrase "turn on a dime" is the catchphrase of bipolar to me because mood shifts are often very sudden and quite jarring. It is a debilitating disorder that poisons every aspect of your life. It is NOT a mental weakness. It is NOT bad behavior. It is an illness, like any other physical illness, that the person cannot control.

Bipolar disorder consists of two polar moods, mania and depression. To me mania, in general, is a period of high energy in which I am anxious, talkative, restless, reckless, powerful, and even euphoric. Hypomania, the less severe form of mania, is actually a pretty positive state. I feel happy, surrounded by a euphoric sense of well-being. It is a truly wonderful state that I dearly wish I could experience more often. Sadly I have only experienced it once, just after I started Paxil and before I began to cycle rapidly, right when I thought I was cured. The entire first half of this book came from that powerful productive boost. I thought I was brilliant. I thought I was the most wonderful person in the world, not in an arrogant or egotistical way. I just thought I was great. I was awash in my own power of being. I thought I was wonderful beyond all measure. I could do anything. Brilliant ideas poured out of my mind, like my own personal muse was sitting on my shoulder. My mind and body were infused with great power and knowledge. No longer shy and demure, I resonated with a brilliance of being, stopping random strangers to start up a chat. Suddenly I was a talk show host able to converse on any topic. I was normally a shy person so my sudden conversiveness was a shock—a clearly mentally induced shock. The world felt orgasmic. It was glorious. I was imbibed with an untapped sensuality. I was happy. I was productive. I was the best form of me.

I wish I could be that me again. Life was easier. Armed with a heightened belief in my own power, the world was mine for the taking. How I long for that. Severe mania (I shall be referring to this type when I use the word "mania" from here on out) is the complete opposite. To me, it is a state of high energy and intense, intractable anxiety. It is more than just one's common worries. It is an entire state of being revolving around anxiety. Every thought I have, every action I take, stems from a distorted mindset. A mindset distorted by anxiety. My mind is no longer functioning like a normal person; it has become a manic mind. I now see the world through anxious-colored glasses, and what a frightening world it is. When I'm severely manic, I am filled with feelings of anger, confusion, and irritation. I feel trapped. It feels like every cell in my body is vibrating at a frequency that I cannot handle. The productive energy I felt in the hypomanic state begins to grow in intensity and turns against me, spiraling into a volcano of anxiety. The world is no longer this vibrant place that I am ready to explore but a dark and dangerous place that I dare not enter. I am no longer glorious but worthless, unworthy to even be alive. The inspirational thoughts that drove me to my greatest ideas are now coming too fast, rushing past me at a rate I can't handle, at a level I can't understand, spinning me in circles, spiraling me down into chaos. The intense anxiety creates confusion, anger, and indescribable terror in my mind, ever so slightly pushing me towards the edge of insanity.

General Symptoms of Mania

My experience with bipolar is not the norm. There really is no norm. There are common symptoms attributed to mania. How many episodes of mania and depression a person has varies for everyone. If you experience three or more of the following symptoms for more than a couple of weeks, you may be having a manic episode:

- Rapid talk, talkativeness
- Racing thoughts
- Easy distractibility
- Sudden mood changes from joyful to irritable, angry, and hostile
- Excessive hopefulness, happiness, and excitement
- Restlessness, less need for or inability to sleep

- Increased energy
- Increased sex drive
- Poor judgment
- Tendency to make grand, unattainable plans
- Inflated self-esteem or grandiosity
- Increased reckless behavior, such as lavish spending sprees, alcohol or drug abuse
- Euphoria
- Anxiety

(Webmd 2012)

My mania rarely passed through the talkative, powerful, euphoric phase. In fact the only time I can remember being in it was when I first started this book. Ideas were flying through my head, and within a couple of weeks, I wrote the first half of this book. I felt everything I touched turned to gold. I suddenly felt like I could do anything I wanted. I could get a black belt in karate. I could become a doctor. I could get a job in the White House. I had the talent, the skill, the drive to do anything in this world. I was under a magic spell, and I didn't want it to end. But eventually it did, and I have never gotten back to it. Instead that energy morphed into irritation, anger, and confusion. Heightened, restless energy made it feel like every cell in my body was vibrating at a frequency I couldn't handle. I felt trapped in an anxious bubble from which there was no escape. The more agitated I got, the smaller the bubble became. I couldn't think; I couldn't breathe. Every sound, every sight, every smell only added to my irritation. *How dare you breathe so loud! Where did that noise come from? What's that smell?* I was living in a state of constant agitation. When the energy got too high, it felt like I was crumbling from the weight of insanity. Chaos rushed upon me. I was drowning in a sea of turbulent, irrational thought.

Depression is the polar opposite of mania. To me it is a period of extremely low energy marked by great sadness and anxiety. It invades every crevice of my life, affecting how I think, feel, eat, and sleep. It affects my ability to function normally at work and in my daily life. Depression is the opposite of OCD: utter silence. The absence of all other voices except my own. A disconnection from others. A disconnection from God. Complete and utter loneliness. A drop in my stomach always signaled the start of a depressive phase for me. It was the omen of dark things to come. It was an unstoppable force knocking me up against a wall and flooding every aspect of my being. An upsetting thought would come to mind. Then another. Then another. Then I would begin feeling off-center, feeling out of sorts. The world begins to look a little different. I look at a glass of water and what once looked to be half-full now looks half-empty. My perception of the world changes. Everything I see, feel, and think comes with a note of sadness. Upsetting thoughts slip into my mind. I feel heavy, like a weight is pressing on my shoulders. A cloud forms above my head, a growing storm dousing me in a chilling rain. Darkness fills me. A deep sadness settles into my chest. I want to cry, but the well is too deep. The world is frighteningly mired in sadness. I search for hope, I search for love, I search for happiness, but I can't find any, not even the smallest amount. And then I feel it, the greatest terror, the deepest darkness, a sadness so old that it outdates the earth. It outdates the sun. It burns as close as my clothes and as far as the most distant galaxy. It stands alone, a single thought, a single fear, the dark truth of the universe, of all existence that life is not made of light and love but of a horror so black that it consumes all matter, leaving a cold touch on man.

To be depressed is to be disconnected from the world, trapped in my own sphere of existence. I stop and the world keeps on moving without me, spinning around my body. I am no longer part of the world; I am merely an observer watching in curious disconnection. But I don't see the happy parts, only the sad ones, eclipsing all my view. The sadness I feel is oppressive, weighing on my chest like a one hundred-pound piece of luggage. Why am I sad? I don't know. There is no reason. There is no cause. The sadness is separate from all that I see and all that I feel; it comes from within, deep within, a carnal truth that draws a single tear, devoid of light, devoid of love.

To be depressed is to be detached from my former self, to withdrawal from all that I was. Things that I once loved, like tennis or a particular TV show, now depress me. The energy, the excitement I once had for life disappears, leaving me lifeless and empty, wasting away on the couch. I can't concentrate, I can't think; all I can do is watch mindless television shows until it is time for me to go to sleep. I think of life. I think of my life, my meaningless, pointless life, and I fall deeper into depression. I think of my death. I think that it is too far away, that I can't wait that long to feel better. So I think about taking my own life, ending the pain, passing into nothingness. And I sit and wonder until I finally pass into sleep.

General Symptoms of Depression

If you experience five or more of these symptoms for longer than two weeks, then you may be having a depressive episode.

- Sadness, uncontrollable weeping
- Anxiety, irritability
- Loss of energy
- Feelings of guilt
- Feelings of hopelessness and worthlessness
- Loss of interest or enjoyment of things you once loved
- Increased sleepiness or insomnia
- Difficulty concentrating
- Difficulty making decisions
- Weight loss or gain
- Thoughts of death or suicide
- Attempting suicide

(Webmd 2012)

Bipolar disorder is actually the most difficult mental disorder for families to understand because they see the actions as simply bad behavior. People just don't realize what mental disorders are like. They think because it is your mind that you can control it, but it is an organ like anything else. It breaks. It gets damaged. It malfunctions. It's like asking me to control my kidney or heal a sore throat. I can't. And that is the insidious thing about it. I think I can control it. Others think, even expect, me to control it, but it is a disorder. It is a condition that I can't control. And what's worse is no one can see it; on the outside I look just fine, marred only by the eczema and worsening acne, which I cover with makeup. No visible wounds, no scars to show the pain I feel inside. Constant, unending pain from OCD, anxiety, depression, bipolar, whatever. Constant pain that has slowly been affecting my body for years, weakening it to the point that I feel like the only thing that is keeping me alive is my will to keep fighting, but I am so much weaker than I used to be. I am so tired. I feel as if I were to let it go that I would just die. Most days I want to die because I am just so tired. With the rapid cycling bipolar, I cycle between deep depression and pulse-racing anxiety five or more times a day. The depression drops are so insidious it is unbearable. I hate to even think of them when I am not in them. I don't want to remind myself of that place, a place so sad and so dark that there is no hope, only a loneliness so intense that I feel disconnected from everyone and everything; even my mom sitting there with her arms around me can't subside the pain, a pain so deep that it feels like a weight in my soul, a terrible pain from somewhere else, some other life, too deep for tears, unreachable by any happy thought.

If one has bipolar, there is a risk of becoming psychotic. Psychotic disorder is a mental illness that causes unusual and often disturbed thinking and perceptions. It affects a person's ability to make good judgments, think clearly, and understand reality. The main symptoms are hallucinations and delusions. Hallucinations are perceptions of things that aren't really there, such as seeing things and hearing voices. Delusions are false beliefs that a person takes on and doesn't give up despite evidence to the contrary. I have been diagnosed to have psychotic episodes, though I find that to be incorrect. Yes, I am afraid to go to sleep because I'm worried in my unconscious state I might do something bad. The doctor can't know what I would do—no one can. It is the unconscious me that I don't know, so I can't know what I'll do. Or I may never wake up. I would get sick and die in my sleep. I'm afraid the world is going to end on December 21, 2012. That isn't delusional; it is a fact. The Mayan calendar ends on that day. It ends! Not to mention that there are only going to be 112 popes before the end of the world, and we are on 111. These are indisputable facts. How could I not be worried that the end is coming? All right, so I am a little psychotic...

<u>Emily's Helpful Information</u>
<u>Quick Facts about Bipolar Disorder</u>

- It is reported that 10 million people currently suffer from it in the US.
- It is universal in its spread across gender, races, ethnic groups, and socioeconomic classes.

- Rapid cycling is more prevalent in women, along with experiencing more depressive states.
- Though it may seem like bipolar appears without any warning, typical onset occurs around age twenty-five.
- It is believed to be a genetic disorder that results from a malfunction of neurotransmitters in the brain that act as messengers to nerve cells.
- It usually runs in families, though it can skip a generation.

(Webmd 2011)

Emily's Helpful Tips
How to Cope with Mania

Severe mania is best treated by seeing a psychiatrist and taking medication, but here are a few ways that I have picked up along the way to help, as well.

1. Shake off your extra energy by taking a walk around the block or going to your local gym.
2. Do not imbibe any substance that is activating. No caffeine whatsoever.
3. If you are having a severe attack, find a quiet spot. If you can't find a quiet spot, squat down, place your elbows on your knees and your hands on either side of your face, covering your ears. This is called my "safety position." Shut your eyes. Breathe deep and rock back and forth on your heels. Find your center. Keep breathing. Keep rocking until the outside world fades away. Find your center, your own quiet space tucked in amidst all chaos of the world.
4. Listen to music that calms you. Try classical music if it's your taste. It just needs to be music that soothes your soul and helps you find your center. I recommend some of the work by Glenn Miller or Enya.
5. Certain anti-anxiety medication, like Valium or Xanax, can be helpful in taking the edge off of a manic episode, but they may also make you feel sedated.

CHAPTER TWENTY-EIGHT
A Bipolar Life

"No excellent soul is exempt from a mixture of madness."
Aristotle

By Fall of 2007, I was nothing more than a ghost on the living room couch. I was a pale, empty shell of the person I once was. The rapid cycling had left me nearly catatonic. Once brimming with life, I was now reduced to a small, fleeting flame. I used to have a fulfilling life. I was enrolled in college, studying for a rewarding career in physics or national security affairs. I had a small but meaningful group of friends that I regularly met for dinner and movies. I spent my time learning interesting skills from ballroom dancing to taekwondo. I was happy. I was healthy. But it was not to last. Now my life consisted of sitting on the couch watching television and doing jigsaw puzzles. Literally, during my struggles with bipolar disorder and OCD, for I can't remember how many years, all I did was watch television and do 1000 piece puzzles on the coffee table in the living room. My room is filled with boxes and boxes of puzzles that I completed. It was the only thing that made me feel calm, feel centered. However, there were times when I couldn't even do that. I would have episodes when I would be too psychotic to do either of those things. The worse I got, the more frequent those episodes. When I would get this bad, I would begin to lose my grip on myself, on reality. My mind would be overrun with chaos. The only thing that would bring the smallest amount of help was riding around in the car with the window down and the cool air brushing against my face.

As things got worse, I slowly stopped interacting in the world. Initially, I just stopped going out once or twice a week. I just felt a little down, a little out of sorts. Then I would stay inside for an entire week, too sad and anxious to face the outside world. Then a week became two weeks. Two weeks became a month. Finally I wouldn't go out for two months at a time. The weight of the disorders kept me planted on the couch, watching hours of mindless television. The anxiety kept my mind racing, making it virtually impossible to perform even the simplest of thought-provoking tasks. The depression laid on me like a blistering winter snow, trapping me beneath its weight, feeling too sad and too heavy to move. I was a waste of space, a worthless lump sitting on the couch. I had no life. I made no contribution to society. I just existed, and that was painful enough.

My only distraction from the hours spent on the couch was sleep, and that was only when I was in my depressive phase. Being depressed is like taking a sedative. My body slows, my mind falters, my eyelids drop down my eyes. I feel sleepy all the time, every minute of every hour of every day. No matter how many hours I sleep, it is never enough. I still feel tired. Ten hours of sleep even left me feeling hardly refreshed. In comparison, when I'm manic, it is hard to get any sleep at all. My mind is racing so fast and my body is so anxious that I am awake for days at a time running on my own internal treadmill. The less sleep I get, the more manic I become until I crash on my bed in a fitful panic.

Entering a bipolar phase is like entering a different universe. The rules of physics are different. The rules dictating how life is ordered are twisted and deranged. How my mind thinks is unlike my regular mind. It is not just my thoughts that are different; it is how I think, how I live, how I perceive the natural world. I think with an irrational light, but I can't see the irrationality, as what is usually irrational is now very rational. What is black is white, what is wrong is right, what is good is bad. Like Alice before me, I have wandered into a great and disturbing wonderland—the wonderland of the broken mind. But where Alice maintains an unspoiled mind, my mind is distorted by the bipolar land.

Walking into the manic land is like walking into a chaotic county fair. The air is electric with anxious tremblings. My eyes are blinded by dancing lights and neon brights. My ears are bombarded by the loud din of hundreds of little conversations and screaming voices. I try to block the chaos. I try to shield the sensory overload. But I can't fight it. The sounds, the lights, the smells all leak in, flooding my body with uncontrollable energy. The cells in my body begin to vibrate, waving to and fro until they resonate with the blaring sounds. I can't contain the vibration; I can't contain the sound. My skin crawls; I feel trapped in my own skin—my own tight, drying, odious skin. My mind races as pulsating lights send psychotic visions into my mind. I am energized by an unholy force, a dark, demented force that pushes me into action. I am no longer joyful but angry and irritable. My mind distorts, twisting my beliefs, twisting my morals, leaving me vulnerable to reckless behavior and ill-advised choices. My moral code is warped, bent beyond all recognition. Bad behavior is no longer taboo. Anything goes in this crazy, jacked-up town. I try to stop myself from these reckless actions, but I can't. They don't seem reckless to me; they don't seem bad. I wonder why I didn't realize this sooner. The most dangerous activities—skydiving, ice mountain climbing, race car driving—seem devoid of fear. I can do anything. I can conquer anything. I have no fear. I have no hesitation. I am invincible. My self-esteem is inflated. Others' emotions mean nothing to me. All that matters is pleasing me, gratifying myself. Steal another friend's boyfriend—why not? Step on my friend's back to reach my goals? Sure. No one else matters. Do what I want; only I matter.

Walking into the depressive land is like walking into an empty medieval castle. The moment I enter, I become trapped within the dark, dank walls. Gates slam down all around me. There are no lights, there are no fires, only the scattered light from the overcast sun. The cold sinks into me, robbing me of all warmth, chilling my bones and burning my skin. The air is sad; I breathe it in like a moisture-laden cloud. It fills me up, racing to my extremities so that everything I touch is imbibed with that same sadness. I can't bear it. I search for someone, for anyone, to tame the loneliness in my heart, but no one is there. I am all alone. The sadness grows deeper. The sky is dark; it casts a shadow on the desolate castle, abandoned for decades. The light is gone. I'm drenched in darkness. All life is gone. All hope is gone. All love is gone. I am alone, always alone, forever alone. I try to think of happy thoughts, think of life outside this castle, but I can't. The distortions in my mind block all goodness. My entire being is wrapped up in this destitute castle where all life goes to die. No one can help me. No one can hear me scream. I am alone, always alone.

It is hard to say which is worse—depression or mania. Both have very offending qualities, and both are nearly impossible to bear at their worst. But I guess I would have to say that the depression is the worst. Mania is much easier to cope with. If I am seriously manic, there are ways to bring me down off that distressing high. Anti-anxiety medication like Xanax or sedatives like Phenergan can take the edge off the mania, bringing it down to a more manageable level. But depression has no corresponding counteraction—at least not any immediate-working.

Stimulants, like over-the-counter caffeine pills, sometimes can jerk me out of a depressive phase, but it unfortunately sends me flying into an intense manic phase, leaving me to take a sedative to calm me back down—not a recommended choice of action. Depression is just too painful to bear.

Poetic Musings

Ancient Foe
by Emily Watson

Oh darkened fiend, ephemeral foe
Of ancient cities long ago
From golden gates I saw you thrown
Upon the lands of fire and stone

In twilight dreams you now appear
Where worldly lines have disappeared
And lands unknown, both new and old
Are opened wide to restless souls

I've seen you on the verdant mountain
Above the grand and wondrous fountain
By hidden forest, ancient lore
Where life had sparked and hope was stored

I've seen you in the olden field
In battles amid good and ill
Where lighted turrets boldly stand
Against the dark, primeval land

I've seen you in the distant night
When tales of terror turn me white
Where shadows dance upon the walls
And conjure fears, unknown to all

By Emily Watson

I've seen you in the eyes of men
Where primal evil stirs within
When deeds unholy blacken souls
And raze the spirit, pure and whole

I've seen you in the days of war
An unseen general in the fore
Inciting purest of all hate
To forge and mold unholy fates

And yet your rival I have seen
In deepest sleep and purest dream
Where fear is but a distant sight
When bathed in warmth and unseen light.

CHAPTER TWENTY-NINE
Manic Minds: Thinking and Talking at the Speed of Light

"When you sit with a nice girl for two hours, you think it's only a minute. But when you sit on a hot stove for a minute, you think it's two hours. That's relativity."
- Albert Einstein

Thinking and talking at a rapid pace is a defining characteristic of mania. One night in college, in an attempt to stay awake to study, I took a caffeine pill. Within a few hours, I was darting about like a little bee, my heart pulsating, my hands trembling, and my lips in constant motion. That is mania defined; only mania is much, much worse. When I'm hypomanic the thoughts come at just the right pace to optimize my normal talents. If you're a brainiac, like me, your analyzing and memorizing skills become perfectly acute like the first day of school. If you're a writer, the words flow out like a bustling current. If you're a painter it's like your hand is guided by an unseen force to a vivid masterpiece. You are always "in the zone." When I'm manic, severely manic, I am anything but functional. The thoughts are moving much too fast, a steam train of thoughts bombarding my mind. I can't think. I can't talk. I can't breathe. I try to shut it out of my mind but to no avail. All I can do is sit in silence and take in each thought like it's a bullet. When it is too painful, I find a dark corner, squat down, place my hands on my head, close my eyes and try to block out all stimuli from the outside world and focus only on sorting the chaos in my mind. Trying to exist in the world makes me feel as if I am going to crack. Any noise was like a speaker in my head adding to an already crowded din. I would beg anyone nearby to stop talking, stop typing, stop watching TV, and even stop eating because I just couldn't handle the noise. My head was already too full.

I am a pretty shy person. When I first meet someone, I am usually at a loss for words. I converse fine with people I know, but I am always quiet around new people. I don't know why really. I guess I am afraid of putting myself out there for risk of rejection. Or maybe I just don't want to seem silly or idiotic. Or, worst of all, I'm worried I will come off boring. Whatever the reason, I keep to myself. But when hypomania kicks in, I am a one-woman talk show, able to converse on any subject with any person. Whatever misgivings I had about my own failings is pushed aside and replaced with an almost pressing need to talk. It is an interesting experience really, putting myself out there like that. My worries about how I might be perceived by others were unwarranted, as most people were receptive to my chatting. Even when my mania was moderately severe, I was still very talkative, although I mostly talked about how crazy and messed up I felt. However, when it got severe, my thoughts were moving faster than I could talk. I quieted down as the insanity began to take over.

CHAPTER THIRTY
Manic Shopping: A Further Blow to Fashion

"Fashion is a form of ugliness so intolerable that we have to alter it every six months."
Oscar Wilde

    As I said before, I love to shop. I'm a girl; it is what we do. Many a lazy weekend was spent at the mall with friends in high school. That being said, is it any wonder I would develop a disorder that involves lavish spending sprees? The reckless pursuit of gratification, specifically shopping, is a major characteristic of mania. It is a compulsive desire to shop taken to the extreme. And I mean shop—big time shopping. One day I walked out of a clothing store $500 poorer than when I walked in. Immediately realizing what I did, I walked over to my dad, handed him the bags and told him to return the clothes because I knew if I went back in I would just buy more. However, I was not always so cognizant of my reckless behavior. My quest for makeup sent me on many a lavish spending spree. I have to admit, I am completely obsessed with makeup. Clothes are great, but they are nothing compared to makeup. Walking into a major makeup store, like Sephora or Ulta, is like walking into a candy store. The eye shadow palettes in glimmering blues and greens, the lipsticks in candy apple reds and cotton candy pinks, the perfumes eclipsing the room in hints of luscious vanilla and exotic muir—it is a festival for the eyes and nose. Oh how I love walking the aisles running my fingers across each little treat, longing to buy everything in the store. And then the moment I find that specific item— oh, the high that envelops me when I head to the register. What pure unadulterated joy! Yet, one is never enough. I have to buy more. I have to sustain that euphoric high. The mania grips me and I spend; I spend myself into debt. In one ill-fated month, I accumulated a $900 charge at Sephora, the makeup mecca. My dad was none too pleased with he saw the bill. I can't help it. I love makeup.

CHAPTER THIRTY-ONE
Little Pills of Happiness

"Thou hast the keys of Paradise, oh just, subtle, and mighty opium!"
Thomas de Quincy

Like I said before, I love narcotics. I knew I had a narcotics problem whenever I heard "overdose of narcotics" in an autopsy on television, and my first thought was "lucky bastard." I should have felt pity or sorrow for their death by overdose, but instead I felt envy. I can't help it. I love narcotics. Ever since I got addicted to them in my early days of OCD, I have fantasized about having a kidney stone attack, going to the ER, and getting an IV of Demerol or morphine. Or perhaps just a tablet—those beautiful, perfectly formed little tablets that could melt right in my mouth like candy. Little pills of happiness. I can feel them, even now—the slow warmth that creeps over my body the moment it first begins to work. The warmth of an intoxicatingly festive holiday home erupting with smells of pumpkin pies and cinnamon sticks. Then, just when I think I can't bear anymore warmth, it blossoms into a state of perfect well-being. I am at peace within myself. Good spirits stretch to every bone in my body and every crevice in my mind. The world is a bountiful treasure chest of riches just waiting to be explored. Life is no longer to be feared but welcomed, caressed like an infant child. It doesn't matter what I do; it doesn't matter what decision I make because I know everything is going to turn out OK. It is love, joy, happiness, and peace of mind, all bottled into a single pill. How could I not desire it? How could I not wish for it when my daily life is the exact opposite? Why should I be denied the happiness that millions of others have?

In the summer of 2007, my addiction to narcotics was given new life. My bipolar had begun to kick in, and my moods were shifting dramatically between deep sorrow and crazed mania. Reckless behavior, like shopping sprees, alcohol abuse, and drug abuse are common symptoms of mania. I had problems with narcotics even before I had mania, so it isn't surprising that it would only further fuel that behavior. I still had a supply of Demerol for my kidney stones. Quickly finishing it up, I was easily able to acquire more, as the doctor hadn't yet realized my addiction. Going through that just as quickly, I tried to acquire more. Dr. Prince now became a bit hesitant and only agreed to give me hydrocodone. I didn't care as long as it gave me that feeling of euphoria that I so desperately needed. Using various lies I was able to get a regular supply of it for about two months, eventually taking up to eight pills a day—a bad idea as the narcotic was mixed with Tylenol. I am fortunate I have no liver damage, but at the time I didn't care. I was happy. My mind was finally clear of my disorders. I could live life again. Sadly Dr. Prince wised up to my deception and cut off my supply, leaving me with no choice but to go through a nasty withdrawal. It is not the worst thing I have ever experienced, but is it not something I would want to go through again. It is seventy-two hours of minor hell. Rampant paranoia, especially of having a seizure and dying, intense loneliness, crying, muscle pain, achiness, panicky feelings, runny nose, suffocating heaviness in the body… It was a virtual who's who of unsettling symptoms, along with vomiting, diarrhea, and psychotic fits that drained me of every ounce of strength I had.

I still don't understand why narcotics can't be used in the treatment of mental illness. My doctor claims it is because it is an addictive substance, but the same could be said of SSRIs. Paxil is the most addictive drug I have ever been on. I have attempted to get off of it more than three times, but the withdrawal was so intense I had to continue taking it. Dropping the dosage sent me into a psychotic fit that my mind couldn't handle. We tried supplementing it with Prozac to help the step down process but to no avail. The withdrawal was one hundred times worse than narcotic withdrawal. So, frankly, that reason is flimsy. Another excuse they use is that narcotics don't cure mental illnesses; they just mask them. So what if they do? It makes people feel better, and there is nothing wrong with that, especially considering the drugs they give me now to cure it don't work. Bottom line: narcotics take away the pain of mental disorders and should be reconsidered as a source of treatment.

Emily's Helpful Tips
How to Deal with Narcotic Withdrawal

Here are a few tips I have discovered to help with narcotic withdrawal. I have gone off narcotics gradually and done it cold turkey.

1. Talk to your doctor if you are dealing with narcotic withdrawal. You don't have to do it cold turkey. The doctor may set up a step-down system to ease you off the pills. Personally, I prefer going cold turkey so that the withdrawal symptoms aren't dragged out over a greater length of time.
2. Keep a bucket next to the toilet because things will be coming out both ends before the end of the first twenty-four hours.
3. If you have to eat, then eat only bland foods like Cheerios, Saltines, Triscuits, and Wheat Thins.
4. Take a couple of Phenergan and just sleep it off.
5. Remember there is an end in sight. This horrible state only lasts seventy-two hours. You can get through it.
6. No matter how hard and how painful the withdrawal is, you will still want narcotics. It's just a consequence of addiction.

CHAPTER THIRTY-TWO
Chords of Depression

"There is a solitude which each and every one of us has always carried within. More inaccessible than the ice-cold mountains, more profound than the midnight sea: the solitude of self."
Elizabeth Cady Stanton

Depression isn't a thought. It isn't an idea. It isn't that sad feeling I get when watching a heartbreaking movie or that punch in my stomach when someone breaks my heart. It isn't temporary. It can't be chased away by a happy movie, by a walk in the park, or by a vacation. It is a way of thinking. A dark poison that floods through every vein in my body controlling the way I think. It is how I perceive the world. It is a malfunction in my brain that causes me to see, feel, and understand the world in a way different from the norm. To be depressed is to feel deeply alone, disconnected from the invisible strands that connect all of humanity together. Unhealthily focused on the seeming futility of life, finding any career, any activity pointless, as in the end, what does it matter? Why does anything matter when we will only die? Whatever we leave behind will perish. Our sun will die. The earth will die. The universe will collapse or expand forever until every star dies and only darkness is left. All is lost. All is forgotten. And what of God? What if there is no God? What if after we die, we merely cease to exist? This is where a depressive person lives.

Depression isn't just a feeling. It is a state of mind, a state of being; it is a way of thinking. It can't be understood, it can only be felt. Somewhere in the icy abyss of despair and the pulsating heart of darkness, I can feel it—lingering, consuming, paralyzing. I can feel it in every breath I take. It's unbearable. Simple sadness is an emotion. It is the result of experiencing something upsetting in life like the death of a friend or family member. Like an insoluble substance in a glass of water, it adds to the volume, but it does not alter the solvent. It can be cured or it can be counteracted through happy experiences and the passage of time. Depression is different. It doesn't come from a sad movie or a bad breakup. It does not come from the environment. It is born within, in the genetic makeup of the body. Like a soluble substance in water, it changes the makeup of the water, creating a new solution. It changes the mind into a depressive mindset. Without any external stimuli, I am weighed down by a heavy sadness. It affects everything I think, everything I do. It changes how I see the world and how I behave in it. It is like rose-colored glasses; only there is nothing rosy about the view. Every piece of information I take in is seen through the glass half-empty.

Depression is hell. It is a darkness so deep and so profound that the sun would fear to shine on it. It is a sadness so intense and so treacherous that even a tear can't bear to shed. To be depressed is to be alone, separated from humanity, isolated from life and love. To be depressed is to be trapped in a terrifying, maddening darkness cut off from all that is light and good. To be depressed is to be so sad, beyond all measure and reason, that happiness is an impossible dream. The worst part of all is that it is inescapable. No matter where I go, no matter what I do, it is always with me—haunting, torturing, paralyzing. Death is my only relief. So in my darkest hours, I long for it. I remember having a conversation with my friend Christine one day, regarding a girl who was left paralyzed from the neck down after a terrible car accident. Her first thoughts were of how fortunate we are to have working limbs and a healthy body. My first thought was a terrible fear that that could happen to me. What if I got into an accident and became paralyzed? What would I do? I couldn't handle that. I am getting a panic attack just thinking about it. That is the depression glasses defined. I couldn't see the positive in that story. I could only see the negative. And that is the gist of it; my whole world view is changed so that I will only see the negative. I have horrible stretch marks. I got them when I gained forty pounds in short period of time (more on that later). I'm very embarrassed by them and can't wear a skirt because of them. I decided to try a cosmetic procedure that reduces if not completely eliminates them. Now it takes four or six procedures to get the desired results, so it is rather slow to see each individual effect. You'd think, though, I should be happy that the doctors think they can get rid of my horrendous stretch marks, but I am not. All I can think about is what if it doesn't work. What if they can't get rid of them? What if I have to live with them for the rest of my life? Despite all the positive affirmations, I could still only focus on the negative. But that is what depression is: always looking at the negative

By Emily Watson

side of things. No matter how much I try to talk myself into seeing the positive, I always end up in drowning in the negative.

Depression is sadness without a cause. Whenever I remarked to anyone that I was depressed, they would immediately ask me why. But I didn't have an answer. I didn't know why I was depressed. When I looked outside of myself, I couldn't see a reason for my foul mood. I received a good education at a prestigious university. I had a loving and caring family. I had a handful of really good friends. And I had great potential for any number of future careers. I had no reason to be sad. But I was. And it wasn't this simple sadness that comes when I watch an upsetting movie or get a bad grade in school. It was a terrifyingly deep sadness from which no light could reach. It was the entire human experience, in all its horrifying sadness, resting squarely on my diminutive shoulders.

All the sadness I see in the world only adds to my burden. The animal that gets hit by a car, the child abused by his parents, the teen girl murdered on the local news—all of their pain is added to my own. I feel their wounds, their deep slashes from an inhumane world, as if they were my own. I am littered with the scars of humanity's forgotten children. The hopeless, the lonely, the tortured all end with me—my beginning, my end. The chain of lost souls reaching across the seas spinning around the world disconnected from the children of the day—the healthy, the happy, the hopeful. I can feel them reaching out for anyone, anyone who cares. I feel them always and somewhere they sense me.

The world is heavy. I can feel it on my shoulders. I can feel it in my legs. I can feel it in every step I take. The world is heavy, and I can't carry it anymore. I am empty. Narcotics fill that emptiness, but the doctors won't let me have them. I have nothing. I am nothing. I don't want to do anything. I don't want to watch any movies. I don't want to read any book. I don't want to call up a friend. I don't want to go outside. I don't want to go to the ocean. I don't want to go to an amusement park. I don't want to go to Disney World. No matter how fun and exciting the activity might be, I still don't want to do it. To everyone else the world is brimming with sunlight, alit in possibilities, but to me it is a gray and gloomy place. The beach is nothing more than miles of sand that get stuck in my shoes and salty water that covers me in sticky grime. Disney World is a hot, sweaty, steamy mass of crying kids and cranky parents. Nothing sounds fun. The world is dark and dreary. It doesn't matter where I go, this darkness, this emptiness follows me always. I can't escape it; I am trapped.

I can't handle the depression phase. It is too intense. The sadness swallows me whole, and I can't breathe. All that stands before me is a rain-soaked sky just waiting to pour on any decision I dare make. I feel like I am walking through a fog. I can't think. I can't breathe. I can't see my way out. I can't clearly think about anything. I have no idea when, if ever, it will clear. It's like running a race with no end in sight. It is easier to endure anything if we know when it ends. The world can never be darker than this. It makes me sick. All I want to do is crawl under the covers on my bed and hide away from the world. If I let one more moment pass in this doomed state, I will break into one hundred pieces. Desperate for any help, I have often, against doctors' orders, taken a stimulant or caffeine pill to try and jolt me back into a manic phase. Yes, the manic phase is horrible, but I can't think about that now. I can only think about getting out of the depressive state. Tomorrow's Emily will have to deal with the consequences.

<u>Emily's Helpful Information</u>
<u>A Healthy Mind versus a Depressed Mind</u>

Healthy Mind:

- It is slightly overcast today, yet still the sun manages to pierce through. Perhaps the clouds will burn off by noon.
- I want to go to the mall to pick up some makeup. I really want to master the art of the smoky eye. I love going to the mall. Shopping is so much fun, especially buying makeup and clothes. I love dressing up and putting on makeup. It makes me feel so pretty.
- I love the mall at Christmastime. Holiday spirit infuses the air, making even the grouchiest spirit alive with joy and love.

By Emily Watson

Depressed Mind:

- The sky is gray. The warmth of the sun cannot even pierce its vast expanse. Another dreary day to add to the thousand before it.
- Yesterday I wanted to go to the mall to search for some makeup. Getting out of the house would be good. But I don't want to get out of the house. Everyone will stare at me. I am so ugly. What is the point of buying makeup? It can't cover up just how ugly I am.
- The sky is sad; I don't want to go out when the sky is sad. I feel alone. I don't want to go to the mall; it will be too lonely. People around every corner, and yet I still feel alone.
- I used to love Christmastime, but now there's nothing. Outside of my parents, I have no one to buy presents for. All my friends have moved on to bigger and better things. No boyfriend, no husband to think of. No reason to put presents under a tree. No reason for a tree at all.

CHAPTER THIRTY-THREE
Trying Times

"Insanity is often the logic of an accurate mind overtasked."
Oliver Wendell Holmes

Six months after starting Paxil, in the winter of 2007, it was evident I had a severe bipolar disorder. As I already said, my bipolar extremes reached their pinnacle on Black Thanksgiving in fall 2007, one of the darkest weekends of my life. It was the culmination of my downward spiral into bipolar hell. My mania and depression were cycling back and forth so fast that I had no time to cope with any one state. I felt like I was on a chaotic roller coaster, only this was unlike any roller coaster I had ever been on. There was no end, I kept dropping and climbing over and over, my stomach in knots, my limbs flailing about. My chest was tight. I couldn't breathe. I couldn't think. I couldn't get a grasp on any one moment; I was in constant change. I began to lose grip on myself, on reality. I felt myself slipping away, disappearing beneath my very eyes. I don't know where I was going, I don't know what I was being replaced with, but I knew I was losing it. Even now I find it hard to explain. How can I slip away? How can I lose myself? The rapid cycling was too much to bear, I couldn't cope. Terror washed over me. I didn't want to leave this life. The cycling had become so rapid that I was lapsing into a psychotic state. Reality was becoming blurred. According to the doctor I would phase out, pass into an imaginary world away from the confusion, away from the pain. In a fleeting glance I would be somewhere else. I was slowly losing my mind, and it seemed there was nothing I could do to stop it. I wish I could remember that state, describe it in full detail but it is nothing more than an afterthought, cloudy and vague. I was barely cognizant of the state while I was in it so remembering it is quite impossible. All I know is that it was bad, very bad, bad enough for the doctor to try to convince my dad to institutionalize me. I was afraid. I couldn't handle being in this state much longer. But no one could help me. Dr. Prince wanted me to go to a mental hospital, but I couldn't do that. I was afraid. I was afraid I would be locked away and I wouldn't be able to get out. I kept picturing the mental institutions of the old days, places filled with crazy people and uncaring doctors, places of frightening medical procedures, like lobotomies and electroshock therapy, places where inmates terrorize each other and doctors turn the other cheek, places where I am so sedated I am virtually catatonic. I couldn't go. I couldn't hand over my life to someone else. It would be the end for me. I knew it would. I had two options, try a mood stabilizer or end up in a mental hospital. I, of course, chose the mood stabilizer. The first one I tried was Zyprexa. If only I were lucky enough to get it right on the first try. Not only did it not work, but it had the rather bad side effect of weight gain. I put on five pounds in five days. Though it did give me the superhero power of immunity to cold. It sent my pulse racing so fast that I could walk outside in 50 degree weather with just a t-shirt and jeans and not feel even the slightest chill. That was an amazing feat for me as I normally need a coat at only 70 degrees. Next up was Depakote. I have no memory of Depakote only the note in my file that it is now considered an allergy. Apparently something went horribly wrong. It made me crazy, worse than I already was.

After two failed tries, Dr. Prince was insistent that I enter a mental hospital but relented after I pressed her to give it one more try. She chose the original pill for bipolar disorder, lithium. The only downside was having my blood checked regularly to make sure it didn't create a toxicity and having to take a drug called Synthroid to counteract lithium's effect on my thyroid. Lithium has the tendency to create hypothyroidism in many patients. Side effects aside, it actually worked…for a time, that is. The clarity for which I had so desperately longed for came on the wings of this small pink pill; I thought, as I had once thought with Paxil, that I was cured. My highs and lows were greatly reduced. In fact, my mood shifting virtually disappeared. For a few short months, I was once again thrust into a deceptively placid lake. But it wasn't long before ripples started to appear. My seemingly dormant depression and mania began to grow. I was once again strapped to that mind-bending roller coaster, and I had no way to get off. Within a few months, it seemed like the lithium had stopped working. The doctor considered upping the dosage, but I couldn't take a higher dose because I would be within the lithium toxicity range. When I am on lithium, I have to have my blood tested monthly to make sure I don't enter this range. It soon seemed as if I wasn't taking any pills at all. How could lithium work in the beginning and then just stop? To make matters worse, my OCD symptoms were back with latent severity. The Paxil seemed to stop working as well. Why weren't any of these drugs working? The commercials say they are supposed to work. When a drug advertises on television, I always see the troubled, depressed woman at the beginning painfully hiding from life, and then once she takes the pill, she finds happiness again. Why doesn't that happen? I have tried so many medications now. Why can't one of them work? With lithium and Paxil no longer working, what was to follow would be a new and tiring range of medications, as we tried to let me lead a normal life. How dark life had become when my only goal was to be normal.

My rapid cycling had dwindled down from every minute to every month. For thirty long days, I was trapped in either throes of a maddening mania or an agonizing depression. In retrospection, mania is the lesser of the two evils, but at the time, no matter which state I was in, the other always seemed better. Though they are at two opposite ends of a pole, their effect is inevitably the same. They both impair me to lead a normal life. I can't perform my daily routine. I can't socialize with friends. I can't work. I can't live. Mania is a state of heightened energy. It is like a shot of caffeine. You want to know what it feels like to be manic? Drink ten cups of coffee on an empty stomach. You might think that would make you more productive, but such large amounts of excited, anxious energy is unfocusable, unusable. My body shakes so badly I can't use a pencil. My mind races with so many thoughts that I can't sustain a conversation. It is like trying to herd a bunch of wild horses through a single one-horse gate. I have all this energy, but I can't do anything with it. I feel out of sorts. I feel sick. Depression is a complete absence of energy. It feels as if every cell in my body has been drained of all its energy. I can't get up from the couch. I just sit there slowly disappearing into its patchwork pattern. I don't have the energy to do anything. I can't perform my daily routine. I can't socialize with friends. I can't work. I can't live. I just sit on the couch and waste away. Sadness flows through every cell in my body, weighting me down like a one hundred-pound weight.

By 2008, my bipolar symptoms were the worst they had ever been. I was perched on the edge of insanity, and I was only inches away from falling in. It is hard to describe what it feels like to lose one's mind, to go insane. I feel like there is all this anxious energy driving me towards a cliff, towards insanity. The anxiety is so severe, it is unbearable. I can't handle being in that state with all that anxiety, all that anxious energy. I start to feel crazy. Little things started to freak me out. Suddenly I became afraid to drink. I was afraid I wouldn't be able to breathe when I drink, so I started having a panic attack that I could no longer drink. I freaked out for a while and then I decided I could drink with a straw. Sometimes all I could do is watch the same movie over and over because it was the only thing that seemed to calm me down in the least bit. One Christmas my mind was so chaotic, and I was so frightened, all I could do was watch White Christmas over and over until I finally drifted off to sleep. My anxiety and depression were so intense that they merged into one fearful entity that set my cells vibrating to such extremes that they were sending danger signals to my brain. My mind starts to crumble from the weight of those two states of being. I start to lose my grip on myself and I begin to panic. Even more heightened anxiety floods my veins and I begin to act erratically. My consciousness starts fading out of existence. Reality begins to blur. I start noticing gaps in my memory and in my thoughts. I feel terror—a deep, unsettling, unholy terror. I am disappearing, but to where I do not know. I am grasping at anything I can to help me remain in this life. But it's not working; I am fading away. So I try more pills and hope that one of them will work.

During winter 2008, I was verging on being psychotic. It is hard to describe what it is like to be psychotic, to lose one's mind. I feel anxious, really anxious, so anxious that I can't breathe, I can't function as a normal human being. Every cell in my body is vibrating at a frequency that I can't handle. Uncontrollable anxious energy spreads through every vein in my body going from the top of my head to the tip of my toes. There's too much energy. I don't think anyone's body can handle that much energy. My body begins to shake. My skin starts to crawl. I feel like I am going to burst out of my skin. All this anxious energy makes my mind start to crumble. Thoughts are racing through my mind so fast that I can't grasp any of them. I can't think. My mind is spinning with loud voices screaming in the background. It is maddening. I can't take it. So I try to escape. My mind begins to check out. I enter a fantasy world away from the pain and chaos. I fall into a psychotic state.

By Emily Watson

Another way to look at mania is as a terrifying thrill ride. I am not an adrenaline junkie in any way, shape, or form. I absolutely hate any ride that causes me to lose my stomach—mainly rides with some sort of drop, like roller coasters. I have only ever been on a few: Space Mountain, Splash Mountain, and the Tower of Terror at Disney World and a ride called Space Shot that my fellow campers dragged me on at space camp. The latter was absolutely the worst, as it shot me straight up in the air racking up four positive Gs and then fell back down at four negative Gs. My stomach leapt into my throat and then left me all together, leaving me feeling utterly disoriented. I left the ride with legs of jelly buckling to and fro as I tried to walk away. The only reason I agreed to go on it was because the cute boy I had a crush on offered to hold my hand. So I guess a minute of distress was worth it. But, high school crushes aside, I rarely go on roller coasters. It had to be a special occasion. My doctor once told me that people who like roller coasters and other thrill rides are often deficient in natural adrenaline, so they seek it out in their everyday lives, whereas others have enough to spare so they don't like thrill rides. I think that makes some sense, and it would explain why I detest them so; perhaps I just have too much natural adrenaline. After all, that is what mania feels like—a shot of sustained adrenaline but not the type that gives me a euphoric high like before my first kiss but rather the terrifying type that floods my body from a horror film or a near-death collision. Every minute of a manic phase is filled with excruciating adrenaline, an unsustainable state that wears on my body.

The phrase "turn on a dime" is the catchphrase of bipolar disorder to me. At the seeming drop of a hat, I can turn from the high energy of mania to the low energy of depression. It is not so much a single catalyst as a chain reaction that causes this sudden shift. Whenever I am trapped in the throes of mania, longing for the quiet repose of depression, it all begins with a single, fleeting upsetting thought. A scene from a movie depicting a lover's heartache…my heart steals a moment of sadness, but then it's gone. The moment passes and I continue on with my life, but something is left behind, something intangible, a worn pathway that spirals down to the darkest depression. I pass a picture, a photograph of me when I was a child, and I long for that innocent euphoria. Sadness and regret grip me, only for a moment, and then it passes. The sadness leaves me, but the pathway remains, and I slip downward. A girl is murdered on the local news; the tragedy strikes me, and then it passes. But I slip further downward—every sadness a catalyst for my further decline. Now the sadness doesn't leave me; it grows heavy, and I slide further down, down to the place where depression lies. The mania I had experienced only moments before has fallen away, and I am locked into a new state, the depressive state. Sadness floods my body, filling every nook and crevice. Once filled with high energy, I am now irritable, angry, and hostile. Darkness consumes me. I'm angry at the world. I don't know why, yet I am filled with such intense rage. *How dare anyone come near me? How dare anyone enter my presence? Get the heck away from me. I hate you all. Do not stand there like fools watching me fume about. Get away, you worthless beasts. No one make a noise. No one disturb me. I hate everything. I hate you. I hate myself. Leave me be.* The sadness stabs like a knife into my soul. Everything is dark. Everything is empty and meaningless.

You might be surprised to learn that hypomania actually has a few positive qualities, specifically an inflated self-esteem. I have always had relatively low self-esteem. Instead of looking inward and finding out what was good about me, I always compared myself to others to the detriment of myself. Middle school and high school were particularly bad, but I imagine that is so for most kids, except, of course, for the lucky few who seemed to have it in spades. But I was not so lucky. I never really thought I was good enough at anything. I was smart, I knew that, but not exceptionally, so there was always someone in the class smarter than me, better than me. Even placing fourth in my graduating class of over 500 students didn't confirm my intellect in my own mind. I knew I wasn't the pretty girl in class however much I wanted to be. Guys didn't flock to me like they did other girls—the ones whose flirty cool stood out. Now I never thought that I was worthless; I just didn't view myself as highly as everyone else did. But that changes when hypomania gets a hold of me. Suddenly I have skyrocketing self-esteem. I believe that I am the smartest, prettiest, wittiest girl in the bunch. I can do anything I set my mind to. I could start taking taekwondo lessons and become a master martial artist. I could place pen to paper and write a young adult novel rivaling Harry Potter. I could learn Spanish and Arabic simultaneously and work for the CIA or the NSA. When I was hypomanic, I would make these grand, unattainable plans because I truly believed I could accomplish them. I had that high of an opinion of my own abilities. Wonderful feeling it is. Wish I could feel that way all the time.

By the summer of 2009, my bipolar symptoms returned in full force. I was trapped in a manic phase that was growing exponentially in intensity for months. I felt as if I was perched at the door of an airplane preparing to jump; my heart was racing, my body was vibrating with anxiety, and my mind was scattered into a million pieces. I was trapped in a single moment of intense emotion that is not meant to be sustained beyond a few minutes. Were I truly on the plane, I would jump, and the heightened tension would pass into the clouds as I spiraled down to earth. But I couldn't jump. I couldn't move. I couldn't release the anxiety.

I begged, I pleaded with Dr. Prince, with the nurses, with anyone to please give me something, anything, to help me. But they couldn't. I was on an accelerating train, and there was no way to get off. They didn't know what to do. I was running through drugs like chocolate, none of them working, none of them easing my mind. The train pushed ever faster. Thoughts, like wintered trees on the wayside, good and bad, moral and immoral, happy and sad, darted though my mind into a dizzying singularity in the distance. But I couldn't grasp them, I couldn't hold onto them; they were moving much too fast. My mind was betraying me; it was failing me. Stop the train, let me think. I cannot grasp the moment. The future and the past are frozen, they are tangible; I can feel their touch, but the present, the present eludes the consciousness. My cells, my molecules, my atoms are vibrating, fluctuating in and out of existence. I can't remain in this state; I can't remain in the present. The train speeds on, dragging me against my will. I can't stop it. No one can stop it. No one can help me. She tried giving me shots. Shooting me up with anti-anxiety medication and sedatives, but they wouldn't work. My mind spun on—the train raced on, speeding ever faster. Coal is piled higher in the hellish engine as my anxiety grows ever more intense. I can't bare it; I can't bare it for a moment longer. I feel as if I am about to explode, erupting like a volcano, tearing my body to pieces. Where's my hero? Where's the cowboy on the golden horse to rescue me from this doomed train? The brakes are gone. The fire is fuelled. The anxiety grows ever stronger. And there is only one way for this train to stop…in the gulley five miles ahead.

That's how I ended up at the emergency room in the wee hours of one terrible morning. I hate going to the hospital, especially the ER. I had been there many times before for my kidney stone attacks, and my memories had not grown fonder. Walking through the ER is like walking through the seventh circle of hell for someone with OCD. It is a teeming cesspool of nasty germs, disgusting viruses, and contagious diseases. People are vomiting, coughing up hordes of phlegm, wiping their noses on their sleeves, oozing out fluids from every orifice. It is sickening, to say the least. I know, I know, I should be more compassionate. The people there are suffering just as I am. But that is the thing about OCD; I can't see the person; I can only see the disease, the contamination, the offending item. All I could think about was being infected with whatever illness they had. And may I add that this took place during the swine flu scare. They gave us masks and hand sanitizers, but frankly I don't put a lot of faith in either when I am sitting next to someone in the worst stage of some flu. Fortunately, even though there were fifteen other people in the waiting room who came in before me, I was called in first. Apparently I was making the other people nervous. I don't remember doing anything outright upsetting. I mean, I was pacing back and forth, just trying to walk off the excess energy in my body. That isn't particularly bad. I suppose I was jerking my arms and head a bit, you know, trying to shake the crazy out of me. And I was conversing with my dad a little louder than I should. But really. Upsetting the patients? Hardly. It seemed like a little bit of an overreaction to me. Unfortunately being called back first doesn't mean I was seen first. Once I was out of the prying eyes of the public, I was left alone until all the other more serious patients were seen. Not that I am complaining now, anyways. I understand the nature of triage. However, at the time I was minutes away from spontaneously combusting from the burning anxiety in my body and quite intolerant to the five-hour wait. By the time the doctor arrived, I was curled up in the fetal position mumbling disjointed phrases. Upon learning I was suffering from a severe manic attack, he seemed most uncomfortable treating me. He was more inclined to transfer me to the psychiatric ward. I, of course, was completely adamant against that. I may not be living in the land of the sane, but I still have some wits about me. No way was I going to voluntarily sign away my rights and enter a mental hospital. I know what goes on in those places; I've seen the movies. Lockdown, forced medication, lobotomies, electroshock treatment…it's more frightening than a Tim Burton movie, the handsome Johnny Depp notwithstanding. Nevertheless, he relented, seeing that I still had some sense about me, and opted for a few shots to calm me. I should probably mention that I hadn't slept for over twenty-four hours by this point, and I was looking for anything to let me get some sleep. He gave me two shots, one anti-anxiety and the other Demerol. I know, I know, Demerol! I could hardly believe my ears. My sweet elixir of happiness was once again within my grasp. I tried to control my elation, acting as if it meant nothing to me, but inside my mind was dancing. Once again warmth spread through me, washing away my worries into the land of forgotten things. But to my distressed discovery, my elation was short-lived. The mania fought back with unrealized strength, tempering my narcotic high. I left the ER mellowed but not cured. I knew it was only a temporary fix and that when I woke up the following morning, I would be right back where I started from.

And I was. Before the end of the month I wound up in the ER two more times. The same routine each time, though each proceeding visit the doctor was more insistent I enter the psychiatric ward. The third time the doctor even considered placing me under the Baker Act—basically having me involuntarily committed. Talk about a frightening prospect. I talked the doctor out of it that time using what was left of my dwindling intellect, but I knew I wouldn't be able to do that a fourth time. If I came to the ER one more time complaining of a manic fit, I would almost assuredly be committed. And I wasn't going to let that happen.

Dr. Prince, feeling in over her head, insisted I try a psychiatrist again. Having had such a bad experience the first time around, I was a bit reluctant, but eventually acquiesced. I went to see a woman named Dr. Rebecca Farinas. The moment I met her, I kept getting this image of a fairy. I had never had such a thought before upon meeting anyone, yet it was such a persistent feeling…fairy, fairy, fairy. But why? There were no fairy figurines in her office, no fairy pictures, no magical paintings, just two orca photographs and a few stuffed animals. So what's with the insistent thought of fairies? She must have fairy energy. What does that mean, you say? I first learned of such a thing a few years ago when I attended a workshop for psychics and mediums in the Florida Keys under medium Dorothea Delgado. I had always been fascinated by the paranormal and was looking to hone any latent skills I may have. In my initial meeting with Dorothea, she told me that I have fairy energy. Fairy energy? Well, I do like fairies. I have numerous figurines on my bookshelves, two cats named Pixie and Tinkerbell, and a propensity for fairy/elf-centric films, but I showed no outward sign or inkling. Even my hair, which used to flow long with a Renaissance feel, was now chopped to my shoulders—a sign more of my current medical conditions than its preferred state. So how could she know? Regardless, she saw something. She sensed something beyond the superficial. But what did her observation mean? According to the book *Earth Angels* by Doreen Virtue, someone with fairy energy or a fairy soul is someone whose soul originates from non-earthly origins, specifically the elemental kingdom where fairies, elves, and unicorns dwell. My soul was once living life as a fairy but reincarnated to a human life, but my soul still bears the footprints, the energy of that life. Thus, I have fairy energy. Now I'm not sure I believe in such fantasy, but it is fascinating to consider. I only mention it now because, all science and logic aside, I did sense a fairy energy from Dr. Farinas. Feeling it was something important, I prompted her if she liked fairies. She did! She liked them a lot. So I swallowed all thoughts of absurdity and told her she had fairy energy. A luminous smile erupted across her face, and she said that made her very happy. I knew right then that I found the right psychiatrist for me. Her office was warm, basked in a soft glow from the one window that was absorbed into the rich wooden bookcases that lined her walls. It was a quiet woodland sanctuary that grew deep green leaves for seats. A little hollow among a sea of austere offices, it eased my tormented spirit. Her voice was soft and lyrical—a much-improved change from my first psychiatrist's office, which bore the cold, blinding white sterile precision of an ER operating room. I knew I was on the right track to getting better.

By that point, in November 2009, my condition had rapidly deteriorated. I had gained forty pounds. My mind was a chaotic mix of garbled bipolar and OCD symptoms. I had stopped showering, washing my face, brushing my teeth, combing my hair, and basically doing anything that involved personal hygiene. I couldn't do it; I was too worn down by the disorders. They had become like a weight on my shoulders, pushing down on me, draining every ounce of strength, both mental and physical, from my growingly frail condition. It is hard for others to understand that a mental disorder can display the same symptoms as a physical disorder, but mental pain is just as real as a pain in any other organ. I have recurrent kidney stones, yet they are nothing compared to the anguish I have felt in my darkest hours of bipolar. But it wasn't just the bipolar I was fighting; my OCD, latent for a short period of time, had returned in greater force than before. What would follow next is another round of new pills.

Dr. Farinas, running out different pills quickly, talked me into trying Geodon. I know, I know, I said I would never try a pill that had a sudden death warning on it, but I was running out of options. I had already tried most of the common drugs used to treat bipolar disorder, and none of them had worked, except for lithium, though in recent months it had ceased to be effective. The intense mania that had sent me to the ER was growing ever worse, and commitment to the mental hospital seemed imminent. I had to try it. Amazingly, despite all my hesitations, it worked. Finally something worked! The symptoms of my bipolar were drastically reduced. Each polar end became much less severe, rendering them impotent in their hold on me. The cycling disappeared from my conscious. Would I only have tried this pill sooner, I probably could have saved myself a lot of heartache. Then again, who knows? It may not have worked then. Nevertheless, I was better; I was much better. The fog of bipolar had lifted, and I could feel the light and warmth on my skin. I was no longer stuck on that accelerating train. The brakes had been fixed, the coal had been stopped, and the lone cowboy walked me off into the sunset. If only the story ended there, for though my bipolar was finally under control, my OCD was as untamed as a pack of wild horses. I thought I knew what it was like to have severe OCD, but I had no idea of what was to come. The stage had been set. The cannons had been loaded. The troops were at attention. And the battle for my sanity had only begun.

Emily's Helpful Information
Medications for Bipolar Disorder (Mood Stabilizers)

WebMD lists the following medications for bipolar disorder.

Ambilify – It was simply ineffective.

Geodon – At first I was afraid to take this pill because it had a sudden death warning, but Dr. Farinas convinced me to try it. Unbelievably it worked. The majority of my bipolar symptoms disappeared. I still have minor episodes of mania and depression, but for the most part I am doing much better.

Lithium – This drug helped to reduce my bipolar symptoms in the beginning, but after a few months, it ceased to be as effective. I continue to take it along with Geodon. Together they help keep the bipolar at bay.

Risperdal - It was simply ineffective.

Seroquel - Ah Seroquel! What can I say? My love affair with this pill lasted for about half a year. I wish I could tell you if it worked, but I was asleep.

Topamax – I take this drug to combat the ravenous appetite and weight gain from the Zyprexa. It also has the strange side effect of making coke taste flat.

Zyprexa – This pill worked to lessen my bipolar symptoms and my anxiety. It also helped me sleep. Unfortunately it made me ravenous thus causing me to gain 30 pounds.

PART VIII: RETURN OF MY OCD

"We do not live an equal life, but one of contrasts and patchwork; now a little joy, then a sorrow, now a sin, then a generous or brave action."
Ralph Waldo Emerson

CHAPTER THIRTY-FOUR
New Battles of OCD

*"Nor ear can hear nor tongue can tell
The tortures of that inward hell."
Lord Byron*

By November 2009 my OCD was the worst it had ever been. I thought it was bad before, but I had no idea how bad it could really get. My mind was filled with a multitude of obsessive thoughts fighting for control. My only hope of quieting them was performing countless rituals that drained me of all my strength, leaving me nothing more than a lifeless figure wasting away on the living room couch. I couldn't do anything but watch television, my mind too caught up in obsessive screams to function in any way.

Obsessive thoughts occupied every square of my conscious mind. Hundreds of voices were screaming in my head, drowning out my ego, my sense of self. They came in waves, formed regiments of soldiers seizing my inner castle.

Is the door locked? I can't remember. I have to go lock it. Is the door locked? I just locked it or did I? I have to go lock it again. I just scratched my eye with my nail. What if I damaged my eye? What if I scratched the cornea? What if I lose my vision? What if I go blind and can't see for the rest of my life? What will I do? I can't handle this. Is the door locked? I just locked it, didn't I? Oh no, I just touched the right side of the sink; that is where I place toilet paper that I touch when I am in the bathroom. It is in the pee zone. What if I have urine on my hands now? I have to wash my hands, but I don't want to. It takes too long. My hands are raw from washing. Oh my eye still hurts. What if I am going blind? I don't want to be trapped in darkness. Is the door locked? I should lock it again; I can't remember. The cat just jumped in my spot on the couch. Didn't she just go to the bathroom? Oh no, there could be traces of urine on the couch now. What do I do? I can't sit there anymore; it is contaminated. I have to take off the covering and put a new couch cover on. The other one will have to be thrown away. My eye still hurts. What if I seriously damaged it? Is the door locked? I just checked a minute ago, didn't I? I don't remember; I'll have to check it again. But I have already checked it like five times. I hate my stretch marks. They look so horrible. I will never be able to wear skirts again. What if I have to live with them for the rest of my life? What if they won't go away? I just want to look pretty. What type of guy is going to marry me when he sees how terrible they are? I'm so embarrassed. Too many thoughts. I can't think; they are all rolling together. Try to separate them out; acknowledge and dismiss them. Is the door locked? I must check it again. My eye still hurts. I don't want to go blind. Oh please, don't let me go blind. What if the cat got urine on the couch; I can't deal with it right now. I just need to sit down and think. But urine could be on my couch! My stretch marks look so horrible, I can't bear it, I can't cope with it. I need them to go away. I can't move on with my life with them there. I can't cope. Stop obsessing over things I can't change. I can just use makeup to cover them up. But I don't want to cover them up. I want them to be gone. Is the door locked? My eye, my eye! Stop talking; everyone stop talking. I can't think. Urine is on the couch! Urine is on the couch! I got pickle juice on my hands from the sandwich I ate at lunch. I washed my hands, but they still smell. I have to wash my hands again; I can't bear the smell. What if the smell won't come off? I don't want to smell of pickles. What am I going to do with my life? I have no career prospects. I'm worthless. What am I going to do? I don't know. I can't think. I can't cope with the voices. What if the cat got urine on me? I picked her up after she went to the bathroom. I didn't know she just went when I picked her up. I found out afterward. Oh God, what if I have pee on me? I don't want to smell of pee. I am contaminated. I have to change clothes; these clothes must be thrown away. I need to get a shower, but I don't want to get a shower. It will be too laborious. I am too tired to perform all my bathing rituals. But what if I have pee on me. I have to get a shower, but I can't. I just can't. Is the door locked? Of course it is; I just checked it. Or did I? I can't remember. I need to lock it again. What if someone dangerous simply walks in because I didn't lock the door? Christine leaves her door unlocked, but I can't do that; I am too afraid. I don't want to be robbed. I don't want to be murdered. Lock the door, lock the door.

Thought after thought, each more obsessive than the last. No break, no time to think, just a constant stream of overflowing thoughts drowning me in their chaotic wake. I can't think. I can't function with the voices screaming in my head. There is only one thing I can do, one thing to make them go away: perform my rituals, my compulsions that the voices call for. Keep getting up and locking the door until I am convinced it is locked. Flush my eye with refresh drops until they ache from aggravation. Throw away any item that is contaminated, or rather that I delusionally believe is contaminated. Scrub myself in the shower until ever drop of pee, perceived or not, is removed from my body. Scrub until my skin is raw. Do what the voices say, barring any bad activity, or they won't stop. And I need them to stop. I need to be able to think; I need to be able to function. My life is now consumed with the compulsions, a broken robot performing the same tasks over and over until I am weak from wear. Please, someone fix me.

Though my OCD didn't fully reveal itself until 1999, upon retrospection I have begun to see little hints, little clues of things to come in my high school years. I was always finicky about being clean, washing my hands a minute or two more than any of my friends, hardly noticeable if I weren't paying complete attention. I just liked being clean. But compulsions weren't really evident at this point. It was the obsessions that caught my attention. I would become fixated on problems to a degree, which was unhealthy and caught the eye of a few of my friends. Any time I had a problem or emotional hardship, it would gather all my attention; I fretted over it until it came to its natural conclusion. Now this was a good thing when it came to my schoolwork. I would focus on math problems, physics problems, and essays, with such intensity that I wouldn't go out with friends or watch television until the work was done. But it was the problems that I couldn't solve—the emotional problems of the teenage years—that garnered the most trouble. I remember having severe acne when I was in high school. It consumed all my attention, making it hard to focus on schoolwork. I would look at myself in the mirror and just sit and cry. How ugly I thought I looked, how unworthy of any boy's affection. I would hide my face in school, covering it with hair or notebooks, putting my head down in class. None of my friends could understand why I was so fixated on my acne when they too were afflicted with the same condition. After all, it was those late teen years when most kids have acne. But I couldn't see that; I could only see the bright red bumps on my face. Hideous. Why was I so unreasonably focused on my appearance? I was obsessed, unhealthily obsessed. But it wasn't just acne; any time any emotional problem came along, I would fixate on it with all the power of my being until the problem went away. Crushes on boys, fights with friends—all were possible obsessions. At the time I just attributed all my actions to puberty, to a hormonal imbalance. Only hindsight has revealed what it really was—the onset of OCD.

By December 2009, the OCD was worse—worse than it ever had been. I don't know if the pills just stopped working or if my symptoms got too bad, but either way, they were rendered ineffective. My compulsions had gone from a minor inconvenience to a debilitating chore. Bathroom activities were by far the worst. No longer an inane bodily function, they were a grand, laborious escapade—an escapade that I had to endure at least three times a day. When did it become such a trying endeavor? When did I lose my way? I can't remember now. I can't remember how things used to be. The worst compulsions I had involved bathroom activities. I feared the bathroom. I feared it because my bathroom rituals were too laborious. Wiping myself, washing my hands, and showering took up too much time. I wasn't always this afraid of the bathroom. I used to go like any other person. I used to wipe myself like anyone else. I used to wash my hands like it was no big deal. How did I do it? I can't remember. I can't remember any of it. Why can't I remember what it felt like to be normal? I want so badly to remember, to be normal again. Why can't I remember? What if I never remember? What if I go the rest of my life living in fear of the bathroom? I won't make it. It has become too severe. It is like a parasite on my back sucking the life blood out of me. I'm too weak now. Years of fighting have left me little more than a shadow of what I used to be. I can't keep going on like this for much longer. I don't have the strength. Walking five feet takes the wind out of me. I am too heavy to go on. I feel like my arms and legs are made out of lead, desperately traipsing through knee-deep mud. There is no vine to help me, no nearby tree to latch onto. I push forward, but it is too hard to move, too hard to breath. There is no end in sight—only miles of desolation. I can't do this anymore. I can't go on. I need help.

As I sit here, typing away at my computer, it is Christmas Eve, the night brimming with anticipation of the neatly wrapped wonders of our youthful wants and needs. The Christmas tree is beautiful, sparkling with joyously colored lights and mementos of years gone by. I should be happy. I should be cherishing all the wonderful people in my life and the great fortunes God has bestowed upon me. But I'm not. My soul dances, but my body is crippled in the chair. My only thought now is of the bathroom. I desperately have to go, but I dread getting up off the couch. I have no choice. The urine will not evaporate from my bladder; eventually I will have to go. But I can't. I do not have the strength. I know what is coming. This is not the bathroom visit that other people have. I will not be out of there in five minutes. I will be in there for an hour laboriously wiping myself until my skin is raw from wear. I try to fight it. I try so hard to fight it, but the OCD always wins out, the incessant voices ringing in my ear that I am not clean, I am not dry. Urine residue is still on my bottom and my upper leg. There is urine on me! There is urine on me! I must wipe myself until I am clean. The voices chant…wipe… wipe…wipe! I desperately try to fight against the screaming voices, but I can't. I can't think with them in my head. I have to eliminate them. I have to wipe myself more, wipe out the drilling voices. Madness descends upon me, screaming, jarring, tormenting madness, pushing out all other thoughts in my head. I relent. I relent to the madness. I relent to the OCD. I go again to the bathroom. But how many more times? I can't keep going. Not like this. I grow tired now, ever so tired. But I can't rest. I can never rest.

Life has degraded down to nothing more than a series of trying bathroom visits. Every time I went to the bathroom, I was in there for at least an hour and a half, not counting showers which were three hours. These bathroom rituals were just so tiring. I would be in there repetitively wiping myself over and over until my skin was raw. To avoid these tiresome rituals, I tried going to the bathroom and getting a shower as few times as possible. When I am not in the bathroom, I am dreading my next visit, counting down the minutes until I have to go again. It is torture—slow, agonizing torture. My only rest comes in the few minutes after each visit, when my bladder echoes emptiness. I can't go on any longer like this. It is breaking me down, slowly chipping off pieces of myself. This isn't living. It is sickness. It is death—slow, agonizing death.

I'm drowning. The OCD is crushing every breath in my body. Its grasp is too tight for me, and it is only getting worse. I'm choking. I'm dying right before everyone's eyes, and no one can help me. Why aren't the medications working? They have helped countless others. I can't hang on much longer. No one could. My time on this world is in its final days. I don't want to go. I don't want to leave my family, but I can't fight anymore. I have no energy left.

<u>Emily's Helpful Information</u>
<u>My Daily Routine</u>

At the worst period of my life, my daily routine was a torturous grip on sanity. I daily fell into psychotic episodes and tantrum fits, so my day was far from ideal.

1. I wake up. Though momentarily refreshed and revived, the weight of the bipolar and OCD fall heavily upon my wilted shoulders.
2. Minutes after I awake, I know I have to go to the bathroom. I dread it with every power of my being. Perhaps I can hold out until I eat lunch; maybe then I will have more energy to go. A risky endeavor due to my bladder incontinence, but any delay to go to the bathroom, I gladly take on.
3. I eat, more than I should as I am trying to lose weight, but I am eating my feelings here, so give me a break. I take my first round of pills.
4. I dreadingly head for the bathroom. Oh God, oh no, bladder spasms. Running to the restroom, I have another bladder accident, leaving my pajamas ruined. Great, more wiping, more cleaning.
5. One hour later I emerge from the bathroom, exhausted, mentally fragile, and ready to sit down.
6. So I am sitting down, trying to relax. I turn on the news to catch up on the daily headlines. Minutes pass and I think about what the heck am I going to do. I can't just sit here all day like this. I have to go out; I have to be active. Doing what, I don't know. I just can't sit here. I have to distract my mind; the crazy thoughts are starting to pour in. Thoughts of OCD, thoughts of

depression, thoughts of anxiety. Unease sets in. What can I do? I start to go crazy, the thoughts driving me to madness. I used to do puzzles, but I can't do them anymore; my mind is under too much duress. What about writing? I could write more in my book. No, I can't do that. My book sucks; I don't want anything to do with it. What about the Wii Nintendo games? No, no, I don't want to play some silly game; I want to be active. I want to have a purpose, a function. With nothing to distract my mind, the thoughts from the OCD and bipolar disorder increase dramatically. Oh God, the thoughts are unbearable. I am going insane as we speak. Full-on psychotic episode in process.

7. In order to calm down, my dad usually has to take time off work to walk with me around the apartment complex or around the mall. Getting me outside and involved in some activity seems to help me calm down temporarily.
8. But when it ends, I begin to grow restless again. My dad can't afford any more time off to placate me, and I can't go off on my own or drive a car, so I am back to sitting on the couch. But soon the thoughts come back—the OCD-laced thoughts, the anxiety, the depression, the chaotic rumblings of insanity, leading inevitably to another psychotic episode.
9. My dad can't take off work this time, so I am left to flail in the wind.
10. Eventually dinner time rolls around, and I am afforded thirty minutes of peace as I bask in the wonderful tastes of the food. I take my second pill dosing of the day.
11. After dinner I relax from another bout of overeating, when the usual array of thoughts descend upon my already tired mind. The thoughts are coming too fast. OCD and bipolar thoughts laying siege on my mind. I can't handle them. I take a sedative to knock out the thoughts and let me rest, only to start the same day over and over again. I call it the cycle of insanity.
12. I have to go to the bathroom again. I can't do it. I am too tired. But my bladder is overflowing. I relent. An hour later I emerge from the bathroom, exhausted, my mind overflowing with OCD thoughts. I give in to the sedative and pass into a restless sleep.

Emily's Helpful Information
OCD Obsessions

Here is a list of my obsessions.

- Contamination obsessions: fear of contamination by
    - body fluids (ex. urine, feces)
    - germs/disease
    - dirt
    - environmental contaminants (ex. radiation, black mold, foul odors)
- Control obsessions: fear of losing control
    - fear of harming or killing myself
    - fear of harming or killing others
    - fear of harming or killing animals
    - fear of having horrible images play out in my mind (ex. images of violence and death)
    - fear of blurting out inappropriate things
    - fear of doing inappropriate things
- Religious obsessions
    - excessively concerned with morality, with what is right/wrong
    - excessively concerned with sinning
    - fear of going to hell
    - fear of the apocalypse
    - fear of demons
- Perfectionism obsessions
    - the need for everything to be symmetrical
    - the need for things to be even and exact
- Superstitious obsessions
    - fear of the numbers 13 and 666 (I don't even like typing them here)
    - fear of a broken mirror
    - fear of a black cat (Ironically, there is a black cat sitting next to me right now.)
    - need to knock on wood whenever something bad is said

Emily's Helpful Information
OCD Rituals

Here is a list of my main OCD compulsion/rituals.

- In the bathroom I would have to wipe myself according to a detailed ritual in order to make sure I was clean.
- In the bathroom I would have to wash my hands according to a detailed ritual to make sure they were clean.
- In the shower I would have to wash myself according to a detailed ritual to make sure I was clean.
- Any time I touched anything unclean, I would have to wash my hands according to a detailed ritual.
- I would constantly check appliances to make sure they were turned off.

Here is a list of a few other OCD compulsions/rituals I have that I have not specifically mentioned in the book.

- Cleaning ritual: I use paper towels to open doors and in general to touch anything that is dirty, like a chair or a magazine.
- Me or my dad would check the refrigerator every time I went out to make sure there wasn't a cat trapped in there.
- Cleaning ritual: If a paper towel is unavailable, I use the sleeve of my shirt or jacket to turn on light switches.
- Cleaning ritual: I use paper towels to turn the faucet on and off while washing my hands.
- Every time I get a shower, I must buy all new bedding for the bed: two sheets, two pillow cases, and one blanket. The old ones don't have to be thrown away; I just simply can't use them anymore. A cover sheet must also be bought to cover the bed with so the animals won't get it dirty.
- Every time I get a shower, I must buy all new towels.
- If any cat lies on the sheets of my bed, other than the cover sheet, I have to put on all new bedding.
- Repeating ritual: I have to press on my door ten times to make sure it is shut tight.

- Mental ritual: I have to recite a tedious prayer every night to make sure no ill will comes to me or anyone in my family.
- I have to put two pieces of furniture in front of the door every night to make sure no one comes in.
- I can't have any curtains/blinds open because I am afraid people are watching me and perhaps even taping me.
- My bedroom is my OCD sanctuary. Everything in that room is clean. No people, aside from me, or animals are allowed in that room without my supervision. I don't even let apartment inspection crews enter my room. Occasionally, I will let my cats walk in there as a treat but not for more than a minute or two.
- I have to put garbage bags over the car seats to make sure a) if it is my mom's car that I don't get dirty or b) if it is my dad's car that I don't get the car dirty. Also, in case I have a bladder accident, I won't get any urine on the seats.
- Checking ritual: I had to recite a checklist with my father every night to make sure he would stop me from hurting any person, including me, or any animal.
- Checking ritual: I constantly checked my hair to see if any more had fallen out and to see how much thinner it had gotten. It, of course, was getting thinner because of the massive stress my body was under from the two disorders, so continually looking in the mirror starring at the bald spots only succeeded in upsetting me.
- Checking ritual: I constantly checked my stretch marks to see if they had gotten any better. I was desperately waiting to see some sign of improvement from the procedure, but it seemed that would never come. Instead I just forced myself to look at gradually worsening stretch marks, which sent me into an anxious fit.
- Repeating ritual: I would turn the reading lamp on and off numerous times until I felt I turned it off just right. If I didn't do it perfectly, I was worried the lamp wires would spark and the house would catch fire.
- Asking for reassurance on everything I think and everything I do.

CHAPTER THIRTY-FIVE
My Bathroom, the Enemy

"A man cannot be too careful in the choice of his enemies."
Oscar Wilde

I dread going to the bathroom. I cannot emphasize enough how much I hate it. The cleaning routines I have to complete make the bathroom time laborious and tiring. I have a specific wiping routine that must be strictly followed in order to be clean enough to leave. Going to the bathroom is a carefully orchestrated endeavor. First is the disposal of the clothing. I pretty much have worn pajamas at all times, for the last four years, at least. I have seen little point in wearing outside clothes as the majority of my day is spent inside on the couch. Besides, I really don't have any day clothes, as I outgrew everything I owned when I packed on a burdensome forty pounds (more on that later). Fashion points aside, it really doesn't matter what I wear as everything goes to the same place—the garbage bin. I am really pretty dirty. I get a shower once every two months, so anything I wear becomes seriously contaminated. By my rules of cleanliness, those pajamas are too contaminated to be washed in the washer and therefore must be thrown away. I know it is wasteful. I know it is illogical, but you can't explain that to my irrational OCD mind. Yet, the fashion graveyard is nothing compared to my arduous wiping process. Fearing any molecule of urine sticking to my skin, I have to wipe my bum and my upper leg until they are red and raw from paper burn. This takes thirty long minutes of constant physical exertion, wipe on, wipe off—thirty minutes of obsessive, compulsive wiping, sweat dripping down my face. Wipe yourself enough and you have your own exercise routine. If I am particularly anxious, I have to wipe myself with antibacterial wipes. That adds an additional fifteen minutes to the equation. My handwashing routine is just as complex and involved, washing two inches past my elbows. I scrub like I am a doctor preparing for open heart surgery, scrubbing every inch of my hand, my lower arm, and my upper arm. I scrub so much that the skin is falling off my hands. It is so exhausting that I avoid going as much as possible. Unhealthy as it is, I restrict the amount of water I drink so that I only have to go to the bathroom twice a day, each visit lasting thirty minutes to one hour and thirty minutes. I leave exhausted, sweat dripping on my brow, my legs shaky with fatigue. It drains me of what little strength I have left. I fear going. I fear the laborious rituals of it. Do you know what it feels like to fear a basic bodily function? It's a fear that I can't escape. I can't run from it. I can't hide from it. I must confront it every day, and it never gets easier. It's strange to say it, but I fear going to the bathroom. But then again, I also fear sleeping, so I suppose it is not that weird. I am afraid to be unconscious, afraid to be out of control. I'm afraid I will die in my sleep, or worse yet, hurt someone. But my body has to go to the sleep, and it has to go to bathroom; as much as I dread it, I cannot fight it. These functions must be done. No matter how much caffeine I imbibe, eventually I will have to go to sleep. But I am afraid, I am so very afraid.

I cannot bear the bathroom rituals any longer. They are too intense. No one should have to spend an hour and a half in the bathroom. Do you realize how much of your life that takes up? That is nearly half the time I am awake. Instead of going outside, leading a normal life, I am hunched over in the bathroom wiping myself raw. No doubt you're asking why I don't just stop, stop the rituals, stop the insanity. But I can't. If I do I will surely go mad. Hundreds of OCD voices are screaming in my head: *I am not clean enough. My bum has urine on it. I am dirty. I smell like urine.* The only way to stop the voices is to clean myself and perform my rituals. If I don't, the voices won't stop; they'll grow louder, stronger, and more insistent. They will scream in my head until I am crouched on the ground rocking in a catatonic state. I must obey; I must or I shall go mad.

I can't go to the bathroom again. I just can't handle it. The wiping/washing process is too arduous, yet I can't stop myself from doing it. If I don't follow my specific routine, then I will be contaminated, and everything I come into contact with will become contaminated as well. But I am too tired to do the routine; the only thing I can do is stop drinking, even if that means becoming dehydrated, but I can deal with that. I just can't deal with going to the bathroom.

By Emily Watson

I had stopped using public restrooms years ago at first just because I noticed my handwashing took longer than others. You'd be surprised how rude some people can be when they observe you behaving just slightly out of the norm. It started with the look—the curious look I get when I dress like I hopped out of a 1980s music video. The look is short and brief and usually lasts no more than ten seconds. Then I get the interested looks—the looks that mark concern and hesitation. Why is this person washing her hands so long? What did she get on her? Is she sick? They see me as puzzle, perhaps a puzzle to be feared, but they don't know. Either way, they treat me with caution. If possible, they choose a faucet far from me or wash their hands quicker than they normally would—all with their eyes fixed steadily upon me. Then came the innocent questions. "Oh honey, you are really washing your hands there. Are you a nurse?" Often I would say yes just to end the conversation. "Did you get something on your hands there?" Quick on my feet, I would respond with some silly story of tomato sauce or tree sap. The longer my routine got and the farther up my arm I would wash, the worst the views would get. They now viewed me with a disturbing eye, contorting their mouths with derision and disgust. What was wrong with me, they didn't dare ask, but their eyes spoke a thousand questions. They just stared, their eyes fixed on me from the moment they walked in to the moment they walked out. They didn't have to say anything; I could see it, I could feel it, and it felt like a knife through my gut every time. I only had one option: stop using the restroom in public and even drinking less when I was out to avoid going. Helpful fact: drinking small amounts of water only makes bladder problems worse.

I have to go to the bathroom. My bladder is swollen with liquid. I can feel it pressing against me, inside of me, spasming in distress. I don't know what to do. I can't go to the bathroom, I just can't. I don't have the energy to perform my rituals. My body is limp and lifeless; the OCD has beaten it down, swing after swing, bruising me beyond repair. But what can I do? Nothing. Eventually I will have to go, lest I pee in my pants. Maybe all the liquid will evaporate in my bladder; maybe I can will it away. The urgency grows stronger, my body is convulsing in protest. Go, go now, I can't win this battle. But I can't. I won't. I must. Please someone help me!

I don't understand why I can't go to the bathroom like normal people. It shouldn't take so long. How is this disorder screwing with my mind? Other people are getting in and out in less than ten minutes. Are they not as dirty as me? Do they not wipe themselves enough? Surely they must. What is their wiping routine? I ask people, try to figure out what I am doing wrong, but they aren't very forthcoming—understandably so. What about handwashing? Are their hands clean enough? I like being different. I like being unique, but not this way. I know some people just simply don't wash their hands. I have seen it a number of times when I used public restrooms. All I can say is "Oh, the horror!" What kind of person doesn't wash their hands? For heaven's sake it is basic hygiene. Gross, really, really gross.

I'm dehydrated. Water is sparse resource in my body. I breathe the wind of the arid desert. I blink the sand of the Sahara. My cells vibrate in protest, sending jarring shivers throughout my aching body. I long for water, for even the smallest droplets of its pristine molecules. I am thirsty. I am so very thirsty. Yet I deny myself this magical elixir. I can't drink. If I drink, I will have to go to the bathroom. I'm weak now; I am much too weak. I can't handle going to the bathroom. I can't handle following my rituals. I'm exhausted. I'm beyond exhausted; I'm deathly tired. Death seems to be my only chance for rest. A simple night's sleep can't restore me. I'm too far gone. I know it's illogical. I know it is bad for me to stop drinking, but I have no other choice. I can't go to the bathroom. I am near collapse. I'll drink enough just to stay alive.

I can't go to the bathroom anymore. It is too hard. Every second I am in there, I feel more alone than any other moment of the day. No one understands. I try to explain it, but my words seem to fall flat. It is not a mere bodily function. It is that test I dread or that jump I fear; it is the worst moment of the day, the one thing I dread beyond all others. I can't do it, I just can't. Urrr, this missing C key is very annoying. I don't know what I am going to do. How long can I hold it? That's silly; I can't hold it forever. I would only be delaying the inevitable. Why does it have to be so hard? I know I am wiping too much. I can see that to some degree, but for the most part, I genuinely feel that I am just thoroughly cleaning myself; I can't imagine cutting anything out of my routine. If I did then

By Emily Watson

I would be leaving urine and fecal matter on my bum. How do people clean it all up with just a few pieces of toilet paper? Oh God, there is no way I am ever going to get a date again after people read all this. I am exposing my bathroom habits, in graphic detail, to anyone who will listen. But I have to talk about it. I have to talk about it so people know the true nature of these disorders. But no one is going to understand; no one will see how truly hard this is. How can going to the bathroom, a basic bodily function, cause anyone such malaise? But it does. It plagues me. I really have to go now; it is only a matter of minutes. I can't do this. I can't go back there. I need an alternative. I need help. Someone please give me a pill that will make all this better. Why do pills work for everyone else and not for me? I can't go. The clock is ticking down. I don't want to go. Please don't make me.

Emily's Helpful Information
My Restroom Repertoire

My Toilet Routine

Now I have debated back and forth whether to place this section in my book, as well frankly, it's gross. It is not commonplace to discuss the intimacies that go on whenever we succumb to our animalistic urgencies, but I have decided the best way to understand my pain is to confront my greatest source—the bathroom. Here is my daily toilet routine:

1. Upon entering the bathroom, I take all my clothes off. It is the only way to ensure that I won't get any pee splatter on my garments, and it offers me more freedom in movement. I then throw away the clothes as they are too contaminated to save.
2. Place toilet paper or sanitary paper on the toilet seat.
3. Get down and do my business.
4. Before getting up, I wipe my undercarriage twice (different paper each time) and each butt cheek once.
5. I stand up. I wipe my left butt cheek multiple times, each time with a different wad of toilet paper, until I feel clean and dry. Each wad of toilet paper must be, at least, ten layers thick.

6. Next, I do the same thing on my right side. I wipe my right butt cheek multiple times, each time with a different wad of toilet paper, until I feel clean and dry.
7. Just in case any pee got on my upper legs, I must also include them in the ritual. I wipe the entire outer side of my left leg multiple times, each with a new wad of toilet paper, until I feel clean and dry, and I wipe the entire inner side of my left leg multiple times, each with a new wad of toilet paper, until I feel clean and dry.
8. Then I do the right side. I wipe the entire outer side of my right leg multiple times, each with a new wad of toilet paper, until I feel clean and dry, and I wipe the entire inner side of my right leg three times, each with a new wad of toilet paper, until I feel clean and dry.
9. I wipe my undercarriage five times, each time with a new wad of toilet paper.
10. If I am feeling extra unclean, then I follow with a few baby wipes or Wet Ones anywhere in the wiping zone.
11. This takes between thirty and ninety minutes.

All right, that wasn't terribly awful, though the word "undercarriage" makes me snicker.

The New and Improved Handwashing Technique

1. I use a foaming hand soap—the bigger the foam the better. I recommend Softsoap in warm vanilla sugar with a hand pump.
2. I press the pump three times to begin washing my hands.
3. I wash an inch past my wrist.
4. I continue pumping in sets of three, adding more soap to my already foaming hands and wash my hands for between ten minutes.
5. Once my hands are thoroughly soaped up, I wash each arm up to two inches past the elbow using three pumps of soap per arm.
6. Once my arms and hands are thoroughly coated in white foam, then I begin the rinsing process.
7. I begin by rinsing only the hands for thirty seconds.

8. Then I start rinsing the left arm. I rinse off the upper arm first down to the elbow. This is done by rotating the elbow beneath the faucet.
9. Next I rinse the lower arm under the facet. I swing my elbow so the water cascades over the arm in one swift motion—three times over the front of the arm and three times over the back of the arm.
10. I rinse the right arm using the same procedure.
11. Returning to the hands, I rinse each side of the hand three times separately.
12. Then I bring the hands together and rinse for thirty seconds.
13. I then separate each hand and rinse top and bottom until the hand feels properly rinsed—usually one minute per hand.
14. Then I bring the hands together once again for the final rinse, thirty seconds.

This being the regular technique for me washing my hands, you can only imagine how involved my shower routine is.

CHAPTER THIRTY-SIX
Revenge of the Bladder

"When sorrows come, they come not as single spies,
But in battalions!"
William Shakespeare

In December of 2009, my bladder problems reemerged with latent severity. My body succumbed daily to painful bladder spasms that left me wearing adult diapers—an absolute embarrassment. I had been having bladder problems since my first kidney stone in 1999. I had the solid misfortune of suffering from recurrent kidney stones, an anomaly for a person my age and gender, though the men in my family had a history of them. But that wasn't my only hardship; I was also diagnosed with interstitial cystitis, IC, a recurring bladder condition that feels like a severe ongoing urinary tract infection, UTI. The IC had tempered in recent years through diet control, but a recent flare-up had left me curled up in pain. The constant spasming rippled through my bladder, burning the walls of the urethra and spilling out uncontrollable urination. Not having control of one's bladder is one of the most upsetting malfunctions to befall the human body. No one wants to walk around fearing the slightest abdominal crunch from a stray cough or sneeze causing urine to leak out. No one wants to go through their day peeing in their pants. It is uncomfortable. It is embarrassing. It is messy and disgusting. And diapers, I must say, are not as absorbent as you think; they inevitably leak onto my clothing…oh, the horror. I can't go out with a condition like this; the slightest spasm, the slightest laugh, and my night is ruined.

I was forced to see a male urologist, to my chagrin, as there are virtually no female urologists. As I feared, the first suggestion he made was an exploratory cystoscopy, an outpatient operation. I am afraid of the hospital, and I am deathly afraid of operations. I don't care how minor the operation is, if there is an IV involved, then I am afraid. The procedure seemed simple enough. Send a camera up my undercarriage and examine my bladder. Now, I am not fond of people looking up my undercarriage. Doesn't have a thing to do with any mental problems; I just don't like people looking there; it is not a theme park attraction. I suppose I am just overly modest, but really, who wouldn't be? Basically they would hook me up to an IV, sedate me, perform the procedure, and then wake me up. Simple enough—that is, if you don't suffer from OCD. There was a whole heck of a lot wrong with that, red flags popping up everywhere. Let's start with the IV. One, I hate needles, especially when it takes three or four tries to get it in. I have very small veins. My arm hurts just thinking about it. Two, I don't like bags full of fluids going in to my veins. It makes me have to go to the restroom, and I don't like doing that. As I have said, most of my OCD problems revolve around the bathroom. I will not use public restrooms, whether it's the hospital or the movies. My bathroom routine is very precise and thus must be done in the privacy of my home. I require four rolls of toilet paper and four containers of Wet Ones per each visit to the bathroom. At the least the wiping process takes twenty minutes, and the washing process takes ten minutes. That time alone prevents me from using a public restroom. If they put an IV into me, that will fill my body up with water, making it necessary to use the restroom at the hospital. I can't do that. They won't let me spend that much time in the bathroom there. Plus, they will not have my soap, or Wet Ones or enough toilet paper rolls. I can't do that. Third, I don't like being sedated. I hate it; I absolutely hate it. I don't like going to sleep; in fact, I outright fear it—another bodily function I fear. It really revolves around the whole control issue thing. I don't like being unconscious. Where do I go? If I am no longer in control, no longer aware, who is? What if I do something bad? What if I hurt someone? I don't know what I would do; I'm asleep. The only things I remember are my dreams, and they are terrifying enough. Disturbing nightmares have plagued me since I was a child. I fear falling asleep into those distorted worlds of shadows and monsters. Worse yet, what if I wake up during the operation and I am paralyzed by the drugs? I can't open my eyes, but I can hear what is going on; I just can't move. It happens to some people—what if it happens to me? I can't be sedated. I can't; it is just too frightening. I can't have that procedure done, but my dad and the doctor didn't listen, putting me on the books for two weeks.

The procedure is nine days away. I can't do it. I don't know what I am going to do. They are going to put me to sleep. They are going to use anesthesia to sedate me. I can't do that. I can't be put to sleep. I am afraid to go to sleep. What if I don't wake up? What if I become trapped in that gray area between sleep and awake? What if the anesthesiologist gives me too much medication and I fall into a coma and die? And the bathroom. God, the bathroom. My OCD is much worse. I am taking an hour in there at a time. They won't let me take an hour at the hospital. They probably won't let me take even fifteen minutes. What am I going to do? I can't do this. But if I don't, my bladder problems may not get better. My bladder needs to be examined and stretched as a part of my treatment. I can't go on like this. My bladder is killing me. The painful spasms take up 80 percent of my day. Every minute I feel like I am urinating in my pants. That is not a pleasant feeling. I have to use adult diapers. This is no way to live.

To ease my pain, the urologist offered me ten pills of Demerol. I know, I know, I should have said no. I should have said that I shouldn't have narcotics, that I have an addiction problem. I should have been strong, but I wasn't. From the moment he mentioned Demerol, my ears perked up with excited glee. I don't remember the rest of the appointment; I don't remember what he said. Once I realized I was getting my sweet Demerol, nothing else mattered. But I ask you, if you were depressed, if you were weak from years of OCD strain, would you not accept the one thing that could make all of that go away? Would you really turn down a happiness pill?

In the end, it didn't really matter, I suppose. The fifty-milligram tablets didn't affect me the way they used to. Perhaps I had become tolerant to the dose, or perhaps the disorders had worsened to a degree that it no longer could counteract. The OCD was the same parasite as the day before. The sadness was just as deep as the previous week. My bladder pain was relieved, but my soul was left dry. I suppose I could argue that was a good thing because it made me less dependent on it. But I had so wanted a few moments of peace.

Oh God, I have to go to the bathroom. I don't want to go. I can't handle it. I feel so lonely in there. I'm all alone. No one can help me. My wiping routine is too much. I want to be able to go to the bathroom just like everyone else. What do they know that I don't? They clean themselves in less than half the time that I do. What am I missing? I can't go on like this. I'm too weak. I need it to end. What do I do? Please someone help me.

A week ahead of time, I chose to cancel the bladder operation. I just couldn't do it. The OCD was much too bad. It was a measure of how truly severe my OCD was that I would cancel an operation that was the only thing that could take my agonizing bladder pain away. I just couldn't do it. I knew what my limits were, and I reached them. I couldn't go to the restroom at the hospital. It would break me. My only choice was to try to get my OCD under control so I could give the operation a try at some later date.

Another bladder spasm. Cursed. What if I peed in my pants? I don't want to go check. I just checked ten minutes ago. But what if I did? It could seep through onto the couch. Then I would have to by new bedding because the old bedding would be too contaminated to wash. That's too much trouble. I don't want to go to all that trouble. But if I don't, I am just going to worry about it. Oh no, I just rubbed my eye with my finger. I haven't washed my hands since I put the eczema cream on them. I could have eczema cream in my eye! That's bad, that's really bad. I should wash my eye out. But I don't want to wash my eye out; it is too much trouble. None of it probably got in my eye. I was rubbing my eyelid. But what if some did get in? What if it causes me to go blind? The label says specifically not to get in the eyes. My foot still hurts. Why is it hurting? Are the tennis shoes rubbing it the wrong way? But I just bought them; if they're the problem, then I just wasted a good one hundred dollars. What if it is my workout? Do I have shock fractures from walking on the treadmill? That is not possible; I haven't been working out very hard. But what if it is? What will I do? I have to exercise. I have to; it is the only way to lose the weight. Why is it hurting? I can't handle another problem. First my bladder, then my eye, and now my foot. The world is spinning. I can't think; I can't breathe. Everything is spinning around me, rushing past me. I'm going to pass out. Stop the spinning. But it never stops. One worry after another rushes past me in a giant tornado, crushing anything in its path.

By Emily Watson

My bladder is killing me! Excruciating spasms punch through my abdomen, leaking out urine in my already filled diapers. I cannot write this book when I am sitting in a puddle of pee. What does changing the diapers do? I will just dirty up another one before the end of ten minutes. Please God, return control of my bladder to me. Let me not be afraid of any movement, lest the floodgates open. I know I need to see an urologist. I know I need that operation, but I can't. Don't you understand I can't? My OCD won't let me. Oh please, heal my OCD so I can get the help I need. I can't go on like this. No one should have to live like this. My bladder tightens, distorts from the pain, and more leaks out. I am in a puddle now. I will never get out. I will never be able to wear regular underwear again. It aches now, a slow burning that radiates up into my body, sending shivers up my spine...

Emily's Helpful Information
What is IC?

Interstitial Cystitis is a chronic bladder disorder characterized by an inflamed/irritated bladder that can lead to stiffening and scarring of the bladder, decreased bladder capacity, and pinpoint bleeding. It is often referred to as painful bladder syndrome. Its symptoms are frequent urination and feelings of pain/pressure/tenderness around the bladder area. Sadly, the cause of this disorder still remains a mystery. To me it feels like a very severe UTI. I feel as if my bladder is constantly spasming, making me urgently feel like I have to go the bathroom or I am already going to the bathroom in my pants. It feels like there is a weight on my bladder, causing discomfort and paranoia. Unfortunately since this disorder is not well-understood, neither is a cure. The main solution lies in controlling my diet to avoid foods that are irritants to the condition, like tomatoes and peanuts. If you think you may be suffering from this disorder, it is a good idea to visit a urologist. They will perform a simple outpatient operation, called a cystoscopy, which basically involves sending a camera up your urethra. Not a pleasant idea, I know, but it will give you a definitive answer.

CHAPTER THIRTY-SEVEN
Boys Have Cooties

"A boy is, of all wild beasts, the most difficult to manage."
Plato

To say that I was well-versed in the art of dating is a gross misstatement. I am a novice, at best. Growing up, boys were never high on my list, unlike most normal girls my age. I had my crushes, of course, daydreaming about guys who would never ask me out. I was the nerd, after all, and not a very cute nerd at that. But most of my focus was on school and my friends.

My junior year of high school, I got asked out on my very first date. An athletic and intelligent senior boy asked ME out to dinner and a movie. My stunned friend standing right beside me said, in shock, that she almost went to the bathroom in her pants. Like I said, I was a nerd, and this was wholly unbelievable. I had never been asked out by anyone before. The closest I ever came was when, swallowing my nerves, I asked a boy to dance at the middle school dance. He, of course, said no, leaving me to walk away in shame. But that was all in the past. Now I was going on my first real date.

I remember him standing at the door, his face lit by the soft glow of the porch light, grinning wildly. His blue eyes danced as he lifted up a bouquet of small but substantial wildflowers. It would seem I found the only gentleman left in modern society. The rest of the date was a frenetic blur punctuated by house salads, awkward driving conversation, and the movie *Titanic*. I agreed upon a second date, but it would be my last. He was quite affable, his old-world manners could charm even the most jaded soul, but I simply wasn't ready. School was the most important thing in my life, and dating would just take time away from that. I didn't know it at the time, but that was my last chance for more than five years to go out on a date.

My next significant opportunity for a romantic rendezvous wouldn't come until my junior year of college, when I caught the eye of a fellow physics undergrad. A fast-talking Latino two years my junior, he towered over my diminutive five-foot-one frame. He was a perfectly suitable date, standing proud as the nerd version of tall, dark, and handsome. But I couldn't reciprocate his advances. I kept telling myself it was because I was too focused on my studies to allow any distractions, but there was something more. Something hidden. Something I only now was beginning to understand—my OCD. All I could think about was he's dirty. *They are all dirty. He's contaminated. How do I know he is clean? Does he wash his hands after he goes to the bathroom? I know only one in five men do according to my dad. Oh the horror!! He could have urine on his hands! He could get urine on me! Dear God, don't let him touch me! How well does he shower? Does he clean himself off well enough? Does he wash in his ears? When was the last time he brushed his teeth? Oh God, I can't stop thinking about only one in five guys wash their hands. What are you, animals? No, I'm sorry; animals clean themselves after going to the restroom. How in the world am I ever going to get married? I cringe at the idea of merely shaking someone's hand. There is no way I am going to be able to date now...*

It is just as they tell you in kindergarten: boys have cooties! That's right, the cootie is back, and it is totally screwing up my love life. One in five! One in five! That statistic is burned in my brain. God, the horror. I really wish I didn't know that. When it comes to OCD, ignorance is truly bliss. If I don't know something is dirty, then it's not dirty, and I can't stress about it. But now I know. How is that even possible? Do they think the sinks are just for decoration? Can they really not know that their hands are dirty? It seems unfathomable that someone could not know that you wash your hands after going to the bathroom. Didn't we learn that in elementary school? Girls are far more sanitary. I would say eight out of ten wash their hands. Women, for the most part, go straight to the sink after leaving the stall. Of course, I think they need to wash their hands much longer, but at least they wash for thirty seconds. I remember one time I was in an airport bathroom, and I noticed a flight attendant didn't wash her hands. I was appalled. I was even more appalled when she was at my gate trying to hand me my ticket. Her urine-covered hands touched my ticket, and she expected me to take it back! Like Jerry Seinfeld when Poppie was trying to hand him that pizza, all I could do was stand there and shake my head in horror. My dad eventually took the ticket and washed his hands with sanitary wipes after I conveyed the whole ordeal. In retrospection, I should have said something.

Apparently people need to be reminded to wash their hands. Maybe I should make up pamphlets describing proper handwashing techniques. I could distribute them at airports and malls. I'd be like the Dali Lama of cleanliness.

The fast talking Latino would be the last guy I would have the chance to date for years to come. I did flirt with a young man in DC. He was one of the students at the Institute of World Politics. He immediately caught my eye. Like the quintessential leading man out of a romantic movie, he was tall, dark, and stunningly handsome. We flirted on and off, well, if you can call it flirting because I clearly don't know how the heck to do it. I was never taught the art of flirting. My attempts at flirting only draw shocked stares and quiet snickering. I try to effortlessly copy the subtle sexiness of Marilyn Monroe with the simple wink of the eye and pout of the lip yet I end up looking like a psychotic idiot. I have no idea if he ever liked me back. Because of my OCD, I obsessed about it all the time, driving my friend Naomi crazy. But after him, I didn't have any more opportunities to date anyone. From the time I left DC, from 2005 on, I spent most of my time in my apartment watching television and doing jigsaw puzzles. I was too sick to do anything else let alone date anyone.

<u>Emily's Helpful Tips</u>
<u>Dating Tips for Guys</u>

WASH YOUR HANDS! FOR THE LOVE OF GOD, WASH YOUR HANDS!

CHAPTER THIRTY-EIGHT
Living with Animals

"Animals are such agreeable friends—they ask no questions, they pass no criticisms."
George Eliot

I love animals. I have had pets since elementary school, starting with a furry little hamster named Doodler and a pure white mouse named Heart to a continual stream of kooky cats. We currently have eleven animals—six cats at our house and three cats and two dogs at my mom's house. The nine cats are Pixie, Tiger, Snow White, Ruby, Blacky, Angel, Tinkerbell, Shadow, and Buddy. The two dogs are Cinnamon and Spice, both pure white poodles. We lost three cats in short order before the end of 2009, one to diabetes (Little One), one to cancer (Mango), and one to old age—the last being the regal Kitty, my very first cat, who lived to the ripe old age of twenty-one. We are very tenderhearted and take in stray animals. Sometimes we get them from shelters, but often we just take them off of the street. We picked up five that were just hanging around our apartment. We picked up one that was hanging around the supermarket. We just took in a new stray kitten a few weeks ago from another supermarket. My dad and I went to shop at another market when we ran into a guy holding a three-week-old kitten. He didn't know what to do with her, and before he could finish his sentence, I offered to take her to the chagrin of my dad, as we already had eight cats. But I couldn't help it. Whenever I see a needy animal, all I want to do is help. She was as cute as could be. She was so young that we had to feed her with a bottle. We'd wrap her up in a towel for stability and then put the bottle in her mouth. She would close her eyes and make the sweetest little sucking noise, of course getting milk everywhere. She is a little hellion, though, when she is awake. She just gets into everything. My family has always had a soft spot for animals of all types. We do what we can for those abandoned, those tossed aside by uncaring owners, and those who felt the lash of a cruel human hand. I detest people who abuse animals whether with direct violence or abject ambivalence. The true character of a man can be seen in his treatment of animals. I am quite sure if I ever witnessed such cruelty firsthand, I would raise my fist in vengeance. How could someone hurt such innocent creatures? How could someone abandon an animal because they've grow tired of it? What worthless, wretched soul could do such a thing? I can't stand to see an animal suffer; I burn up in a fit of rage. I wish I could help all the animals of the world, all those quietly suffering in the unseen shadows. I wish I had the money to build a big shelter to house all of the hundreds of abandoned animals wandering the streets. But I don't. For now I will have to help one animal at a time, taking in strays or finding them other suitable homes.

Unfortunately, having animals is very detrimental to the health of someone with OCD. Animals, by their very nature, are dirty. They shed, they get slobber everywhere, and they don't wipe themselves with toilet paper. Cats are probably the best, relatively speaking, as they are self-cleaning. I never have to give a cat a bath. Still, our house is filthy; cat fur is everywhere. Little tumbleweeds of cat fur, litter, and dust blow by as we walk. The cats don't wipe their bottoms or their paws after they go to the restroom, so traces of pee and poo are tracked throughout the house. Two of my cats like to spray around the house. I was shuffling through some books one afternoon only to discover they were covered in urine. Medication, specifically Prozac, curbed their spraying but didn't stop them from peeing outside the box. A few cats peed out of the box, while another cat went pooh out of the box. The dining room was constantly splattered in urine. I felt like I was living in a public restroom. The disgusting smell perforated every piece of furniture, every patch of fabric, weaving its odor throughout the small room. The smell was disgusting. Sure, I could clean it up, but five minutes later another pee spot would appear. The dining room was changed from a place of eating to a public restroom for cats. I hate walking though it on my way to the kitchen. Furthermore, cat hair and dander was spread all throughout the apartment and littered on every piece of furniture. I suppose this is the price we pay for having six cats in a small apartment. But despite all evidence it was hurting my condition, I couldn't give them up. All six were abandoned animals that we took in from the outside. Their owners already abandoned them once; I couldn't do that to them again. I just had to learn how to cope with that situation. Besides, they have some very positive qualities. They are entertaining to watch, especially when they were kittens. I could watch Pixie climbing up and down the Christmas tree, flying off branch limbs, for hours. It is calming to have one sit in my lap purring while I gently stroke her back and forth. It doesn't matter if the negatives outweigh the positive; they are a part of my family and I love them, so I will just have to deal with the consequences.

Emily's Helpful Tips
How to Cope with Living with Animals

Here are a few tips that helped me cope with living with animals.

1. Designate an area in the living room, bedroom, and any other major room that you are in a lot, to be animal-free. Then train your animals not to enter that zone. It is easy to train dogs, as they are often taught not to get on the furniture, but cats can be taught too. I have six cats; it can be done. I trained them not to get up on the living room sofa.
2. Always keep Wet Ones and Clorox wipes around to clean up any messes.
3. Buy organic litter; it not only smells better, but it doesn't get tons of litter dust floating in the air.
4. If possible, replace any carpeted areas with a hard surface like tile. It is much easier to clean than carpet, and it also doesn't trap any hair and pet dander.
5. Try to focus on how much you love your animals, not how much trouble they cause.

CHAPTER THIRTY-NINE
Control Issues

*"Know how sublime a thing it is
To suffer and be strong."*
Henry Wadsworth Longfellow

"The supreme excellence is not to win a hundred victories in a hundred battles. The supreme excellence is to subdue the armies of your enemies without even having to fight them."
Sun Tzu

    Embedded deep within OCD is one of its most primal elements: the need to be in control. Generally speaking, all people want to be in control of their lives, in control of their own fates. But it is only when it enters the obsessive realm that it falls under the banner of OCD. Consider one of my greatest fears: going to sleep. Being asleep is the epitome of lack of control. When I am asleep, my conscious mind is no longer in control. How very frightful, the absence of consciousness. What happens during this time? What part of me is in control? Where do I go? Worse yet, what if I do something terrible during this time? If I am not conscious to control my actions, who is? What if I hurt someone? What if I hurt my parents? What is I hurt my animals? What if I kill someone? How can I monitor my actions if I am asleep? I must be in control of my actions 24/7 if I am to prevent myself from doing something bad. The only logical thing to do is not to sleep. But as that is impossible for more than a night or two, I am left with only one alternative: to worry about it until I am gray in the face.
    If only my control issues stopped at sleeping. But, alas, that is not so. The need to be in control impacts every aspect of my life, preventing me from having any level of normalcy. Take my fear of flying. Why don't I like to fly? What stops me from boarding a plane? Fiery death comes to mind, but it is more than that. When I step aboard a plane, I am handing over control of my life to two pilots and a handful of mechanics. Whether I live or die is in their hands. How can anyone agree to such a

charter? Are they mad? As long as I am on the ground, I have at least the illusion of control that my fate, my destiny is in my own hands. I can't give up control; my only choice is not to fly. If I need to get somewhere within the United States, I can simply drive. Well, actually someone else would have to drive me, as I am unable to take the wheel. My OCD is bad enough to make me a danger on the road. Besides, I have about six psychotropic drugs in my system—a cocktail no one should drive under. Riding the open road is a long alternative to the speed of flight but worth the price of my sanity. As for the lands beyond the oceans, for now at least, they are out of reach. It's odd when I think about these disorders, how they, in effect, change my thought process, my very mind. I wasn't always so frightened of flying. In fact, I racked up quite a large number of frequent flier miles during my four years in high school, traveling all across the country. I had no more control over my fate then as I do now, yet it didn't bother me. Well, it did bother me some but not to the degree it does now. I actually liked flying—the cozy cabin, the preprepared little meals, the rush of adrenaline when I'm taking off, the mystique of flying high over miniature lands, the excitement of travel. Every time I boarded a plane, I felt like I was taking off on a great adventure like Indiana Jones. The air was rich with possibilities. How could I love flying a few years ago and now fear it so desperately? Nothing's changed. The lack of control remains the same. How can OCD make me suddenly fearful? It is just so strange.

It isn't just flying. I fear any type of ride, from a small Cessna to a rollicking roller coaster. As I have already mentioned, I detest roller coasters. Nowhere is one's lack of control more evident than strapped to a mind-bending, stomach-twisting, hair-whitening roller coaster. Like a rag doll from my youth, I am pushed, pulled, dropped, spun, and tossed about without any ounce of say. Adrenaline burns through my body, elevating my pulse rate, rattling my stomach, and nearly giving me a heart attack, yet I can do nothing to stop it. Who would find such a ride pleasurable? Who would wait in a two-hour line for such a monstrosity? I remember going to Busch Gardens, primarily a roller coaster theme park, during spring break of my senior year of high school. I spent the entire day holding my friends' purses as they excitedly road nearly every coaster in the park. Not that I am complaining, as nothing short of a presidential call would get me to ride one of those deathtraps. I opted for the lazy flume ride with only one minor drop. Give me Disney World any day with their child-friendly, slow-moving rides.

I have to be in control of every aspect of my life. But there's the catch: OCD makes me want to be in control, but it also prevents me from doing so. With OCD my life is not my own. My actions are dictated by my rituals. I don't want to spend one hour and thirty minutes in the bathroom, but I have to. I have to complete my rituals. I hate them. I wish I didn't have to do them. They bring me no joy. OCD controls me. It controls what I think. It controls how I act.

CHAPTER FORTY
Growing Up

"Be not afraid of growing slowly, be afraid only of standing still."
Chinese proverb

It hurts to grow up. No one ever tells you that, but it does. You watch all these movies when you're young, with amazing heroes and heroines, and you think you are going to have your own epic story. You don't think you are going to be the sick secondary character who gets killed off in the first act, but that is who you are—the sick character—the character who doesn't matter. One day you just grow up and realize your life isn't going to be anything special.

I'm a nerd. I'll admit it. I am a huge nerd. I was always the "smart, quiet one" in school. Instead of going to the beach in the day and partying at night, I was in my room studying. Getting good grades was the most important thing to me in those late teen years. I had a plan: make good grades, graduate top in my class, get into a great college, and become successful in my job. I nearly made straight As my entire high school time, graduating fourth in my class. I would have graduated second or first had I taken two more AP classes senior year instead of yearbook and study hall. But no regrets; it would have been too traumatizing giving speeches to my entire graduating class. Such thoughts aside, it should be evident that I was a brainiac. My mind was my one great skill. I couldn't sing. I couldn't play a musical instrument. I couldn't draw. I couldn't paint. But I could think. I could solve complex mathematical equations. I could analyze the magnetic field of a current in a wire. I could study the wave function of an atomic particle. That was what I was good at. That was who I was, the "smart girl." But like some insidious thief, that was stolen from me. OCD and bipolar stole my mind. What was I to do now?

I had so many dreams growing up. Daydreaming was my favorite pastime. I would sit in class, my head resting on my hand, and wonder what my future could be. Would I become an astronaut and be the first woman to step foot on the Red Planet? Would I become a paleontologist and dig up millions of years old dinosaur skeletons on the dry hills of Wyoming? Would I become a CIA agent working to protect the country from terrorist threats? Would I study Egyptian at the foot of the Sphinx? Would I be a world traveler, leaving my footprints from the Sistine Chapel to the Great Wall? Would I be a mom with a baby on each hip? Would I be the first woman president? The possibilities were endless. I had the potential to do anything. OK, well not anything. I can't sing; actually I'm really awful—dogs howling awful. I can't play sports; my shining moment in flag football being when I scored a goal against my own team. Oh, that was so embarrassing, though not quite as embarrassing as being picked last for team sports. Why do they have to divvy up kids like that? Talk about a self-esteem crusher. I can't be a biologist. I can't dissect animals, I just can't. I can't be a lawyer; I hate to argue. Plus there is that whole "fear of public speaking" thing. So, all right, there are a lot of things I couldn't do, but I think you should get the picture. My future was unwritten, and I was ready to pen a great adventure. Little did I know that somewhere inside my body, deep in the interworking of my cells, in the pages of DNA, my fate was already written—a nightmare I had never imagined.

I can't do this. Someone please help me. I'm afraid. I don't know what's wrong. I don't know how I feel. There is too much going on to make sense of.

Why is all this happening? I don't mean to whine, but I don't understand. My friends have all moved on past me. One has her own real estate company, one is a writer at a newspaper, one is a high school math teacher, and one is studying for her doctorate in Egyptology. Two are married. But me? I am doing nothing, just wasting away. I am but a tragic shadow of the vibrant character I used to be. My hair is falling out in monstrous chunks from anxiety. My skin is dull and lifeless from lack of washing. My once slender physique is now a heavy mass hanging off my petite frame like a chunky sweater on a wire hanger. Why do all of my friends get to succeed while I remain trapped in a single moment in time, unable able to move forward, unable to even see forward, only able to look back? I have always been the successful one. I got a BS in physics, arguably the hardest major out there. I got accepted into graduate school at Florida State University, the University of Florida, the Institute of World Politics, and Georgetown University. I'm smart and hardworking, and after all my years of hard work, I deserve to see the fruits of my labor. Yet nothing. I remain frozen in a single moment of terror—my hands cusped against my head, a single scream touching off my lips, and ice all around me.

CHAPTER FORTY-ONE
Mourning the Loss

"Gone - glimmering through the dream of things that were."
Lord Byron

    I miss myself. It has been so long since I have been me—the me prior to all these mental illnesses. It has been so long, I am beginning to forget. What a poor thing memory is; we retain so little of our entire human experience. I don't remember the last time I was myself—maybe four years ago when I was in DC. There are a few flashes of me, though I had already begun to spiral out of control. I would have to go all the way back to high school to find a time when I was completely free of my disorders. That is ten years ago. Hard to believe. It seems like it was only yesterday—cliché, but true. This past summer, the summer of 2009, we had our ten-year reunion. I didn't go, for obvious reasons. I had always imagined that at this point in my life I would have a successful career, a loving husband, and a couple of babies on the side. I thought I would walk into that reunion proud and happy. I never thought I would walk in like this—mentally unstable, haggard from the strain, barely garnering the will to live. Pathetic. I amounted to nothing. I'm living in the same apartment I have lived all my life with my parents, no less. I am not an adult; I am a worthless child.
    I miss Washington, DC. I miss my apartment, my first apartment—the cozy den with a window nestled beautifully above Embassy Row. I miss the historical underpinning of the city awash with fortuitous monuments. I miss the noises of the city seeping through my window in the wee hours of the morning. I miss who I was when I was there. I miss that girl, the girl who could turn the world on with her smile, the girl who tossed her hat in the air as she walked through the city with the whimsy of a child. OK, so that was Mary Tyler Moore, but you get the picture. I miss me. I missed how independent and brave I was. I was on my own, living in my own apartment, leading my life as a grown-up. I walked the city streets alone, unafraid of the dangers, blissfully walking from the National Cathedral to the Lincoln Memorial. I was working toward a prestigious career in national security affairs, heading toward a job at

the CIA or the NSA. I had dreamt for years about being a secret agent at the CIA, using my intellect and skill to thwart the evildoers the entire world over. Cracking secret codes, exposing terrorist plots, protecting the weak all in a day's work. I just wanted to help others. That is all I have ever wanted to do. But I can't—not as a CIA operations officer, at least. No one would hire a mentally unbalanced person to handle such dangerous matters. The mental strain would undoubtedly unseat a person like me. I wouldn't even pass the physical.

I miss my freedom—the ability to travel of my own volition wherever I could walk or wherever a taxicab could drop me. I didn't need a car; the city took care of me. I wish I could do that now, but I can't. The OCD has left me completely unable to drive a car. Even if I thought I could, I shouldn't because of all the medication I am on. I am left having my parents drive me wherever I need to go. I'm so afraid to drive. I am worried I would hurt someone. I can't handle such large machinery; I would surely get into an accident. Yet I drove for many years, from ages seventeen to twenty-four without injuring anyone. I did hit another car once. A mom and two kids were inside, but no one was hurt. I mean, I was only going five miles per hour in rush-hour traffic. I looked down for one second and bam, bumper-to-bumper action. The kids did not miss a beat playing on their handheld games. I have only ever been in one other accident, and it only involved my car. I was driving to visit some friends at FSU, when uneven roading caused my tire to pull away from the hubcap, sending me in an uncontrolled 360-degree spin. Scary, just a bit. I remember letting go of the steering wheel and letting fate take control. Fortunately I was unharmed, though the car took quite a beating, ending up at the bottom of a hill beside the road. But did I let that scare me away from driving. Absolutely not. I picked myself up and kept driving, fear not even a glimmer in my rearview window.

I miss the life I lead back in high school, back before anything was ever wrong. I miss my life before I had OCD, before I had bipolar, before I had bladder problems. I can't live the way things are now, not for much longer anyways. I can't live the rest of my life with OCD. I can't deal with never ending stress about cleanliness and the bathroom. I can't live the rest of my life with bipolar. I can't deal with periods of agonizing depression and unbridled anxiety over and over. I can't live the rest of my life with bladder problems. I can't deal with an unstable bladder and perpetual bladder accidents for the rest of my life. I just can't deal with it. I can't. It's too much. It's not fair. I can't handle it. I would rather die.

Poetic Musings

Without Vision
by Emily Watson

Angel from unearthly realm
Why have you left my aging helm?
Leaving me in time of need
Without divine and knowing lead

No longer do you guide my path
I'm off the course, exposed to wrath
No longer do you light my way
Now in the dark, I'm left astray

Offended thee? I implore
Won't you visit just once more?

CHAPTER FORTY-TWO
Shooting for the Stars

"If one advances confidently in the direction of his dreams, and endeavours to live the life which he has imagined, he will meet with a success unexpected in common hours."
Henry David Thoreau

"All that is gold does not glitter; not all those that wander are lost."
J. R. R. Tolkien, The Fellowship of the Ring

"Do not go where the path may lead, go instead where there is no path and leave a trail."
Ralph Waldo Emerson

Ever since I was a child, I wanted to be a scientist. I wanted to be an astronomer studying the heavens. Or a physicist searching for the grand unified theory. Or a paleontologist digging up millions of year-old bones. I wanted to do so many things, be so many things. But my heart always settled on physics. I wanted to be a great physicist, searching for answers to life's deepest questions. How did the universe begin? Is time travel possible? Is there life on other planets? While other kids where struggling to find their identity in high school, I already had my plans set in stone. I was going to go to a prestigious university and get my doctorate in physics, or perhaps astrophysics. Then I was going to get a job at NASA or another government department or maybe SETI. I remember I was at a birthday party for a friend in sixth grade where her mom was videotaping everyone and asking them questions. She asked me what I wanted to do when I grew up. I remember saying quite assertively that I planned on being the first woman to walk on Mars. High aspirations I had there. I can't believe I ever thought I could do that. I mean, really, can you imagine *me* in the space program? I would surely flunk out of basic training, probably on the very first day. The minute they put me in a space suit, I would have a panic attack from claustrophobia. But back then I was hopelessly idealistic, and I thought I could do anything. It wasn't until I started college in 2000 that everything fell apart. It was the end of my freshman year, after having taken two semesters of physics courses, when I came to the unsettling realization that I didn't like physics. I thought perhaps I didn't like it because it was too hard and that I just couldn't cut it. So to prove to myself that I could do it, I stuck it out another year. By then I was absolutely miserable. I was making straight As, so I knew I could handle the workload, but I just wasn't enjoying what I was doing. Sure, I still liked the broad theories of physics, but I was getting bogged down in the day-to-day workings of it, complex mathematical equations and obscure theorems. I hated it and I hated how much of my time it took up studying to maintain an A average. I wanted to switch majors, but I couldn't. It had been my dream for so long to be a physicist that I couldn't give up on it. I kept thinking that maybe I would start liking it. So I toughed it out for another year. But things got worse. I didn't just dislike it; I loathed it with every fiber of my being. How could I feel this way about a major I had grown up loving? I think perhaps I had a romanticized view of physics, spending my time solving the grand mysteries of the universe. I didn't see the day-to-day work of physics in which you're trapped in a sea of mundane equations. I should have switched majors then, but I couldn't. This had been my dream for so long that I couldn't give up. But I was miserable. The anxiety I felt over remaining in a difficult major that I hated was unbearable. That, along with my burgeoning OCD and bipolar, made me an absolute mess. My hair was falling out. Red patches of eczema were appearing all over my skin. My acne was breaking out. I was engaged in countless OCD rituals from washing my hands for ten minutes to neurotically arranging my research folders over and over. I was deeply depressed, not wanting to go to school and work, prone to fits of tears and screams. I had developed the crazy eyes—those wild, shaking, unblinking eyes that warn others to stay away. Mental deterioration aside, I decided to stick it out for one more year; after all, it was my dream. I finished my degree in the longest four years of my life. I had the bachelor's in my hand, which I had sought for so long, yet what was I going to do with it? I couldn't go on to get a doctorate in this major; I was too miserable. How I wished I loved that major. Why couldn't I love it? Whatever the reason, it didn't matter; physics and I were to part ways. I was losing my dream, but more than that, I was losing my identity.

By Emily Watson

Since middle school I labeled myself a future physicist. That was who I was. It was my identity. But after college I lost that, and I didn't know who I was. What do you do when you lose your identity? I didn't know what to do. I was lost. My confidence was shattered. I was worthless. Who would ever want to love me when I have no career? I've always believed that we are each destined to follow a specific career path. Some are destined to be real estate agents, others teachers, and others scientists. If you're lucky, you figure out what you are meant to do early on like I thought I did. But what do you do when you can't find your path? What do you do when you're lost? It has been six years since I graduated with my physics degree, and I still haven't figured out what I am meant to do. Granted, the OCD and bipolar make it difficult for me to discern that, as each path seems filled with anxiety and depression. But still, I thought some light might shine through. Right after I got my degree, I thought I wanted a career in national security affairs. I wanted to work for the CIA or the NSA. I moved up to Washington, DC, and enrolled in the Institute of World Politics in 2005. I was perfectly poised to get a position in the intelligence sector. But I quickly learned that career wasn't meant for me. Besides, even if I wanted to do it, I couldn't, as my OCD and bipolar were so severe that I had to give up school entirely. Since then I have been trying to find my path, but the OCD and bipolar make it difficult. As for right now I really can only take jobs where I can work from home. I thought about becoming a photographer. I went out and bought a nice camera and began taking pictures around town, mostly of the beach. I thought if I was meant to do it I would have some natural skill, but alas the pictures turned out to be most uninspiring. I thought about becoming a makeup artist, but that would require at least another year of school, and I am not mentally stable enough to return to school, though I certainly practice enough on my own, as I absolutely love makeup. I thought about becoming a writer. My friends and family have been telling me that for years. It would be an ideal career as I can work out of my own home, and it would be fun to write fictional stories, but I don't think I have the skill to be one. Anyways, I am left without a career path; maybe if I was without the OCD and the bipolar, I would be able to find one, but as for now they control my decisions.

For now, I have lost my identity and am struggling to come to terms with that. It is unfortunate how we define a person's identity based on what they do instead of who they are. My friend Naomi reminded me of that when I called her just the other day. She is one of only two friends that I have kept up with since high school. I've known her since middle school. Hard to believe that is about twenty years ago, as we are both now heading for our thirtieth birthdays. She knows me in a way that only childhood friends can know each other. Knowing each other back to when we were pure, unburdened by the trials and tribulations of life. Back to when we were happy from just the simple joys in life. It had been over a year since I last talked to her, being too wrapped up in my own problems to want to talk to anyone. But as with good friends, it felt like no time had passed. She excitedly told me about all the new things in her life from a new career as an international business woman to travels in Eastern Europe and the Middle East. I listened with joy for her but sadness for myself, as I could never do such things, not with the OCD at least. I then tearfully told her all about my misfortunes. She reminded me that our identity isn't wrapped up in the career we have, but rather it comes from who we are inside. What we do doesn't define who we are. But I don't know who I am. I have been suffering from OCD and bipolar for ten years now. They have become a huge part of me, and more than anything else, they define who I am and what I am about. I can't separate them from myself. I am manic/depressive. I am obsessive/compulsive. I am completely and totally crazy. But Naomi looked past all of that. She reminded me that I am sweet, funny, and intelligent. It's nice that someone can see something good inside of you when all you can see is the bad.

Kind words aside, I still feel lost. I miss my identity as an up-and-coming physicist. I only wished I actually liked the job itself. As a child, I used to have so many dreams of what I was going to do when I grew up. I was always told what great potential I had. I liked to think of myself as Joe from *Little Women*—the girl you just knew was destined to do something special. She had all the talent in the world and an adventurous spirit to take life by the reins. I thought surely that was me. I never imagined I was actually Beth, the sickly sister who dies before the final act. She was a sensitive, gentle soul, limited by her frail body, who only wished to be with her family. I'm not Joe at all. I'm Beth. Despite my best efforts, I am trapped in a body that is ravaged by OCD and bipolar. My body, worn down by years of stress from these disorders, is

By Emily Watson

weak and frail. And amidst the darkness that I am trapped in, my only desire is to be with my family because that is the only thing that really matters. I only hope I don't die before the story is done.

PART IX: THE CRUEL MIRROR

"It is amazing how complete is the delusion that beauty is goodness."
Leo Tolstoy

CHAPTER FORTY-THREE
My Expanding Waistline

"There is no love sincerer than the love of food."
George Bernard Shaw

By the summer of 2009, I had gained over forty pounds, though it felt more like one hundred. My entire life I have had a svelte frame, not overly thin or excessively chubby, just perfectly healthy-looking. Gaining weight had never been an obsessive fear of mine like it is for many girls because, frankly, I thought I would never let myself become fat. I prided myself on having a slightly comely appearance. Was I vain? Perhaps a little. But in today's society with so much emphasis being placed on beauty, it is hard not to be. Appearance meant a lot to me. Images of full-lipped, long-tressed, curvaceous beauties attacked me in every major media forum. I was a product of the modern world spoon-fed the belief that if I want to be successful, have an exciting life, and nab the man of my dreams, then I needed to be beautiful. The greatest heroines of the big screen, Vivian Leigh in *Gone with the Wind* (who, coincidentally, was also diagnosed as bipolar), Ingrid Bergman in *Casablanca*, and Kate Winslet in *Titanic*, all had the look that men desire and women envy. If I wanted to be a great heroine too, then I had to be beautiful. If I am not beautiful, then I don't matter. Every magazine, every television show, every movie espouses the singular belief that only the beautiful lead successful, adventurous, amazing lives. Think of your favorite movie. Are the leads good-looking? Think of your favorite television show. Are the characters handsome? Society is telling us that you have to be beautiful to get good jobs. But it is not just good jobs; it is relationships as well. Pick any romantic comedy and you see only the pretty girl catches the handsome suitor. But I am not pretty. I am far from it. I tried hard to be. I pored over images in magazines, desperately trying to morph myself into one of those captivating starlets. I highlighted my hair to a golden blond hue. I taught myself the art of makeup, transforming my face from ingénue to full Hollywood icon. I bought the latest trends in fashion. I was the product of modern Hollywood, and I was perfect. But that all came crashing down. Forty pounds heavier and ghastly pale, I resemble the villain rather than the heroine of the epic tales.

It's funny, really. I didn't notice the first twenty pounds, nor did I really notice the next ten. I just woke up one morning and discovered, to my great horror, that I had gained about forty pounds. Sudden panic set in as I raced to the mirror to find, yes, yes, I had actually gained forty pounds. How did that happen? I swear, I looked thin just the other day. The only explanation is that sometime during the last year I had just checked out of reality. The anxiety, the mania, the depression—at some point they just became too much to bear, so I gave in. Or gave up. I just couldn't stay in the fight any longer. I let go of the world and receded to a cozy corner in my mind. People asked me how I could I simply let go. What did that actually mean? What am I letting go of? I guess it is a hard concept for people to understand—at least people who have never had a mental disorder. It's no different than an athlete running race until he collapses just feet from the finish line due to extreme exhaustion. That's what mental illnesses are: a race, a terrifying and disturbing race, but one with no end. At least no end that we can see. We just keep running, keep fighting, but the cure never comes; the race never ends. At some point we fall down and instead of getting up and keeping on running what seems to be an endless race, we stay down. I stopped caring about my hair looking nice. I stopped caring about my makeup being perfectly done. I stopped caring about the size of my waistline because none of it matters any more. All the side issues that have been consuming my daily life have fallen by the wayside. Only one thing matters now and that is living to fight another day.

I am nothing! I am worthless! No one will ever love me. Staring at myself in the mirror is punishing. I can't look at myself. I can't look at what I have become. I hate myself! I need to be punished. I need a knife. I need a sharp kitchen knife to cut the ugliness out of me! I despise myself! I despise myself! Where's the knife!

I'm ashamed to say that I underestimated how difficult it is to lose weight. Being thin all my life, I just assumed that anyone who was fat was merely lazy. But it is really very difficult. I have to look at food as an addiction; however, unlike any other addiction, the offending substance is everywhere. I have come to the realization that I have addictive tendencies. I openly admit that I am addicted to narcotics. I absolutely love them. Just the thought of them raises my pulse and dilates my eyes. I've lied to get my hands on them; I have conducted little ruses. Were I braver, I would attempt to get them on the black market, but alas, I am too cowardly. Really the only thing stopping me from taking them all the time is the relative difficulty in acquiring them. Unfortunately the same can't be said of food, my other big addiction. Walking through a grocery store is like walking through a store full of narcotics. Everywhere I turn there are drugs, precious food, delectable cupcakes, savory pastas, and succulent steaks. How am I to fight my addiction when I can get my fix at any local store? Food is everywhere: in my kitchen, at work, at the grocery store, at the bookstore, at the mall. It is everywhere, calling to me, begging me to swipe a taste. But it is never just a taste; it is an inhalation of anything tasty, a never-ending desire for more food. I eat till I am full, and then I keep eating until all the plate is gone, overstuffing myself to the point of explosion. The urge is too strong. I can't deny it; I can't only appease it. The emptiness burns my stomach; I must fill it. I must fill the void. My appetite is unrelenting. Why am I so hungry? Why am I so addicted to this substance? Is it because of the disorders? Am I trying to fill the emptiness? Eating makes me happy; it settles the chaos in my mind, if only for a moment. Every time I'm sad, every time I'm anxious, I can simply go to the store and raid the cookie aisle. Momentary happiness lies inside a crème-filled treat or generously powdered donut. Do I keep eating to extend that moment, to make it last as long as possible, to stay wrapped in happiness? It makes sense. It is the same reason I love narcotics—the high, the state of pure unadulterated happiness. All addictions, all longings for the joyfulness I once had. In the darkest hours, it has been the only happiness I could afford myself. For a few brief moments while I was eating, I could think only of the tasty delights dancing across my tongue. There were no worries, no sad thoughts, no manic fits, just joy. But it came at a price, a big price.

Get this fat off of me! Get it off! I hate you! You let this happen. You let yourself get fat, and now look at you—a soft, fat mass hanging off a skeleton. You disgust me. I'm never going to lose the weight. I am going to look like this for the rest of my life. It is all my fault. Damn you! Burn in hell! Get this disgusting lard off of me! Burn, burn!

I had to lose weight. I had to get the chubby lard shell off of my body. I needed to cut it out, slice the layers of fat right off me with a jagged kitchen knife. The mass mocked me, all the while suffocating my petite frame. Burn the fat, burn it off me. Use any weapon to cut the ugliness out of me. Every day was a dangerous balancing act between self-mutilation and self-improvement. It is normal to want to lose weight in order to be healthy and fit. It is not normal to become so obsessed with my weight that I resorted to harming myself. But how could I not be obsessed? Now that I was aware of my weight gain, it was all I could do to not think about the mass of forty pounds now crushing my tiny five-foot-one frame. I could feel it. I could feel every pound. How could I let this happen? How could I let myself go? I began counting every calorie, every morsel of food I ate. It was discouraging to see how quickly my calorie limit for the day was reached. I would spend five terrible hours waiting for midnight to come so I could start my calorie clock at zero. Every minute of every day I spent thinking about food. After all, food was my only weapon to chase away my anxiety and depression. But I couldn't eat. I had to lose the weight, and my mental disorders fought back with prejudice.

I hate myself. I catch a glance of myself in the mirror. I am hideous. My eyes are too small and close together. My skin is sallow and gray. My lips are so small that they might as well not even be lips. My face has ballooned from the extra weight. I look disgusting. I want to be pretty. I want to look like the girls in the movies. They are all so elegant and beautiful. I am nothing more than the ugly stepsister. I was OK-looking once. At least I think I was. Other people would affirm it. I looked like an elf from Lord of the Rings. *My golden blond hair fell down to my waist in soft, flowing waves. My skin was as white as the newly fallen snow. Clothes draped over my petite five-foot-one frame, with the precision of a Hollywood-tailored gown. I was OK-looking. I only wish I would have realized it at the time. I was too busy focusing on my flaws, my minute imperfections. Comparing myself endlessly to the newest Hollywood "it girl." But now, that was all gone. Will it ever return? Have I reached*

By Emily Watson

my peak and everything else is downhill? It doesn't matter now. I am nothing. I can't stand to see my face in the mirror. I want to take a knife and cut up my face. It is too ugly. I can't bear it. It must be destroyed. I need to cut out all offending features. STOP STARING BACK AT ME IN THE MIRROR!!

Desperate to lose weight, my only choice was to cut back my calories and start exercising. I decided to join the local YMCA. It was embarrassing going at first, as I was utterly out of shape. My fifty-nine-year-old mother could lift more weights than I could on every circuit machine. More demoralizing was seeing the petite old woman trotting along on the treadmill at twice my pace. Despite my embarrassment, I made the decision to plod on. But I didn't just make it that day; I made it every day. That is the thing about losing weight; it isn't just some resolution I make amidst noisemakers and glowing confetti; it is a continual choice I make when I'm ordering my dinner or floundering about exercising because I am just too tired. That is what makes it so hard. I have to keep making the decision anew.

I began working out at the gym in late December 2009. I have never been much of a gym enthusiast. I had a member ship in 2002, and I barely ever went. Of course, I really didn't need to go then, as I was as thin as a supermodel. The fact is I simply don't like working out. It is mind-bendingly boring. Walking or spinning on stationary machines while staring at other people working out is surprisingly unexciting. Sports never excited me, in general. Gym class was always the black mark on my day, getting me all sweaty and sticky before class. I mean, really, who thought up the idea of having gym in the middle of the day? I don't want to wear out my deodorant and then go and give a class presentation. Besides, I was never much of an athlete, my shining moment being when I scored a goal against my own team in flag football. I was wondering why the opposing team wasn't trying to stop me. But previous experiences aside, I had to start exercising; the fat wasn't going to magically disappear. But my mind was unable to stay focused on one particular activity for more than ten minutes. How can people stay on those treadmills for an hour, plugging away like it is the easiest thing in the world? Five minutes in, I want to shoot myself just to stave off boredom. Looking at other people working out is just demoralizing. Worst of all were the tons of tiny bopettes (my word for tiny teenage girls who work out as their ponytails bop), dancing away on the ellipticals, putting everyone else to shame. How do they do that? Ten minutes in, I am sweating like a fat man in spandex—not a pretty sight. Red-faced and dripping with sweat, I look like I am about to hyperventilate. But my dislikes aside, I started to exercise. I had no choice. If I was ever going to get back to my pre-disorder weight, I had to put in some major effort. I opted for the treadmill—much easier than the bike, the elliptical, or the stepper. I found that listening to my iPod improved my performance. In a shock even to myself, I managed to walk along for an astounding forty minutes. I've never walked that long even when I was healthy. Now I was actually getting somewhere. Forty minutes can actually pull some weight off, unlike my previous ten-minute trials. Eventually we bought a treadmill, making it much easier to work out being in the comfort of my own home. I had an easier time splitting up my workouts into twenty-minute intervals three times a day. It helped to manage the boredom; so too did the television, as I could now watch movies while I worked out. I still don't like working out; it is just something that I don't enjoy. Each day I have to make myself get on the treadmill, make myself work out. I have to take it day by day, or I get upset thinking of all the workouts to come.

I wish I could remember when it happened—when I gave up. I would go back and change it if I could. I lost too much that was important to me. I lost my health. I lost my beauty. I lost me. I lost everything that I was. I know it's terribly vain, but I miss being OK-looking. I always wanted to be the most beautiful girl in class, the one getting all the attention from the boys. Of course, I never was. That place always belonged to someone else. The blond-haired starlet of my high school years. The angel-faced princess of my college days. I wasn't even second best; I was far down the line. I longed to be at the top. But at least I was pretty—pretty enough to get a glance or two from a passing guy. And for a brief, beautiful time, I was the prettiest girl in one of my college classes. Then again, my major was physics, so I was just the only girl in the class. It's not the same thing. All of my other classes were filled with girls, so I fell back down to my usual place on the list. But how could I give my spot up, far down as it might have been? How could I let myself go? How could I give up what little beauty I had? I don't remember making that decision. I don't remember giving in to my disorders. If I could, I would go back in time and stop myself. But time travel isn't possible—well, not yet anyways. I don't remember. I just remember the day I realized I was fat.

Emily's Helpful Tips
Weight Loss Tips

1. Keep a diary of everything you eat and the corresponding calorie count. Find out how many calories your body needs to maintain a certain weight and make sure you don't go over that calorie count. It really is very helpful.
2. Don't go on a sudden strict diet; you won't be able to stick to it. Instead, start out small. Try removing a few bad items on your list, such as sweet snacks or sugary beverages. Once you get adjusted to that, try removing a few more and so forth until you reach your ideal meal plan. Whatever you do, don't eliminate all your comfort foods; it will just lead you to binge later on. We each need a treat every day to give us something to look forward to.
3. Exercise at least three times a week for forty minutes at a time. I know, I know, exercising isn't fun. Personally I hate it. It is mind-numbing to walk on a treadmill or spin on a bike for an hour. Unfortunately, it is an essential part to weight loss. There is no way around it. Believe me, I have tried. You just have to grin and bear it.
4. Try to walk 10,000 steps a day. It is helpful to buy a step counter so you can track the steps. It is also good to buy one that keeps track of the calories you burn. I have a Fitbit. It tracks the number of steps I take, the miles I walk, the calories I burn, and the amount of sleep I get. It is very helpful.

CHAPTER FORTY-FOUR
The Fall of Hygiene

"Beauty is but a vain and doubtful good; a shining gloss that fadeth suddenly; a flower that dies when it begins to bud; a doubtful good, a gloss, a glass, a flower, lost, faded, broken, dead within an hour."
William Shakespeare

By the start of 2010, I had stopped showering with any type of regularity. I couldn't do it. I didn't have the energy anymore. The shower rituals had become too laborious, and after years of being beat down by the OCD, I didn't have the strength to complete them. I know it seems contradictory that being the clean freak I am that I would give up showering, but I just couldn't keep up with the ritual of showering; it was too difficult. It took too much energy and work to shower because of the OCD, so I just stopped. I let go of being clean and gave into the OCD. I forced myself into the shower stall once every five months. For three to four long hours, I would scrub myself from top to bottom until I was convinced every inch of me was clean, washing and rewashing my body, stuck in an endless loop, until my skin was red and raw. I was nothing more than a robot—a broken robot stuck performing the same task over and over. No matter how much I pleaded with myself, how much I screamed at myself, I couldn't stop the cycle. I only made it worse. So I just let go. I let go of showering. I let go of being clean. How can anyone go five months without showering, you're probably repeating to yourself in shock? How could I let myself get so filthy? Well, it wasn't as bad as you might think. Granted, I looked pretty gross, my hair slicked back in oily, knotted lumps, my face sallow and gray, and my skin a bumpy stretch of trapped dirt and pet dander. I looked like a zombie. OK, maybe it is as bad as you might think. But I didn't care. I couldn't shower. I didn't have it in me.

It was bad enough being dirty, but I really didn't want to smell. Though even if someone told me that I did, I still probably wouldn't have gotten a shower. I was just too weak. But despite not showering, I still don't think I was that dirty; after all, it wasn't like I was out rolling in the dirt or playing sports in the humid summer heat. I just sat on the couch most of the time. I did go to the gym, but I didn't get that dirty there, just a little sweaty. And I kept my hands clean; they were always clean.

Even though they were months apart, I still dreaded every shower. A week ahead of each shower, I would begin a slow panic attack, my mind racing, my body shivering, and my stomach turning. Everyone takes showers; in fact, most people take them every day. They aren't afraid. They aren't worried. It is a simple daily task that causes no distress. And I sit hyperventilating over one that is a week away. How did this happen? How did it get to be so difficult? I can't even remember what it is like to get a normal shower. How crazy I must seem to someone else, freaking out over a little shower. Besides, what was the point of getting a shower, what was the point of being clean when my environment was filthy? My house was a pig pen but for cats. Our entire dining room had become a public restroom for the cats, urine and pooh littered along the walls. It was impossible to stay clean in this dirty house, so I might as well have been dirty too.

I feel alone. Even if there were one hundred people surrounding me, I would still feel alone. No one can touch me. No single person can offer a hand of comfort. They can't reach through the invisible prison I am in. I long for their touch. I hunger for it. The calming touch of my mother. The protecting grip of my father. All are miles from me.

Brushing my teeth was equally a laborious activity. Every tooth had to be brushed a specific way and then re-brushed over and over until I was content each was clean. Brushing my teeth may seem like an easy activity, even mundane in its simplicity, but that is for the hearty masses. A healthy mind can't possibly understand how such a simple task could be so trying. To everyone else it is just a normal part of life. But to me it is a black patch on my day. Faced with performing such a laborious task on a daily basis, I just opted to give up brushing altogether. I can't even remember the last time I picked up a tooth brush. It must have been at least two months ago. A permanent yellow stain marks my teeth, reminiscent of the pirates of ancient lore. My gums are inflamed from lack of flossing, overflowing with particles of previous meals. My once cavity-free smile is laced with open sores, tarter, and gingivitis, bleeding out into my mouth. But I don't care. I can't care. It is too hard to keep up with personal hygiene. I don't have the energy. The OCD rituals zap me of all my strength. Caring hurts. I can't carry the weight of caring; it is easier to just let it go. Let go of showering, let go of brushing, let go of the hassles of living and focus only on the rituals of OCD.

I have to get a shower next Wednesday, a full six days away. It's too soon; it is much too soon. I don't have the energy. I can't do it. I won't. But I must. It has been over five months since my last one. My body is starting to decompose. My hair, drenched in oil, is stringy and stiff. My skin is dry and gray, flaking off in large patches like dandruff of the body. My pores on my face are clogged with dirt and oil, turning my once smooth skin into a mountainous terrain. Do I smell? I don't want people whispering behind my back that I am the smelly girl. I must get a shower. But how can I do it? I am too fatigued for three hours of hard labor. How am I going to do this? I wish I had a Demerol; it would make things much easier. Why won't the doctors let me have it? It cures my OCD. It cures my bipolar. It lets me lead a normal life. Why are the doctors keeping it from me? I would never deny help to someone who is suffering. Six days, six days until the shower.

Hard as it is to believe, during the entire year of 2010, I only got three showers. No doubt your jaw has dropped open in shock and you are cringing in disgust. I can hardly believe it myself, but it is true. Each shower was an epic activity lasting from three to four hours. That is three to four hours of constant washing, scrubbing, and rinsing. It was exhausting. I just couldn't do it that often. It was too hard. Worse yet, I was worried I would leak out pee in the shower. My bladder had gotten much worse. I could only hold my bladder for two to three hours thus, as my showers were longer than that, I risked pee leaking out in the shower. If that happened, I would have to clean myself extra good to get the pee off, which means being in the shower even longer. I feared going pee in the shower. I dreaded having to wash myself so much in the shower. So, I showered as little as possible, which is how I ended up doing it only three times in 2010.

CHAPTER FORTY-FIVE
A Distorted Body

"There is no excellent beauty that hath not some strangeness in the proportion."
Francis Bacon

Dr. Farinas didn't understand my obsession with my appearance. She observed that I might have a twinge of body dysmorphic disorder (BDD) in addition to my OCD. The two disorders are related, as both involve repetitive checking, and often occur together. The main difference is that BDD sufferers' obsessive/compulsive behavior revolves around their appearance, often causing them to go to severe measures to change their appearance, such as cosmetic surgery. Now, I'll admit I have OCD, and I'll admit that I am a little obsessed with my appearance, but I hardly think I qualify for this one. Now what is BDD you ask? Let us examine it in more detail. Put on those science goggles and slap on that lab coat; things are about to get logical. BDD is a mental illness whereby people are obsessed with a minor defect or imaginary defect in their physical appearance. Like OCD, this leads to ritualistic behavior revolving around the perceived flaw. The most common trouble areas are body weight, facial features, hair, and skin imperfections. A person views himself or herself as ugly, avoiding social interactions and seeking out plastic surgery.

Common symptoms of body dysmorphic disorder:

- Engaging in ritualistic behaviors revolving around the perceived defect in an attempt to hide or cover it up, such as looking in the mirror or picking at skin.
- Continually seeking reassurance that the defect isn't too obvious.
- Repeatedly touching, measuring, or looking at the perceived defect.
- Consulting with cosmetic surgeons to improve one's appearance.
- Not wanting to go out because the person is too self-conscious.
- Developing problems in school, relationships, and work because of the obsessive focus on the perceived problem.

Like OCD, it is likely caused by a malfunction of the neurotransmitters in the brain, but it can also be caused by some societal pressures. It can be treated through psychotherapy and medication (Webmd 2012).

Now I don't have a distorted view about my appearance. I am analyzing and quantifying my appearance with the precession and skill of any trained scientist. I am not imagining my body any differently than it appears to others. Yes, I obsess, but that is because I am unhappy about how I look, and I must seek to correct things. I am deeply flawed. I'm ugly. I know I am. I am not imagining myself so; it is a verifiable fact. Society has dictated who's pretty and who's not, and I fall in the latter. There are certain standards by which beauty is ranked. Think about the women in Hollywood. They all invariably have the same look: full, long, lustrous hair; flawless skin; svelte body; pouty lips; and big eyes. People who don't fit that palette aren't considered beautiful. I know it is true; that is how our society is. My hair is thin and short. My skin is dull and covered in pock marks. I'm forty pounds overweight. My lips are thin and colorless. My eyes are small and hooded beneath a sparse brow. I don't tell myself I am ugly; society does. I merely agree. Granted, I have a few of the symptoms. I do look at myself in the mirror constantly, trying to wish away my flaws, and I do have a tendency to pick at my skin with an obsessive flair but not too terribly much. I do hide away, not wanting to be seen in public, too embarrassed even to see my friends. I am having some minor cosmetic procedures done but only to fix horrendous flaws, specifically some very unappealing stretch marks. There is nothing wrong with seeing flaws and wanting to correct them. I don't have a distorted view of my body.

CHAPTER FORTY-SIX
Chronic Stress

"We walk in circles, so limited by our own anxieties that we can no longer distinguish between true and false, between the gangster's whim and the purest ideal."
Ingrid Bergman

Since the moment I first developed OCD and bipolar disorder, they have gradually been taking a terrible toll on me physically. My once healthy body is now sickly and overweight. People often don't realize that mental disorders have a physical component. The stress of fighting these disorders is very detrimental to the body. Living with a mental disorder can be extremely stressful. The strain of fighting for my sanity every day can lead to chronic stress. Constant stress can have a destructive effect on your physical body. The following are some of the major health problems you can develop:

- depression
- hair loss
- hyperthyroidism
- anxiety disorder, e.g. OCD
- tooth and gum disease
- diabetes
- heart disease
- obesity
- sexual dysfunction
- ulcers

(About 2011)

My hair was thinning, my skin was turning gray, and inflammation spread through my body, injuring muscles and pulling tendons. The most offensive symptom to me was hair loss. As I have said many times, I am afflicted with vanity. Having a pleasing appearance is important to me, no matter how impossible it may be. But it is not just me; hair is very important in our society. Thick, long, and lustrous hair is associated with youth, beauty, and goodness. The brave heroine always as has long locks, tossed about seductively in key scenes. You rarely ever see a bald protagonist. Everyone wants to have great hair. Why do you think men are so consumed by hair loss? Not a day goes by that I don't see some commercial on television promoting the newest thing in hair growth technology. Men want thick hair as much as women. Why do you think some women buy hair extensions and hair pieces? Many movie stars have extensions put in to thicken their hair. My hair has been thinning for the past eight years. Once a minor inconvenience, it is now a serious problem. I used to have beautiful hair—thick, golden brown waves cascading down to my waist. I wanted to emulate a Renaissance woman, the long-tressed woman in movies of knights and wizards. But all that fell away, strands of hair trickling down my back, sometimes in singlets, sometimes in lumps. There is barely enough left now for a ponytail. It settles now just below my ears—a thin, lifeless expression of all that once was. I don't look like me; I look like a disorder. Will it ever grow back? I hope so, but first the stress must be removed. And until the disorders are cured, the stress will remain.

My hair is falling out again. I guess it never really stopped. I just stopped paying attention, trying not care, avoiding feeling my hair. But then I slipped and felt how small the ponytail was beneath my fingers. It broke my heart; another piece of me was slowly falling away. I desperately want to regain my vision of myself in the future, but what am I to do? Get a wig? I've thought about it; in fact, I would really like to get one, but how would I explain it to someone? Yes, my thinning hair is a result of a medical problem, but not the ones people are commonly used to. Most people don't realize that mental illness is a physical illness that not only affects the mind but the body too.

Depression and anxiety I already have, though I guess it's like a circle, each one causing the other. I am overweight, and I have hair loss. As for the rest of the symptoms, well, I don't have any of those—not yet at least, though I do think stress has had other effects on my body. I have regular stomachaches and regular nausea that drains my appetite and feeds my depression. Cells bounce around my stomach excited by the anxiety and stress. My muscles ache, trembling from the weight of these disorders. My skin is sallow and lifeless, marred by patches of red, flaky scales of eczema. I resemble a ghost more than a live young woman.

PART X: THE DARK AGES

"And I looked, and behold a pale horse: and his name that sat on him was Death, and Hell followed with him."
Revelation 6:8

CHAPTER FORTY-SEVEN
A Lifetime Ago

"It's a poor sort of memory that only works backwards."
Lewis Carroll

I remember when I was young, not even really young, as late as high school, I always thought I was destined for something special. I thought I had some singular purpose in this life. Maybe I would become a renowned physicist and prove the grand unified theory. Maybe I would become an international spy and save the world on a daily basis. Maybe I would become a doctor and cure cancer. Maybe I would become an archaeologist and discover the Ark of the Covenant. The possibilities were endless. The future lay open before me, and I was ready for a great adventure. But all that changed…in a day…in a hour…in a minute…in a single second. I remember it clearly. It was the day after my high school graduation back in 1999. I awoke as I always did around eleven a.m. My room was the same as it had always been, neatly organized, draped in the warmth that only a childhood home can create. Yet something was different. I was different. My Grandmother Maude came to talk to me, yet I was not in the mood. I yelled at her. I never yelled at my grandmother. But something was wrong. I could feel it. I didn't know what, but I could feel it. I was frustrated. I was confused. I was angry for no apparent reason. Something wasn't right. The world was the same, but I was different. There was a change, a switch, a switch in my body that had been flicked on. My biology was different, my cells distorted. Something in my DNA was awakened, and I was afraid. I stood there, rage dripping down my fingers. Something had gone wrong; something had gone very wrong.

Dear God, everything is spiraling. It's spinning too fast. I can't bear it. Everything is moving too fast. I am still and the world is spinning around me. I reach out to try to stabilize, but my hand is brushed aside.

I wish you could have known me when I was young. I was always brimming with positivity, the go-to girl to make others feel better, a mini-Dear Abby. Every day was filled with sunshine. Of course, I lived in Florida, the Sunshine State, so maybe it was just good location. I spent six months living in DC, and I have never seen so many dreary days. I developed a little seasonal affective disorder. But, in all seriousness, it really wasn't the weather; I just had a positive outlook on life. The world was my playground, a land of childlike fun and epic adventures. Oh how I loved adventure. I was fearless, or if I did have fear, I was too busy to notice. How else do you explain the fact that I scuba dived in a tank with six-foot sharks? Can you imagine me, frightened little me, swimming alongside the most ferocious fish in the sea? I spent the previous winter diving in one of Florida's many icy springs alongside the gentle giants of the sea—manatees. I can't imagine doing that now. I'm scared of large bodies of water. OK, medium-size ones too. Oh heck, I am afraid of puddles. Do you know how many viruses live in them? Oceans are deep, dark, death traps filled with sharks, jellyfish, and undertows that will drag me out to sea and drown me in its icy depths. Lakes are no better. Oh sure, they don't have dangerous riptides that could kill me in a single tug, but they do have poisonous water moccasins, killer alligators, and enough parasites to back me up until next Tuesday. I almost got bitten by a water moccasin once. I was canoeing—that's right, I knew how to canoe—when I stepped out on what I thought was a dry rock. I nearly put my foot on a curled up camouflaged moccasin, perfectly poised to pounce. Did I panic? Absolutely not. I calmly got back in my canoe and paddled down to another landing. It was not my first time in a canoe. One summer I kayaked down the white water rapids of the Colorado River. Afraid of dangerous rapids? Not a chance. I scaled those rapids with the skill of a seasoned adventurer, paddling to and fro until an unusually strong wind turned my kayak over, trapping me in the icy turbulence beneath. No light, no air, only the onrush of freezing water sucking the shoes right off my feet. I struggled beneath the overturned kayak, cold water piercing my bones, my life jacket preventing me from reaching the small air pocket, terror in my heart, but did I panic? No, I instinctively tried to free myself from this watery deathtrap before an equally strong gust of wind sent the kayak flying off my head. I faced death, yet I remained ever strong. How could that have been me? I was so brave, so daring. I could never do that now. I'm so afraid. But I did it and so much more. I didn't just conquer the seas. I took to the air flying from Hawaii to Turkey. Teeming cesspools of germs that regularly crash going hundreds of miles per hour into the unforgiving landscape…no problem. I was invincible. I even took a handful of flying lessons for fun one summer. Ironically, the instructor commented on how calm and relaxed I was at the helm. Me, relaxed? I get the shakes just thinking about being on a plane now. How do they even stay in the air? They weigh hundreds of tons, and they are gliding atop minute particles of air. They could fall out of the sky at any moment and tumble miles below into a raging fireball as they smack painfully into the unforgiving ground. And if I am fortunate enough to teeter on the edge of clouds, I will be killed by the thousands of germs that are circulating through the recycled air on the plane. How I could fly so carefree is unimaginable to me. But I did. I flew the tempestuous skies; I paddled the turbulent seas. I combed through the dirt of Wyoming to find dinosaur bones. I swam with dolphins in the waters of the Keys. I trekked across the ruins of Italy and the mountains of Greece. I stood before a wall of fears and knocked it down as if it were children's building blocks. I lived life the way life should be lived, with boldness of spirit, logic of mind, and joyousness of heart. Now I live in fear. How could a mental disorder so drastically change my personality? How did I live without fear? That, I can't remember.

I used to be such a happy person. I had a great life. I had two loving parents. I had a houseful of pets. I had a group of great friends. I was top in my class at school. I had a wonderful life. I was wonderful. I had a light inside me that just radiated outward. I remember when my best friend Christine and I took ballroom dancing classes one summer. We both had this sudden urge to dance, and we went with it. It was so much fun. We learned everything from the cha-cha to the waltz to the swing—the last being my favorite because it was such a high-energy dance, and we could do lifts and tricks. It was great. But what I remember most, as I have since forgotten many of the steps, is how happy I was, how filled with light I was. Christine reminded me the other day of just how wonderful I am, and she pointed to those months of dancing when I radiated so much that I was virtually the center of attention every time we were there. She remembers how much the other people there were drawn to me. Even the handsome male instructor was smitten with me, and that never happens. At least I think he was. The world was so filled with light and love.

Now, everything is so dark. The world is filled with despair and sadness. I can't remember the light. All is dark. I am dark. I am filled with such unrelenting sadness. It's not born from any one source but comes from deep inside my soul from something older than the sun itself, something eternal, an absence…of what…of light, of love, of God himself? It is a dark recess that one should never know about, should never experience. Yet that is where I live now, and I can't escape. I desperately want to be happy again. I see everyone else living in the light, living happy, healthy, normal lives. How I long for that. I just can't find my way out of the darkness. No one can help me out. No one can lead me out of the darkness. I am all alone. Separated from all other life, I am separated from all those who live in the light. They can't help me because they have never been there before. They don't know the road out. So I stand alone. But I know a way out. I just try not to think about it. But there is a way out; there has always been a way out. I can end things now. I can end the darkness, the sadness, the terror. I just have to take my own life. That's the answer. Just one slit of my wrist, and it is all over with. The pills aren't working, the therapy isn't working; this is the only way out. Just gobble down a handful of pills. And then it is over. But I can't think on that. I must not think on that. I just can't see the light. I can't see the end.

I can't remember what it is like to be normal. I can see a picture of myself, a still photograph of who I used to be. But I can't remember how I acted. I can't remember how it used to take me only five minutes in the bathroom and now it takes two hours. I can't remember why I was happy to go to sleep and now I'm not petrified to do so. I can't remember why I thought the world was a wondrous place to be when now it is something to be feared. I wish I could remember. I need to remember if I ever am going to be normal again.

By Emily Watson

Poetic Musings

Beginning of the End
by Emily Watson

Somewhere in a distant year
I work away without a fear
Joyful as the day goes by
I lie beneath the clear blue sky
Yet in the sky appears a light
Whose burning flame is twice as bright
As flaming sun in still of day
Or shinning stars perched far away
When all the world lies fast asleep
And I alone sit up and weep
For light which sits so far away
Will bring the world untimely day
When poisons fall from up above
To end the world that we all love.

CHAPTER FORTY-EIGHT
A Life of Fear

"I will not fear. Fear is the mind killer. I will face my fear, I will let it pass through me."
Children of Dune

I used to be fearless. It's a shame I didn't realize it at the time, but looking back now I can see it. Sure, I had my little phobias like every normal person, but they were small and few. They didn't control me. I controlled them. I was brave and brilliant, my own superhero. I was invincible. The world was a wonderland of unknown adventures and magical possibilities. It was not to be feared. It was to be explored. I lived life with the vigor and joy of a wide-eyed child. Fear was not my enemy. It was an afterthought amidst a curious mind. But somewhere along the way that changed. Somewhere along the way fear crept in, slowly growing in the deep recesses in my mind until it seeped into every aspect of my life, poisoning my soul beyond repair. What happened? Where did this fear come from? What was causing it? It is like a parasite latching onto me, tainting my blood with fear.

Get it off of me. Rip it from my body. It is taking over. It is consuming me. My veins are black with fear. The world isn't joyous; it isn't wondrous. It is frightening. It is terrifying.

As I said, I was quite the adventurous tomboy in my youth, my fears years away. I don't think I even knew what true fear was then. I went about my life like I was invincible. I climbed trees, rode bicycles, and swam in many of Florida's waterways. Every summer I went to Kingsley Lake. I jumped off two-story platforms into the murky lake below, a lake that housed such predators as alligators and snakes. I did what? But that's insanity? What of my fear of heights and dangerous animals? Not to worry. I wasn't afraid. Alligators and snakes are in every Florida lake and river. You just have to be vigilant when you swim. Besides, it was the local watering hole with slides and docks—enough activity to keep any creatures away. Key note: if you are ever being chased by an alligator, run in a zigzag line. But I wasn't worried, nor was I worried when I scuba dived with six-foot long sharks in a tank in central Florida. OK, I was a little worried, but I didn't let that stop me, though I could have done without a diving buddy that insisted on swimming right next to the ferocious beasts. Seriously, I was diving all alone, so I was assigned a buddy, who as fate would have it, liked to swim right next to the six-foot-long man-eating beasts. I ditched my buddy and maintained a good five-foot distance. When not in the water, I took to the air, tossing a few flying lessons under my belt. I bravely took the controls and soared through the air in a tiny plane no bigger than my room. I was fearless then. I wish I could be that way now.

I'm afraid. I'm always afraid. Others may not see it, but I do. I know the dangers that lurk around me in the shadows.

I've been haunted for a lifetime. From my earliest childhood memories, I can recall being tormented by ghoulish nightmares. My dreams were filled with terrifying images of demonic beasts and demented worlds that would frighten even those in Wonderland. What spurred this nightmarish existence? What brought forth this unholy state, I cannot say. I avoided horror movies; I never partook in ghost story games. I lived on the princess-themed movies and cartoon ramblings of Disney. Nevertheless, I slept in terror. Even to this day, I cry out in the middle of the night for someone to help me, free me from the prison I am trapped in. Is it any wonder I so deeply fear sleep? I am uncontrollably dragged into the darkness of mankind, to worlds of shadows and fright, to realms unperceived by the eye, unfelt by the body, linked only to the mind. Dorothea thinks I must have been tortured many lifetimes over. I would really rather not remember them; I would never sleep again. My dad thinks I am simply having visions of parallel worlds. Judging by the content, I don't think these are worlds I'd like to visit in my daily life. Regardless of where they come from, my nightmares have at least lessened in recent years. I still go through periods of intense activity, but they are fewer and farther between. I don't really know what that means. Maybe the pills are working to block those dark thoughts. But still I fear sleep. I fear it because I know what lurks behind one's closed

By Emily Watson

eyes; I know the darkness that steals me in my sleep. I know the terror that draws me into another world, a world of abject fear.

I'm not crazy. I'm not. What if I am? Oh, God I am! It can't be normal to see things that aren't there. But they are there, in the shadows; we just can't see them. The darkness, the beings of the darkness, demonic beings bent on our destruction. They're all around me, they're coming for me. I see them in the corners of my eyes. Oh God, demons are coming for me. Save me, save me God from their embrace. The voices are everywhere, the voices wishing me to do harm, biding me at their pleasure. No! No! I will do no such thing. I will never harm anyone. I will never harm any animals. Stop flashing before my eyes. I'm afraid. I'm so very afraid. No one believes me. No one believes they are there. But I have seen movies; they exist and they are laughing at those who don't believe. Oh God, I am crazy! Such things do not exist. Yes they do. I know they do. I'm not crazy. I'm not crazy. I just see the truth. While everyone else is living their self-diluted lives, I see the truth. Demons are out there. They are coming for each and every one of us. Now would be a good time to be afraid.

I am a bit superstitious. How is that different from my other fears and phobias? Well, superstition is a general fear of the unknown and a trust in magic or chance. For example, I believe that anytime I say something bad about a potential future event I must knock on wood to prevent it from coming to pass. If wood isn't around, any hard surface will suffice, though wood has the most magical powers. How silly you must think I am, but superstition has a place in many cultures and many religions. Think of our own, for example: the notions that breaking a mirror causes seven years of bad luck, the four-leaf clover is good luck, black cats are bad omens, opening an umbrella inside causes bad luck. All are fixtures in our society, and many still believe in them. Though, I don't believe that black cats involve anything negative; they are just cute little animals. OK, right, just had to knock on wood after typing that—point null and void. Maybe I'm more than a bit superstitious.

Once brave and bold, my life is now consumed by fear. I fear everything from the kitchen sink to a giant asteroid. No really, the kitchen sink. I am afraid my finger is going to get caught in the garbage disposal.

Not that I have any intention of putting my finger in that hole, but what if it happened by accident? What if I tripped, my hand plunged into the sink, my finger slipped into the hole, and in an attempt brace myself, I grab at the shelf on the wall and instead I hit the switch of the garbage disposal? It could happen. But the sink is really the least of my fears. There are far too many others on the list to quibble over just one: fear of germs, driving, odors, and bugs. But my phobias are the worst. A phobia is basically a fear that is so strong it impedes my ability to lead a normal life. Let's take a look at the top eleven shall we.

Coming in at number eleven are the dreaded spiders—little creepy crawlers with eight legs and numerous eyes darting here and there in every building, in every car, in every patch of nature all over the world, carefully spinning their webs of death, lurking, waiting to attack. I know what they are thinking. They want to crawl on me and take a bite of my flesh. They're after me; they're all after me. When I see one in my house, I run screaming in the opposite direction. I run from them. I hide from them. I jump out of moving vehicles when one appears before me. The last sighting of one resulted in my absolute refusal to get back in my dad's car, leaving me stuck on the side of the rode until my mother drove her car over to pick me up. Needless to say, I have a bit of a phobia, but I think justifiably so.

That brings me to my number ten fear: sleep. I am afraid to go to sleep. If I am asleep, my conscious mind isn't in control. I am fearful of my own subconscious, even though my conscious mind would never do terrible things. Who is in control when I am asleep? My subconscious? But what does that mean? Is it the same as my conscious mind but only the sleepy version? What if I do something terrible under its supervision? I couldn't bear it if I caused pain to anyone, even the smallest of animals.

At nine is my fear of hurting others and animals. I have been convinced that I would hurt someone or some animal. I can't go to bed at night until I instruct whoever is around to check on me frequently while I am asleep and stop me if I try to hurt anyone.

At number eight is anything to do with flying. I used to love to fly—the excitement of the airport, of everyone rushing about to some grand adventure, the thrill of flying, my stomach dancing at that first lift-off, the joy of flying high in the sky, soaring above the birds, through the clouds into a sky so blue it looks as if it has been painted on. And the food, oh the food, little meals all set up before me like my own personal room service. The view made it taste oh so good. Little prepared meals that the astronauts would eat. Flying was an adventure all unto itself. I miss that…now, all the joy is gone. Now I fear it with the same passion I used to love it. Flying death traps, they are. It's almost impossible that they fly at all with all that weight bearing down on the tiny particles of air. You could hit a patch of turbulence and fall through the sky to unceremoniously end in a ball of searing flames. A bomb could go off in the plane, ripping apart whole sections in a fiery dance through the air. Sitting on the plane, death is just a breath away.

    I'm afraid of showers. Showering is my number seven fear. Strange to fear something as mundane and harmless as a shower, but I do. I fear the amount of time the shower takes, the endless scrubbing and rinsing and scrubbing again—two to three hours out of my life in senseless laborious work. That's why I avoid the shower, and I mean seriously avoid it; it is a compilation of all my fears. Once every five months is the best I can do. And even that sends me into a panic attack days ahead of time.

    Terrorists slide into the sixth spot. I think after 9/11 everyone is afraid of terrorists but not to the same crazy obsessive degree. I mean how can one not be frightened knowing that there are people out there actively working on ways to destroy us? There people out there plotting our murder. I fear going to any public place for fear that they might set off a dirty bomb there, or worse, a nuclear bomb. Our ports aren't safe, our airports aren't safe, and our borders aren't safe. The doors are open for any would-be terrorist to get in and strike. It's not a question of if we will get hit again but when.

    At number five is my phobia of demons. They are out there, you know, hiding in the shadows, hiding in the filth and waste of humanity, watching us, studying us for any sign of weakness, and then they attack. I sense them. In the quiet moments of life, I feel their presence, the moisture of their warm echoing breaths. They're here. They have us surrounded. Light keeps them at bay, but it can't be light all the time. Eventually darkness falls, I will pass into sleep, and I will be vulnerable. It is only safe to sleep in the day when the radiant sun burns their eyes. I can't sleep in my room, in my nice comfy bed, for fear of the demons in my closet. I can't be in the room with the door shut; I must sleep in a more open area, in the living room on the couch. I haven't slept in my room for years; I'm afraid to even be in there alone. I hate being left alone at night when everyone else is asleep. They know I am a weak target. They will lay siege on me while everyone else dreams. I don't know how to fight them off. I'm afraid, so very afraid. You don't believe me, I know you don't, but it is true; they are there. And one day they will come after you.

Coming in at number four is the ever-present fear of contamination. Germs, viruses, dirt, urine, odors—anything that could contaminate me I am afraid of. Smells are by far the worst as I am terrified of being smelly. I dodge smells with the skill and precision of a dodgeball player. If I become enclosed with a foul odor, I will break down into a complete panic attack until I am free. Of course, then I am worried the smell attached itself to me like a parasite. How could I not? I was trapped with it. Oh, I don't want to smell bad. Get these smells away from me. What if I start smelling of urine? Our house positively reeks of it; surely the smell will attach to me. I will be walking around covered in the stench of pee to disgusted onlookers. How do I stop the smell from attaching to me? Oh God, I don't want to stink. But it is not just smells; it is germs, diseases, viruses, all at my fingertips on surfaces, on walls, on doors, and in the subtle breath of the contagious. There aren't enough Wet Ones in the world to protect me. The only choice is to avoid people, sit locked in my little apartment away from the world, away from the dangers. But what of the contamination in my own house? What shall I do? Nothing. Nothing can be done. I've surrendered to the stench of my house; I cannot fight it anymore.

Number three is the bathroom, rather more specifically urine and pooh. I fear going to the restroom. I fear a basic bodily function. You would too if you spent one hour and thirty minutes wiping and washing yourself. It is the black mark on my day, and I try to do it as little as possible. I greatly restrict the amount of fluids I drink so that I only have to go twice a day. Not exactly the healthiest thing to do, but I don't care; I can't handle that ritual. It is a laborious, tiring endeavor that feels more like a workout at the gym, except with urine. Oh how I fear urine, that foul-smelling liquid; it disgusts me. I hate wiping it off me; I hate touching it. One of my greatest fears is being covered in urine or pooh.

By Emily Watson

I get stressed out by the fact that urine residue is all over the apartment because my cats step in urine and track it all over the house...on the floor, in chairs, on the couch. Oh the indescribable horror of it all! I try not to think about it otherwise it will drive me insane. It is just one of the downsides of having animals. Besides, the amount of urine spreading over the house is probably miniscule, at least that is what my dad tries to tell me. I am just really terrified of getting urine or pooh on me, especially urine. I hate going to the bathroom because of it. I hate getting it on me, which happens frequently because I have accidents in my pants due to my bladder disorders. I hate having bladder accidents. They are messy and disgusting. Urine gets all over my bottom and my upper legs. It is horrible. One of my greatest fears realized. I can't live my life with my bladder problems like this. Something has to give.

My number two fear is the fear that I will be hurt by others. I am desperately afraid that I will be maimed or killed in a sequence of unfortunate events. The world is filled with danger more than anything else. You think I am wrong? Just watch the news for a few minutes and see if you don't have a panic attack. Nuclear bombs, terrorists, rapists, murderers...the world is going to hell, and no one seems to be very afraid. I pray every night for God to keep me safe, but I am not. Safety is an illusion; it's a promise from the government that can't be upheld. I have just as much of a chance of being killed on my way home as I do of returning safely. Car accidents happen on every corner. Rapists live next door. Murderers roam the city streets. Terrorists are plotting deadly strikes. Countries are building nuclear bombs. Somewhere someone is being assaulted, someone is being raped, and someone is being murdered, and somewhere there's a girl typing on a small computer alerting the world to this dangerous state. How can I go on leading a normal life when all this is happening? It's all converging to a single point, a single event, a single moment in time where the world's stage falls dim and the end is upon us.

The apocalypse is coming, and so is my number one fear. Humanity's end is approaching. Pain and devastation are all we have to look forward to. Mark your calendars: December 21, 2012. Are you ready? I guess no other phobia, no other fear really matters; all others pale in comparison. What does it matter when we are all going to die?

I fear sleep. I fear closing my eyes and drifting out of consciousness. What happens when I go to sleep? Where do I go? I lose consciousness. I lose control. I can't remember anything. Only dreams. Terrible, traumatic, frightening, nightmarish visions of a world I hope never to inhabit. But what of my mind? Where do I go? Am I still in control of my actions? What if I hurt someone while I am asleep? What if I hurt my father or my mother? What if I hurt my animals? I have visions of hurting them. Terrible flashes of killing them. What if I do this while I am unconscious? What if a switch clicks one day, and I am no longer there? I couldn't bear it if I ever hurt anyone or any animals. I couldn't bear it. I couldn't bear hurting my animals. I couldn't bear injuring one hair on their heads. And my parents, I could never hurt my parents. I love them. But what if I do when I am unconscious? Am I in control of my actions while I am asleep? What if I am not? What if I do something bad? I would never forgive myself. The only thing I can do is not go to sleep. I don't want to go to sleep. I'm afraid, not just of hurting others, but of going into the darkness. I'm all alone when I sleep. I am all alone in my dreams. My parents aren't there to help me. They aren't there to fight off the demented villains that haunt my dreams. I am all alone. I don't like being alone. I am afraid. I am so very afraid. I can't go to sleep. I can't. I have to stay awake. I'm afraid to shut my eyes and pass into darkness. What will I find beneath my eyelids? Vivid images of murderous demons, frightly ghouls, or dastardly beasts. Apocalyptic visions, nuclear bombs, raging fires united in a demented dance on my sleeping stage. Will I find only darkness? No shred of light, no ounce of warmth, only deep, unrelenting darkness. Will I become trapped? Will my soul lose direction and become lost in the chilling night, never to awaken again, destined to wander the earth alone forever? Will I hurt someone? When my conscience falls to sleep and my unconscious awakens, will I do something bad? When I am not in control, will I hurt someone or some animal? I couldn't live with myself if I hurt anyone or any animals. I can't go to sleep. I'm afraid. I must stay awake. I need a caffeine pill. I need coffee. Stay awake. Stay alert. I can fight the sleep. But for how long? Eventually time will catch up to me, and I will have to sleep. God help me, I don't want to go to sleep.

By Emily Watson

    As my bipolar slowly came under control, my OCD and anxiety grew ever worse making my fears worse. One not so particularly extraordinary day, I was seized by the most intense paranoia. All that was normal became contorted into madness, and I was lost in terror. I was drinking from a cup of water when suddenly I forgot how to breathe. Everyone knows how to drink and breathe at the same time. It is pure instinct. Somehow I lost that knowledge. Every time I tried to take a sip, I felt like I was hyperventilating. Do you know what it feels like to not be able to drink? It is terrifying. I had to drink or else I would die, but every time I took a sip, I stopped breathing. I was in a complete and total panic. How could I forget such an instinctive behavior? But it didn't stop there. Suddenly I was afraid that if I didn't consciously swallow, I would stop altogether. My mouth became unbearably parched, and it became very difficult to swallow. No matter how much water I drank, it would evaporate in mere seconds, leaving behind an arid desert, no doubt a result of one of the medications I was on. Unable to swallow, I fell into a fitful panic. I shouldn't be stressing over these things; they should all come instinctively. Most distressing of all was that I was paranoid to go to sleep. Every time my head touched the pillow and I closed my eyes, a deep sense of terror would grip me, and I would sit straight up. What did I fear? Many things. Mostly the loss of control. But it was more than that. I feared sleep paralysis. That is a state of being in which you know you are asleep and you want to wake up but you can't move. You can't open your eyes. You are paralyzed. I have had that happen to me a few times in my life, and I absolutely hated it. It is terrifying to be paralyzed like that. I once read that if you ever find yourself in that situation, don't try to make big movements. Instead start with something small like trying to move your pinky finger, and then the rest of the body will follow. I was also afraid of being trapped in my dreams. I knew I was in a dream, but I couldn't wake myself up. More than that I feared the nightmares and disturbing dreams that had plagued me ever since I was a little child. Every night was a Stephen King novel come to life. Strange, as I don't watch horror movies or anything even the least bit scary.

Emily's Helpful Information
A List of My Main Fears

FEAR - An intense aversion to or apprehension of a person, place, activity, event, or object that causes emotional distress and often avoidance behavior.

Fear of…

My dad getting hurt	Driving	Nightmares
My dad dying	Shadows	Emptiness
My mom getting hurt	Vampires/Zombies	Falling
My mom dying	Needles	Heights
Hitting animal by car	Mom's car	Dog drool
Getting into an accident	Scary movies	Knives
Snakes	Labor	Cigarette smoke
Losing my mind	Public restrooms	Food poisoning
Stretch marks	Private restrooms	Being ugly
Being blind	Toilets	IVs
Being deaf	Medical operations	My animals dying
Being deformed	Never falling in love	Roller coasters
Being paraplegic	Dying	Water slides
Being disabled	Drowning	Sky diving
Being quadriplegic	Burning to death	Car crashes
Black holes	Being fat	Facial damage
Asteroids	Suffocating	Losing a limb
Comets	Failure	Sharp objects
The sun dying	Disfigurement	Dirt
Carnivorous fish	My OCD	Hostile nations
Carnivorous animals	Germs	Fire
Mosquitoes	Meteors	Flesh-eating bacteria
Not getting better	Earth losing orbit	Getting burned

By Emily Watson

Murderers	The moon losing orbit	Armed robbery
Rapists	Nuclear bombs	Not being able to have kids
Crime	Radiation poisoning	
Serial Killers	Breast cancer	

PHOBIA - An intense but unrealistic fear that can interfere with the ability to socialize, work, or go about everyday life, brought on by an object, event, or situation.

Phobia of…

Smelling	Contamination	Airplanes
Flying	The ocean	Being harmed
Urine and feces	Losing my hair	Hurting someone
Demons	Darkness	Killing someone
Devil	Being alone	Hurting an animal
Hell	Hospitals	Killing an animal
Spiders	Sleep	Driving
The apocalypse	Evil people	Public speaking
Dec. 21, 2012	Evil animals	Monsters
Bad odors	Sharks	Terrorists
Showering	Going to the bathroom	Being hurt/killed

CHAPTER FORTY-NINE
An Unclean Environment

"You must not lose faith in humanity. Humanity is an ocean; if a few drops of the ocean are dirty, the ocean does not become dirty."
Mahatma Gandhi

    I like being clean, the crisp, fresh fragrance of spring emanating from my skin, the silky smooth texture of my body, the soft curls cascading down my face. I revel in my own purity, an Olympian goddess of ancient Greece. Yet, I hardly ever attain that state. Instead I dwell in dirt and grime, wallowing in my own putrid stench. I can't shower regularly. I can't clean my own body. Ironic, as I am obsessed with cleanliness. But that, in fact, is the problem. Maintaining proper cleanliness involves endless tiring rituals. My handwashing routine alone takes twenty minutes. You can imagine how long it takes me to clean everything else. Just one simple shower takes me three to four hours. Three to four hours of intense labor to make sure my body is free of any dirt and disease. Three to four hours of rigorous scrubbing. Three to four hours of endless rinsing. It is not enough to simply be clean. I have to have the sterile cleanliness of a hospital operating room. I have to be purified of any contaminant, of any foul odor. It is much too tiring of a task. I can't keep it up daily. I can't keep it up weekly. I can't keep it up monthly. Once every five months is the best I can do. Why do I need to be clean anyway? My house is a pit of filth and disrepair, worn down by years of messy cats and my mom's relentless hoarding. I can never be clean and live in that apartment. It's one or the other, and as I can't afford my own place, I choose the latter.
    As I have said before, my family and I are bleeding hearts when it comes to animals. We cannot turn away any animal in need, especially abandoned strays. We only ever bought one cat, my first, Kitty when I was in second grade. Original name, yes, I know. She lived to be twenty-one years old. All my other cats were strays we took in off the street. Having animals is naturally a dirty business. Though cats are arguably the cleanest pets one can have, even if I only have them, I am still basically letting the barnyard animals roam around my house. That's right,

horses, goats, cows, all wreaking havoc on my just-washed floors. Cat fur and dander lingering on all the furniture and floating through the air. Slobber dripping onto fresh clean linens. Littered boxes scattered through my house like furniture, with granules tracked all throughout the house. And forget any potpourri or air freshener; no man-made product out there can cover the stench emanating from an unclean box. Dear God! It is a nightmare for anyone suffering from OCD. But the worst of all, the real kicker, is that my cats don't know how to properly use the restroom. They were strays, grown-ups unfamiliar with litter boxes, so I don't blame them. But the constant puddles of urine and mounds of poo did weigh heavily on me. That's what I want: wake up in the morning, step out of bed, put my slippers on, walk to the bathroom, and wam! I step right in a pond of pee. Oh, the horror! Having terrible flashbacks now…my shoes, my beautiful wooden gladiator slingback heals dripping in pee, the shoes I wore with every outfit, the ones I strolled down Rodeo Drive in, ruined. That one really stings. Let us take a moment to mourn. Sadly, those were not the only shoes to fall prey to the dreaded urine puddles; many more fell before the dawn of 2010.

Over the past few years, my once pristine house has fallen into disrepair, now resembling more of a public restroom than a cozy home. It is the price of having many animals, I suppose, though I don't remember any of my friends' houses, who also had animals, being this bad. I hate public restrooms…urine-covered floors, clogged toilets, no soap, and a stench that could knock down a full-grown man; I grow nauseous just thinking about them. I avoid using them if at all possible, structuring my outings around my own bathroom schedule. Funny, really, when you consider I live in one. I am not exaggerating. I am not stretching the truth to make a point. I am being honest; my apartment is a public restroom, at least for the cats. For years two of my cats sprayed all over the house from the walls, to the furniture, to my high school diploma—the last one being the most offensive. I can't replace that. Somehow it had gotten mixed in with my mom's belongings, the countless boxes and bags she littered and stacked all throughout the house. More than once I have sat down on a chair only to discover a puddle of urine underneath my bum. God, the horror!

As I recounted earlier, Mom is a bit of a hoarder. She keeps everything from the jewelry she got from her mother to the napkins from the corner donut shop, all lumped together with no prejudice, in giant masses in every room, save my own. It is a flea market of trinkets mixed in with junk. Items are stowed away in overflowing bags and boxes that reach from the floor to the ceiling—a hidden cave of junk. She knows not to put her belongings on the ground, as they will be a prime target for spray, but she doesn't listen or rather she can't help herself and leaves things as they are. From an old sunscreen tube to childhood pictures to my precious diploma, the piles have been drenched in spray, creating the ruinous aftermath of a flood. But no flood could create that smell; no river water could leave that odor, the stomach-cringing, eye-watering, nose-raping, urine-soaking stench of a Porta-Potty at an outdoor rock concert. This smell can't be covered up, it can't be cleaned; it is stained into every item in its wake, burned into the cushions of the couch, absorbed in the pictures of my youth, seeped into the scraps of fabric my mom obsessively stored for the fabled quilts she would one day make. I couldn't bear it. I feared being in that room. I feared that being trapped in that apartment day in and day out, for I feared I too would begin to smell of urine. I couldn't leave the house, afraid that my smell would reach the noses of others. The only way to get the apartment clean was to throw the sprayed items away, which my mom was completely opposed to, but it had to be done. Like I said before, one week when she away, I took on the Herculean task of overhauling the entire house. Seven long days of back-breaking work with my head right in the spray zones, inhaling every disgusting molecule. I threw away the trash of which most of it was and cleaned off the treasured items. My mom was, of course, furious when she came home, but she wasn't going to do it, and for the sanity of me and my dad, it had to be done. The house did smell remarkably better afterward, and the cats were given a medicine that stopped them from spraying, though it didn't last long before my mother began hoarding anew. I don't know where she gets all that stuff, but like a black hole, the world's trash seemed to end up on our front door. Despite my best efforts, our apartment didn't stay clean for long.

I just walked in the kitchen to get something to drink when I spotted a pee puddle behind the chair. In the kitchen? In the kitchen! They've never peed in the kitchen before…the dining room yes, but the kitchen no. What am I going to do? I can't handle this! I can't handle the cat jumping on my computer as I am trying to type. I love you, but please leave me alone. I need some peace. Why did one pee in the kitchen? I just can't deal with that right now. I already have a very high anxiety level from my withdrawal from Paxil. I have to take Phenergan just to calm down.

Though the cats had stopped spraying, they still peed on the floor. The dining room was one big litter box with puddles of pee and droppings of poo taking the spots once marked by furniture. The damage was mostly confined to this one room, though one would rub his butt throughout the house, leaving poo pellets in his wake. Regular fear of stepping in urine or getting feces on my belongings is deeply stressful. But there is nothing I can do. We tried training the cats to use the box but to no avail. Cats are very obstinate. Friends suggested that I just get rid of the cats, but I couldn't do that. They are a part of my family. I love them. Besides, they had all been abandoned by previous owners; I couldn't do that to them again. I just had to accept my environment, accept the lot that I am in right now. So what else could I do? If my environment wasn't clean, and it takes too much effort to keep it clean, then why should I bother being clean either? I might as well just be dirty. It is easier just to be dirty—be as dirty as the house. It is the only way to deal with my environment. I don't have the ability to change my environment, so I have had to find some way to live in the house I have. So, I don't shower. There is no point. I would just get dirty right away. I don't have the energy to deal with the stress of constantly maintaining my own cleanliness. So, I shower once every five months. I do my best to hide my smell. Lots of deodorant is a must. Baby wipes and Wet Ones are useful as mini-showers. Dry shampoo is good to use on my hair to sop up the extra oil. Changing my clothes every few days helps make me feel fresh. But for now, I remain unclean. Has anyone else gone so long without a shower? Am I the only one who so grossly violates the rules of good hygiene? I have crossed the bridge out of the modern world and back to the Dark Ages. I would fit in quite with that lot. My hair drenched in oil piled atop my head like a squirrel's nest in disrepair. My skin painted with oil and dirt, dead cells freely flaking off my body. My mouth overflowing with trapped food particles, tartar, and gingivitis, with my gums bleeding down my lips. My teeth's yellow color matching perfectly to my graying skin. I am what many fear, what many long never to be…the smelly kid in class. Yes, I would fit in nicely in those dank, dirty, dreary Middle Ages showering only once a year. Not exactly a goal of mine.

    I don't really know where this obsession with cleanliness comes from. It is almost absurd to think that a misfiring in my brain could cause me to fear dirt and germs. I mean, why stop there? How about another misfiring that causes me to fear the color purple? It is all so seemingly random. It couldn't have come from my childhood; I had no fear of all that is unclean. I practically reveled in dirt. I spent many weekends camping in state parks across Florida. My mom took me camping when I was in elementary school, sparking a lifelong love of the outdoors. Hiking through lush forests, canoeing in natural springs, sleeping in tiny pitch-up tents, I immersed myself in nature. But now, sadly, I could never do such things. Even the thought of them sends shivers of panic up my spine. How could I do them then and not do them now? How could a disorder completely change my view on life, even in the smallest details? Now I cringe walking through the smallest patch of nature. Fear of bugs, especially spiders, crawling across my arms and legs stops me from walking in the grass or leaning against a tree. I can no longer take an idle ride in a canoe, fearing alligators and snakes would surround me. Why do I have this fear? Where did it come from? How does OCD cause this? I used to love paddling around in the little steel canoes, skating on water across a sizeable lake. Threats of alligators and poisonous snakes, both common in Florida's waterways, barely registered a thought in my mind. Even a near miss with a coiled water moccasin didn't faze me. I just didn't think anything bad was going to happen to me. How I long for that sense of security, that childlike fearlessness that got lost somewhere along the way. And the dirt, oh the icky, bacteria-laden mush, how I reveled in it. Rolling across the ground in childhood games of tag and hide-and-go-seek. Sleeping in tents with less than an inch of fabric between me and the ground. No OCD episodes. No panic attacks. No all-consuming fears. Just life, in all its glory, devoid of the disorders that now bind me. And spiders, far from running for them, I actually went looking for them. We called them jewel bugs because of the way their eyes lit up in colorful tones whenever a flashlight was passed on them. Looking for spiders? Was I mad? Or was I sane and now I'm mad? Now if I see a spider I run screaming into another room, tail firmly tucked between my legs. I used to love sleeping in tents; there is something so comfortable and reassuring about those small little houses, my mom's snoring aside. Now one step inside one and I am overcome with claustrophobia. Why does OCD make me so afraid of everything?

Frankly, I blame *Seinfeld* for most of my OCD issues (sarcasm activated). I wouldn't fear the transference of bad odors if it wasn't for the episode of the smelly car. Up to that point, I did not know smells could transfer from object to person or person to person simply by being in the same area. Now I am afraid that if I pass through a bad smell, it is going to attach itself to me. The smelly car contaminated Jerry and Elaine. They couldn't get if off them. It was like a parasite. What if some foul smell attaches to me? Oh, the horror, the horror! But it wasn't just this episode that involved OCD-like behavior; numerous others assert the fact that Jerry was a bit finicky when it came to cleanliness. Remember the episode where Jerry dropped his girlfriend's toothbrush into the toilet? In retaliation she said she put one item from his house in the toilet, but she didn't tell him which one. He went crazy wondering what the offending item was, eventually throwing everything away because he didn't know what item was contaminated. That is exactly what I would do. Jerry clearly had a bit of OCD. He corrupted my mind. It's all Seinfeld's fault.

Emily's Helpful Information
Rules of Cleanliness

1. Anything that has been, ever was, or may be in contact with urine or feces is to be immediately disposed of, no questions asked. This is the primary rule, and it must be followed to the strictest measures, unless it is a highly valued item, like a diploma or a picture. These items have been irreparably damaged, and they cannot be saved. They have been contaminated. Urine is the enemy! If you have animals, this will be a constant concern. Your best bet is to make sure your belongings are not within ten feet of the litter box.
2. To prevent urine from being a major problem in the bathroom, follow these few rules: A) Keep all urine-tainted materials (aka

toilet paper, Wet Ones, baby wipes) in a specified area like on an over-the-toilet shelving unit. B) If you touch anything after your hands have been in contact with urine, such as a cabinet or a doorknob, those are to henceforth be listed as contaminated areas and should be avoided at all costs. The only way you can erase their status is to clean them with Clorox wipes. C) If you use an unclean hand to turn on the sink to wash your hands, you must use a paper towel to turn off the water when you are done washing your hands because your hands are now clean. Otherwise, you will recontaminate your hands upon turning the water off. D) Always use paper towels to dry your hands, as they are more sanitary than hand towels, which accumulate germs by continual use.
3. Animals should not be allowed on kitchen surfaces. If they get up there frequently and cannot be taught otherwise, then the surfaces should be labeled as contaminated zones and never be used, as it would be too time-consuming to clean them on a bi-daily basis. This leads to the inability to cook in your own kitchen, so it is beneficial to gather a number of take-out menus.
4. Train your animals only to get up on certain furniture, thereby allowing you a contaminate-free seat. It's is very hard to do, but it can be done.
5. If you don't want your animals to dirty up your couch or your bed, then buy a cover sheet to put over those areas when you are not on them.
6. Door knobs can be very dirty. Use paper towels to open and close doors in your house. If you are in a public restroom, use paper towels on the doors there too. If they don't have paper towels, use an item of your clothing like your dress or your sleeve to open the door. Grab the bottom of the door handle because that is the least used part of the handle. Also, use paper towels to turn the faucet off when you are done washing your hands. The faucet is dirty because you turned it on with dirty hands so you can't turn it off with your hands after washing your hands clean.
7. Carry Wet Ones in your purse or backpack to make sure your hands are clean. It's a dirty world out there my friends.

8. Use trash bags to cover the seats in your car. I do this to prevent myself from getting dirty when I sit in my mom's car because it is dirty. I do this in my dad's car to prevent his car from getting dirty from me sitting in chairs outside of the house which may be contaminated because you don't know how dirty the person was who sat in them. I know the chairs in my house are clean but I don't know about the ones in other places. Plus in case I have a bladder accident, I don't want it to get on the clean seat. My dad's car is relatively new. It is only two years old.
9. I use a hand towel to cover the seat on my recumbent exercise bike because the cats sit on the seat and get it dirty.
10. I keep the door to my bedroom shut at all times, so that no cat could get in. It was necessary for my sanity to have one room in the house that was cat free and thus not contaminated. I kept the room as clean as possible so my clothes were clean, my furniture was clean, my bed was clean, my belongings were clean, and my floors were cleaner than the rest of the house. It was my sanctuary.
11. When my dad touched anything dirty or contaminated I made him wash his hands.

CHAPTER FIFTY
Showering

"He that hath no rule over his own spirit is like a city that is broken down, and without walls."
Proverbs 25:28

It has been almost four months since my last shower. I can't believe it has been so long. It is almost unimaginable. I've reverted back to an earlier era in which bathing every few months was commonplace. Now it is just taboo. I just don't have the strength in me to go through another shower. My last one was a tiring four hours long. I had to keep washing and rewashing over and over until my skin was raw from wear. So I put it off, first one month, then two, then three, and now an unbelievably four months. I thought if you went so long without a shower you must be filthy and smelly, but surprisingly I am neither, at least if you can believe what others say. I go to the hairdresser about once every three weeks to keep my hair clean, which has the result of making me look clean all over. And most astonishing, I don't smell. Everyone around me tells me I don't have any bad odors—hard to believe. If I started to smell, I don't know if I would get a shower or not. I really don't want to be known as the smelly adult. I guess I would force myself to do it.

I have to get a shower. I am way overdue. It has been five months since my last shower. But I can't do it. I just can't. It's too hard. It's four and a half hours of scrubbing and washing and scrubbing again. It is just too tiring. I can't do it. Plus there are my bladder problems. My bladder is acting up, or rather my IC is acting up, and I don't have bladder control. What if I pee in the shower? Can you imagine how much washing I would have to do to get pee off of me? I would be in there for at least another hour scrubbing myself raw. What am I going to do? I can't get a shower. I don't have the energy. You don't know how tiring it is working that hard to get myself clean. And what if I lose bladder control? The horror, the horror! I can't do it. But I must. It has been far too long. What am I going to do? I am so stressed out. This is making me so anxious. I can't do this. I can't sleep. I can't eat. All I can do is worry about the upcoming shower. How am I going to get through this?

It's Halloween night. I've just gotten my first shower in five months. Last time was the Fourth of July. How quickly the months go by. I'm clean, I'm finally clean! Rejoice, good people, rejoice! The village idiot has at last bathed! What a wonderful feeling it is to be clean, to have my body purified. I'm like a goddess perched high on Mt. Olympus, awash in the purest of waters. I comb through my hair; it is as silk cascading down my neck and glistening in the morning sun. I touch my skin; its softness sends goose bumps down my spine, tingling across my body. Notes of warm vanilla play off me, filling the room in my perfume. Perfection. But it came at a price. I spent four hours and thirty minutes in the shower. All the washing, the scrubbing, the rewashing, the rinsing tired me out. I was so worn down by the end of the shower that I fell down upon my bed and went to sleep. Nevertheless, I did it. It's over with.

Well, no more five months without showering. I have been ordered by the psychiatrist to shower every month. I don't know how I am going to do that. It was hard doing it every five months. How am I going to do it monthly? I know you must think I am mad; after all, you probably get a shower daily. You no doubt don't understand how something you do so easily can be so difficult for me. But then you're assuming that I am the same as you and that my brain functions the same as yours when in fact we're miles apart. Our brains are nothing alike; mine is broken while yours functions perfectly. But, I suppose after you have read this book, you understand that now. Showers are hard for me, second only to bathroom visits. Four and a half hours of scrubbing and washing is very exhausting and very stressful. It is hard to do. I don't know how I am going to do it monthly. I can't believe she ordered that. Well, I guess I should be happy she didn't order every week, or worse, every day. But frankly, after having gone so long without a shower, I learned a few things. Mainly, the body doesn't get as dirty as you think it does, unless, of course, you have a job that gets you dirty or you work out hard every day. But for most people, you just don't get that dirty on a daily basis. I really don't think you need to get a shower more often than once a week.

CHAPTER FIFTY-ONE
Recluse

"It's a dangerous business going out your front door."
J. R. R. Tolkien, The Fellowship of the Ring

My hideous physique and my comorbid disorders kept me chained inside my own house, sheltered within the dark shadows. Comorbid just means having more than one disorder at a time. I couldn't go out. It was just too hard. All of my energy was spent on the ritualistic behaviors of OCD. The bathroom alone took up half of my waking hours. I barely had the energy left over to sit upright on the couch, drowsiness weighing down my weary eyes. Life was divided into two states, life in the bathroom and life out of the bathroom, usually spent worrying about when the next visit would be. My bladder problems kept my mind fixed on the obsession at all times. A moment rarely passed free of thinking about the bathroom. But it wasn't just my bladder; it was all my obsessions burning holes through my mind, an incessant din of countless obsessions robbing me of my life. I crumbled upon their weight. I just sat on the couch and thought the thoughts of an unstable mind. My once lively wardrobe dwindled down into pajamas and sweats as I sat shackled to the living room couch, my eyes blankly fixed on the television.

Like I said before, I wasn't always the recluse I am nowadays. Once upon a time I used to be an adventurer, traveling the world over for new and unique experiences. I studied astronomy in the mountains of Arizona, biked down volcanoes in Hawaii, swam with manatees in the crystal springs of the Florida, and I even spent two weeks strolling through the streets of ancient Europe. My friend Christine and I were looking for adventure our freshman year of college, and the countries of Europe stood ready for the challenge. For two blissful weeks in the summer of 2001, we travelled from the ancient city of Rome, to the whitewashed islands of Greece, to the desert lands of Turkey. But the most fascinating aspect of this trip was not the rich history of the countries or the majestic beauty, but the fact that I managed to go on such a trip at all. Now I certainly couldn't do such a thing, but just a few years ago I could, without blinking an eye. I wasn't the fearful creature I am now. It is amazing how fully life changes in the briefest of times.

Back in the summer of 2001, when traveling to Europe, I wasn't as fearful of flying as I am now. I had reservations, of course, about taking a flight, any flight, let alone one that was nine hours, as I was afraid of crashing. Horrible way to go that is, falling from the skies into a blistering ball of fire—very frightening. But I didn't let that stop me. I couldn't; it was the trip of a lifetime. So I swallowed my fear and boarded my way to potential disaster. Fortunately, all worked out, and I arrived in the capital of Italy unharmed and excited. Rome was much how I imagined, living history next to modern art, a festival for the eyes and ears. I remember our first day there, sitting beneath a sun umbrella on the sandy beach of the Mediterranean Sea. Oh, I have been to the ocean hundreds of times before, a consequence of living in Florida, but this was different; it bore the subtle mystique of ancient travelers all the world over, merchants braving the seas with airs rich of frankincense and myrrh, touched by gods and goddesses ruling over the tempestuous lands—a needed relief from the hours of travel. Ancient ruins were nestled in and out of modern buildings—a reminder of the greatness that once was back when gladiators stood heel to heel before emperors and kings. I pressed my hand against the Coliseum, its old energy flowing through my veins, and I could almost see the battles of thousands of years ago. We walked the streets of the Roman Forum, stopping to pose as vestal virgins to the bemused onlookers then grabbed a mouth-watering cheese pizza amidst serenades from the native waiters. But all paled in comparison to the exquisite masterpiece that is the Sistine Chapel—the touch of God illuminating the trials of man, brilliant hues of blues, greens, and reds painting man in the rich tapestry of life. I could stand for hours beneath that pale blue sky and still never fully grasp the skillful beauty of it all. I would say Italy was my favorite. All that history was amazing from the Coliseum to the Sistine Chapel. I remember standing there under that ceiling completely in awe of what I saw, silenced by the officials, which was quite a feat, as Christine and I were quite the chatterboxes when we were are together—a problem that constantly got us in trouble when we were ballroom dancing. We roamed the streets of Florence, grabbing a slice of pizza and plenty of delicious gelato while walking the store-lined bridges and touring local museums. Oh how I miss the gelato. I

By Emily Watson

can't go back to regular ice cream. We toured the ruins of Pompeii in the shadow of Mt. Vesuvius, imagining what it was like all those years ago when ash rained down on the innocent villagers. We spent the night in the beautiful Sorrento where we got a room with a brilliant view of the ocean and the mountains. We were the only ones in the group to get such a view. I remember staying up late that night falling asleep on the balcony, with music from the local bar softly singing me to sleep and the cool ocean breeze caressing my body. From the ruins of Rome to the shops of Florence to the sunflower fields of Naples, my friend and I were like children on the playground. The moods of bipolar years away, I joyfully jumped into each new situation, documenting it with crazy pictures along the way. Though Rome was king of ancient ruins, I have to say that Capri was the queen of beauty, one of the most enchanting places I have ever been lucky enough to see. Whitewashed houses were nestled amongst lush plant life, rising from crystal blue waters to towering mountains glimmering in the noonday sun. The island was majestic, a watercolor painting of vibrant turquoises, lush emeralds, and crisp whites. It was magical. We took a ski lift to the top of the highest peak to get a 360-degree view of the magnificent landscape, the entire island visible right below our feet. That's right. I took a ski lift. It was such a peaceful ride, the cool wind blowing in my hair, the rich greenery beneath my feet, and the beautiful mountain waiting at the top. I stood on the apex of the highest mountain, my fear of heights years ahead. We goofily posed for pictures, drawing onlookers by our girlish antics. High up, beneath the clear blue sky, above the gentle turquoise riddled sea, nestled on the rocky mountain peak, life was in full bloom, the air was rich with magic, and I was happy, truly happy. It was the sight of a lifetime, wind brushing against my body with all the world down below, a bird on the highest peak. Greece was stunning too. The ruins at Delphi were absolutely breathtaking. Nestled in the cliffs of a towering mountain, they were quite a climb but definitely worth the effort. Now, if I had been sick back then as I am now, I wouldn't have been able to enjoy what I saw. I would be consumed by bathroom troubles, always looking for the nearest restroom, stuck inside for hours at a time, missing out on all that beauty, my obsessions and compulsions controlling every waking thought, hiding the sights of the city from me. But this was 2001, and my OCD was nothing but a shadow in my wake.

On the Edge of Insanity

Our trip included a three-day cruise though the Grecian Isles, stopping in Rhodes and the Turkish port of Kusadasi. We sailed the deep blue waters of the Mediterranean Sea, walking the ruins of ancient cities in the day, gorging on endless buffets at night, the gentle waves rocking us to sleep—perfect days on a perfect trip. The world at our feet, the edge of greatness laid out before us, a world before unknown. But now, now that is just a dream. I could never do that now. I could never get on a boat. Strange, as I have been on boats numerous times in my life, riding the waves along Hawaii's Na Pali coast and cruising the Atlantic's Bermuda Triangle. Let's stop and address that bombshell for a moment. I went into the Bermuda Triangle. The Bermuda Triangle! Hard to believe as I am the queen of superstitions and irrational fears. Just watching a special on the Triangle now makes my stomach turn—all those strange occurrences and unexplained disappearances. How could I sail through it? I don't know; one day I was OK with it, while the next day I was afraid of it. This disorder is so bizarre. Needless to say, I felt perfectly fine sailing through it back then at least four separate times. No panic attacks. No crazy freak-outs. Just the sun, the pool, and me in my bathing suit. The Bermuda Triangle aside, I fear all boats now. I fear the ocean. I fear sharks lurking beside our ship waiting for us to sink. I fear its carnal power producing rogue waves, tossing us to our death. I fear being swallowed whole by the ocean's unpredictable waves, which by the way, a thirty-three-foot rogue wave recently struck a cruise ship off the Spanish coast, so they do exist. How I used to love to sail. But I was healthy then; my mind properly functioned, and the only thing I had to worry about was if I had enough film to capture all of my great experiences. I long for those days—days free of worry, free of sadness, free only to be me.

All other fears aside, my greatest enemy, the one that would stop me from enjoying such a trip—the bathroom—was nonexistent at this time. How would I be able to travel to the ruins of Pompeii if I was stuck in the bathroom for hours at a time? How would I be able to walk the streets of Ephesus if I was consumed by washing my hands after every dirty ruin I touched? I couldn't. If I were sick just ten years ago, I would have missed out on the trip of a lifetime—for what, a few nonsensical fears. But as it was, I didn't have to worry about the bathroom. I was in and out in five minutes. If you think that was shocking, you'd be even more surprised to know that when I went on dinosaur digs in the hills of Wyoming, I actually went to the restroom on hillsides—no bathrooms in sight, just miles of rolling hills. Seriously, no toilet, no toilet paper, no faucets; I was a true adventurer. Can you believe it, using the restroom without a toilet? I just pulled up alongside a nice-looking hill, made sure no one was in sight, and let my bladder loose on the dirt-covered terrain, making sure of course the wind was at my back. I made that mistake only once. Now, to be honest, I can't go pee outdoors by myself. I have tried. I just get pee all over myself. So I cheated a little. I used a device, a funnel and tube type of device, that let me pee standing up like guys. So that let me pee outside. Of course, I couldn't pee outside now, mind you. I get a panic attack just thinking about it. Frankly, I don't even know how I managed to do it then. But I did. I didn't like it—I prefer a nice porcelain seat—but I did it. Real outdoors woman I was. Didn't even have to use any toilet paper; the arid Wyoming wind just dried me right off. Brilliant.

But all of that changed with the onset of OCD and bipolar. The trips of yesterday were long past. I am confined to the house now, and I am miserable. How could I only a few years ago travel to the other side of the world, and now I am afraid to walk outside my front door? How could things change so drastically? How could a mental disorder do this? I don't understand. I am missing out on so much now. My friend, Naomi, just got back from Jordan and Israel. She saw the ruins at Petra and the Temple Mount. What amazing sights to see—once-in-a-lifetime sights. How I long to see such things for myself. But I can't. That would mean stepping outside my front door. That would mean getting in a car and traveling a great distance. That would mean getting on plane filled with potential terrorists. That would mean flying over a massive ocean and at any moment falling out of the skies. That would mean going to the most dangerous place on earth, the Middle East. I couldn't do that. The risk is just too great and so I remain sitting on my couch with the illusion of safety. I am a recluse now, a lonely hermit, and I am terrified.

CHAPTER FIFTY-TWO
January Nightshades

*"Be what you would seem to be—or, if you'd like it put more simply—
Never imagine yourself not to be otherwise than what it might appear
to others that what you were or might have been was not otherwise
than what you had been would have appeared
to them to be otherwise."*
Lewis Carroll

I am born. Or rather I was born in January 1981. I hate birthdays, but then again past the age of twenty-one, I think most people hate birthdays. What are they really? A reminder of all we are not and all we have not done, and of course, the ever-present reminder that we are one year closer to death. Birthdays were always great fun growing up, as I eagerly looked forward to being one year older, one year more mature, counting the days until I got my driver's license, until I graduated, until I could vote, until I could drink. They were celebrations of the joy of being young. One of my nicest birthdays was when I turned sixteen, I think. My best friend at the time, Chrissy, threw me a surprise birthday party. I was elated. I couldn't believe that anyone cared that much, outside of my family, about my birthday. All my closest friends gathered around a table at the local Applebee's. I was happy, really happy. Little things like that mean so much, even now, fifteen years later. But now, birthdays bring no happiness. All my friends have moved up and gone on with their lives, leaving me alone in their dust. My parents always sweetly give me presents, but none that are what I really want: to get better. No one can give me that, not even the doctors.

Sometimes I think that those with mental disorders are merely too empathetic. They simply feel too much pain to belong solely to themselves. They must be feeling the pain of others. My heart weeps for reasons I cannot fathom. My mind dances with the anxiety of fears I've never known. My sorrow is not my own. I feel the pain of a trampled plant. I feel the saddened rage of an animal being abused. I feel the terrible fear of those murdered worldwide. I take this pain on as if it were my own, crushing me beneath an ever-growing weight, the weight of the entire world. Driving me mad, tormenting me every waking hour, every dreadful minute, feeling all the world's pain and sorrow. Driving out every laugh, every smile, every warm feeling I ever had. Driving me to the brink, to the brink of insanity. Why? Because I feel too much. Are our fellow soldiers, those in the fight against mental disorders, are they merely undiscovered empaths? What were psychics or mediums before they realized their gift—disturbed schizophrenics? Maybe this is all a strange dream thought about one particularly mournful day. But what do you feel when you go to bed at night?

Sometimes when I am sitting alone on the couch, I wonder about other people. Who are all these people I see walking around each day living their lives? Busily darting here and there, going to work, going to the movies, going to loved ones' houses. Are they OK? Are they happy? Are they living the American dream? Are they living normal lives? Or are they like me? Are they suffering from some medical disorder? Are they in pain? Do they long for normal lives too? Do they even know I exist? Or am I hidden beyond their awareness, lost behind a cookie-cutter apartment, faded into darkness? Forgotten by ambivalence. Left alone like Boo Radley. But there are others. Somewhere in a quiet town is a teen weighing a half a ton. I see him in the darkness; when I'm quiet I can feel his pain. Somewhere in a bustling city is a woman battling cancer, fighting for life in the ICU. I hear her heart beating in line with mine. The darkness parts, hundreds of stories, hundreds of voices, all lost against the din of everyday life, the life of the normal. The life of the healthy, the happy, the content. The life of those who dwell in the light. But we dwell in the dark, in the absence, the helpless wanderers of the night, searching for hope amidst the crushing shadows. We all cry out, and my loneliness tempers. Let us not be forgotten. Let us not be alone.

I'm desperate for a drink. I'm desperate for the sweet relief of alcohol that so many partake in for their nightly troubles. What must I imbibe to erase the pains of OCD? What drink will wash away all my worries? I need relief. But I abhor the taste. Sweet wine, tangy vodka, smooth rum—all are a sickness to my senses. But there must be one out there I can tolerate, one that can soften all my troubles. I see it regularly taming the misdeeds of the day for hundreds of souls—the jubilant bloke at the bar, the mellowed actor on TV, the giddy girl at a party. They are all mellowed and uplifted by a single sip of alcohol. How I long for that. How I long for that piece of mind. I know perhaps that I am delusional. Alcohol isn't the answer to mental problems. If it were doctors would prescribe two drinks a day. There wouldn't be groups for people addicted to the substance. But people make drinking look so much fun, so relaxing. I can't watch an hour of television without seeing someone down a few beers. Next scene they are all relaxed, or they are bouncing off the walls with jubilation. Who wouldn't want to taste the sweet nectar of that joyousness? I must find my drink.

I'm not getting better. It is the first time I have said it out loud, the first time I have really come to terms with what that means. I'm not getting better. The innocent words make my skin stand on end. The pills aren't working. I have tried dozens of SSRIs, mood stabilizers, and antipsychotics, yet I remain the same. No uplifting notes for my depression. No calming chords for my mania. No rest for my OCD. I remain unchanged. Probability alone would dictate that at least one of them would have worked. These pills have clearly worked for millions of others, so why not with me? What special trait has left me unhealed? There are so few left now. What if none of them work? Am I to spend the rest of my life in this hobbled state?

I can't see the future. I can't see what my life will be like in the future, five years from now, ten years from now. I can't see myself married. I can't see myself having children. I can't see myself in any career. I see nothing. It scares me that I cannot see it. I don't know why my vision is impaired. Does it mean that I have no future? Am I meant to die before any of those things comes to pass? Or are the disorders blocking my view? I can't tell. I can't see. I can't even dream of tomorrow. I used to sit daydreaming hours on end, imagining what a wonderful future I would have. I pictured myself sitting in an austere lab pondering the questions of the universe. I pictured myself on an archaeological dig in the arid heat of the Egyptian sun. I pictured myself at the CIA analyzing security data in an office at Langley. I pictured myself in an epic romance that would span the rest of my life. And kids, I pictured myself the proud mother of four beautiful children, two boys and two girls. I pictured the American dream in all its glory. It was meant to be. It was going to be. I could dream it into existence. But now, now it has all disappeared. The dreams are lost, faded into nothing. Replaced with nothing, only silence, only darkness. I stay as I am now maybe for a few weeks, maybe for a few months, maybe a few years, and then time stops. The future ends. I end. And what have I left behind? Nothing. I have done nothing worthwhile in the small fraction of time I had on this earth. I have squandered precious years in my selfish pursuit of my own glory, desperately searching for my own way to make a difference in this world. But I have done nothing. I have changed nothing. When I die the world will go on as it always has, unfazed by such an insignificant loss. My parents will cry for me, but no one else. I have not left my imprint on anyone's life. I wish I had done more. I wish I had time to do more. But I can't see it. I can't see the future.

Why am I writing this book? What's the point? In a few years everyone will be dead—or at least most people. No one will be left around, or at least no one that cares. The world is coming to an end, and there's nothing we can do to stop it. The signs are all there: the growing conflict in the Middle East, the rise in terrorism, the proliferation of nuclear bombs, the failing economy, the escalating tension in numerous countries. The world is going to hell, and no one seems to take notice. Where is Superman? Where is Batman? Where is the lone vigilante who arrives in the eleventh hour to save us from ourselves? The end is coming. The Mayans saw it. Thousands of years ago they saw it, and they gave us the date: December 21, 2012. The Catholics saw it. St. Malachi saw it. He gave us a number 112. There will only be 112 popes and we are on 111. The end is coming, and the trials and tribulations of one girl mean nothing.

CHAPTER FIFTY-THREE
An Unfortunate Collision

"We must never despair; our situation has been compromising before, and it has changed for the better; so I trust it will again. If difficulties arise, we must put forth new exertion and proportion our efforts to the exigencies of the times."
George Washington

"Noble souls, through dust and heat, rise from disaster and defeat the stronger."
Henry Wadsworth Longfellow

My dad and I were driving up to visit my mom in St. Augustine. He was driving, as I'm still unable to drive, when a large pickup truck smashed into the back of our compact Saturn. Some punk-ass kid, who only turned eighteen two weeks before, was too distracted to put his foot on the brake and slammed into us accelerator full on. He was also too distracted to get out of his car and see if we were all right, to which my father got out and gave him a good talking down to. Meanwhile, I was still coming out of a daze and nursing an injury to my head. My memory of the whole incident is rather foggy. I remember staring at my dad when the impact occurred and seeing him violently jerk forward. Strangely, I don't remember the sound of the crash, which was heard at the BBQ restaurant less than a mile up the road. As for me, my head was throbbing after having hit the back rest just a little too hard. It was the worst car accident I had ever been in. I had only been in two prior. The first can hardly be considered in accident, as I hit the car ahead of me going no more than five miles per hour in deadlocked traffic. I still maintain the only reason the person called the cops was because her husband was a cop. I had to go to traffic school for that. I am still a little miffed. The second occurred when I was driving by myself on a four-hour trip to visit a friend of mine out west. My tire got pulled away from the hubcap when hitting some uneven road and sent me into an uncontrolled 360. I desperately tried to regain some control, but it was out of my hands. I let go of the steering wheel and just waited for the chips to fall where they would. I spun up on two wheels and flew off the side of the road down into a large ditch and up the other side into a large forest before I finally came to a stop. People nicely stopped their cars to see if I was all right, and one helped me change a tire. Luckily I was OK, and surprisingly my car, a tough little Saturn, only sustained minor damages. I just hopped back on the road and continued on my way—a little shaken but OK. Back to the most recent crash, though. It was by far the worst damage-wise. The whole back end of the Saturn was smashed in. By the time the cops arrived, I was bent over with a throbbing pain in my head. They advised I get in the ambulance when it arrived. I had never been in an ambulance before, and I felt rather silly being in one then. My injuries weren't life-threatening. I just had a little bang on my head. Needless to say, everyone was of the better-safe-than-sorry thinking, so I just went along with it. They strapped me up to a gurney and asked my dad a bunch of questions as we road through the city. It was actually a rather peaceful ride as I had no worries because I knew the hospital would make sure there was nothing wrong with me, so I didn't have to stress about my head. When we arrived at Flagler Hospital, I felt like Cleopatra riding in on that gurney high above the ground. And once again I didn't have to wait in the ER; I got rolled right into a room. Brilliant. Two hours later I strolled out with a clean bill of health—well, however clean I could be being a crazy bipolar OCD freak who needed continual reassurance from the doctor that I was all right. I could see him slowly edging out of the room to get away from me seeing there was no end to my incessant questioning.

Over the next few weeks, I began feeling pain and numbness in my extremities. I went through the usual CAT scans and MRIs and suffered another trip to the ER to check for blood clots, but everything turned up normal. Next stop was a month-long stint in physical therapy to treat residual unidentified symptoms brought on by the violent impact of the crash and the atrophy in my muscles resulting from dormancy from my inability to exercise due to my disorders. Unfortunately, my car didn't fare any better than I did. It was totaled. I was heartbroken. I loved that car, but there was nothing we could do. It was too badly damaged. We had to buy a new car. My dad bought a lovely red Honda Insight.

CHAPTER FIFTY-FOUR
Continued Bladder Problems

"The first wealth is health."
Ralph Waldo Emerson

"A healthy body is a guest-chamber for the soul;
a sick body is a prison."
Sir Francis Bacon

My bladder problems are in dire need of some resolution. The pain is unbearable, burning spasms jerking me out of my mental prison. I have little to no bladder control left, leaving me to relieve myself in a diaper like a baby. You cannot imagine the stress upon my body: every cough, every sneeze, every tense muscle an impetus to my bladder to open the floodgates. I can't ignore it any longer. I have to have a cystoscopy and soon. I don't know how I am going to do it. Maybe the doctor will take pity on me and give me some Demerol to get through it, though even a tablet of Demerol may not be enough to deter a panic attack worthy of Oscar himself. The minute they put an IV in me my damaged bladder will begin filling up, meaning that in an hour or so I will have to go to the bathroom—bad—which means I will be forced to use a restroom at the hospital. I can't do that. I spend thirty minutes to an hour in the bathroom every time I go. The hospital staff won't let me do that. I probably won't even be allowed fifteen minutes. My bathroom ritual is too involved; fifteen minutes isn't possible. Worse yet, what if I have an accident before I even make it to the bathroom? Loss of bladder control with all the world to see. No, I can't do it. I absolutely can't, but I must. And the anesthesia? Being forcibly put to sleep? That's madness. I can't be sedated; I am afraid of sleep. I am afraid of being put to sleep. I can't be unconscious. And worst of all, I will be exposed; my undercarriage will be on view for all the world to see. People will be messing around down there sticking tubes where they don't belong. No, I can't. I absolutely can't. But I have to. I just don't know how I am going to get through it. Fortunately the doctor understands psychiatric illnesses and is willing to work with me. He thinks it is best to try me on a few medications for bladder control problems before subjecting me to a cystoscopy that most likely will come up clear of any major problems. Plus, he gave me some hydrocodone for the pain. Jubilant festivities begin! It's only a week's supply, but it is always better than none at all.

My bladder is killing me. Every minute of every day is focused on this temperamental organ, as I am always peeing in my pants. My bladder control muscle is out of commission. I am subjected to constant spasms, which disable the dam on my bladder. A day strolling the ancient streets of St. Augustine ruined by a sudden leakage. A night on the town scrapped as I began peeing in my car. I can't go out anywhere or do anything. My world revolves around my bladder. How does someone live like this? How am I supposed to function in my daily life? Even at home I am not free from my bladder. Though I have a bathroom nearby, my bladder often lets loose before I reach the toilet, splattering pee everywhere. Like I didn't already spend enough time in the bathroom cleaning and wiping, now I have to clean up a pee mess on the floor, on the toilet, and on my legs and bum. My bathroom visits were already an hour in length, and now with this whole mess, I am looking at an additional thirty minutes. I can't do this. I can't spend that much time in there. I'm too tired. I'm too tired to do this anymore. What am I going to do? What can I do? I have to go to the restroom; it is an inherent part of life. But I can't; it is too tiring. Maybe I can't stop going, but I can stop how often I go. I will just have to drink less—reduce my liquid intake until I only have to go twice a day. That's a bad idea, I know; dehydration makes bladder problems worse. But I don't have a choice. I have to do something, and this is the only thing that I can do. The urologist is no help. The second time I went to see him I could tell he had already written me off as a mental case. He didn't recommend any procedures, as he didn't think they would show anything. He never said it outright, but what he did say made it evident that he thought most of my bladder problems were caused by anxiety. He got wind that I am under psychiatric care and assumes, like many doctors, that all my problems revolve around my mental illness. Do I think that perhaps my anxiety is making my bladder worse? Absolutely. But do I think it is the cause of my bladder ails? Absolutely not. My bladder problems started long before any of my mental disorders began showing. I've lived with anxiety long enough to be able to distinguish between what is caused by it and what is not. But do they treat me as a perfectly rational adult? No. Once they see that I have mental problems they write me off as crazy. It appears even doctors are not immune to this stigma. Who's going to help me now?

CHAPTER FIFTY-FIVE
Juries of the World

"Forbear to judge, for we are sinners all."
William Shakespeare

I'm tired of having to justify myself. I am tired of having to prove to others that I am really sick. I am tired of having to plead my case as if I were on the witness stand. Why do we have such a negative view on mental illnesses? Why do we think they are imaginary? Why do we think they are mental weaknesses? Why don't we see them for what they are…an illness, a devastating illness that corrupts the mind and damages the body. The only way to fight these stigmas is to talk about them and educate others on what mental illnesses really are. We need to come out of the shadows, come out of our hiding places, and stand tall against the world. We are not weak. We are not crazy. We are strong. We are brave. We are warriors in the battles of our minds.

Why do I have to prove I am sick to others? Why can't they accept my word? If they lived with me 24/7, I wouldn't have to say a word because they would bear witness to the true horror of it all. But they don't and so they don't see the sickness; they don't see any scars on me that bespeak any illness. I am tired of explaining myself, tired of explaining what these disorders are and what they do, so I wrote this book. Let it be a manifesto. Let this single piece of work be a loudspeaker for these disorders, enabling all those who wish to know me the ability to understand my pain. Let henceforth this book be the key evidence in my trial. Let it fall at the feet of the juries of the world. Let it speak for me when I am too weary to plead my case. I am not weak! I am sick, as sick as anyone with a physical illness. I am beaten. I am bruised. I can barely stand. But I can't give up. I will never give up. I will fight until my last breath. Let the juries of the world here me now. I am strong and I am going to beat this. Let it stand forever as a monument to the warriors of OCD and bi-polar. Let it stand as a symbol of truth in a courtroom of doubt and lies.

CHAPTER FIFTY-SIX
Heightened Anxiety

*"Some of your hurts you have cured, and the
sharpest you still have survived,
But what torments of grief you endured from
the evil which never arrived."*
Ralph Waldo Emerson

    I wandered into purgatory the other day when I found myself trapped in an ER for a grueling nine hours. Seeing an urgent care physician over a simple leg pain earlier in the day sent me on a weekend visit to the hospital to check for blood clots until the wee hours of one desperate morning. Nine dreadful hours of waiting…waiting for an answer that seemed would never come. The faces of the other fifty-two patients lining that hall were blank, dulled by their own suffering, lost in a sea of their own pain. Fifty-two souls waiting for but one thing, their name to be called, a nurse walking through those big double doors bidding them to come back to wait in another smaller, yet cozier, room. At first merely strangers, they became a strange sort of family. People united in a common bond of suffering, looking to each other for support in their time of need—all desperately waiting for someone to call them back. But they didn't come. For hours on end, they didn't come. We all just sat waiting with no hope. With no end in sight. Just waiting. For a seeming eternity. Many left. The poor woman with the new-born baby and young child who spoke broken English. The little boy with an injury to his head and his father. Should they have stayed? Who knows? I hope they are OK. I almost left myself numerous times. But the fear of having a blood clot kept me in my seat. We finally got to see the doctor around three a.m., and my fears were allayed. It looked more like I had a pinched nerve in my back because half my leg was asleep. I'd say that was nine hours wasted, except for the fact that they gave me a low level narcotic called Darvocet. I know! Can you believe it? I didn't even have to ask for it; they just gave it to me. And that urgent care center—you know, the one that sent me to the hospital—well, they called in a prescription for me too, for hydrocodone. Ah! What joyousness! I was swimming in a sea of narcotics. I could forget about my illnesses. I could throw out my obsessive thoughts. I could rid myself of my sudden mood shifts. For two weeks I could be completely and perfectly happy. Right?

Wrong. By the time I made my epic visit to the ER, I was already waist-deep in the worst anxiety episode I had ever been in. I was once again strapped to that runaway train. Coal was being piled even higher as I sat there unable to move, unable to stop it. The coal dust in the air was suffocating me. The anxiety was suffocating me. I couldn't breathe. My life force was being drained from me. The coal was piled higher. I couldn't catch my breath. Please stop the train. I needed to breathe. I couldn't think. My mind was spinning, racing, turning. Please stop. The coal was piled higher. The wind tossed through my hair with a maddening rage. The heat from the fire singed my skin. The anxiety couldn't go any higher. I couldn't bear it. I just couldn't bear it. I couldn't contain the energy inside of me. I felt like I was going to explode. I needed someone to please help me. I couldn't do this alone. The coal was piled higher. The train raced on, speeding past the union station, past the scenic overlook, past the signs reading slow down, turn back, end of the line…it kept racing, going ever faster, but to where? Where would it end up, where would it go? Where would I go? I couldn't hang on much longer.

I found myself the sufferer of a drunken blackout the past two weeks without having imbibed a single drop of alcohol. That came courtesy of Ativan. Dr. Farinas was looking for some way to reduce my anxiety, so she tried me on this new class of drugs. I think it might have actually helped a little, but to be honest I can't really remember. I literally can't remember the majority of what happened those two weeks. It is a strange feeling, really, to have people say that I said and did all these things and not remember a single one of them. I have never gotten drunk before so I guess this was my experience. I sent emails, talked to people on the phone, had friends over—all things I can't remember. I even played two rounds of mini golf, which I haven't played since middle school, yet I can't remember them either. Weird feeling really. Worse yet was what would come to be known as the "Walmart Excursion," an event I have to be continually be reminded of. I was shopping at Walmart with my dad when I caught a glimpse of myself in the mirror. I was so horrified at what I saw that I plopped down on the ground—well, actually on a package of paper towels, as the floor is rather dirty—and refused to get up. I was too upset to continue shopping. My dad had to call my mom to come and sit with me so he could continue shopping. I can't believe I did that. I have no memory of doing that. I'm really embarrassed by that. Alas, none of those reasons are why I stopped taking Ativan. That reason solely belongs to the horrid side effect of incontinence. Now, I am not talking there is a little leak in the dam that is causing a small amount of liquid to collect on a maxi pad. Oh no. No, I'm talking the dam has burst, the frightened villagers are running for their lives, and that little maxi pad is about to drown. And did this conveniently happen when I was near the bathroom? No. It waited and happened when I was walking around the apartment complex during my daily exercise when I was ten apartments away from my own, right there in the middle of the freaking street. My bladder let loose, and I found myself jogging home with pee running down my legs. That is why I'm never taking Ativan again, or any other drug in that class, which is a shame because they really did help a little.

    My OCD is out of control. Every cell in my body is vibrating at a frequency that I can't handle, poisoning my body with anxious energy. It is wound around me like a snake, squeezing all the breath out of my lungs. I am slowly being consumed by anxiety, and there is nothing I can do to stop it. Other people must feel anxiety too. They have to. It is a natural part of life. It's easiest to see in kids, the little anxieties of childhood: worry over an upcoming test, worry over giving an oral presentation, worry over getting a bad report card, worry over being accepted by your peers. Anxiety gives way to moody behavior and bouts of tears. But adults, they hide their fears. They control their anxiety. My friend Christine is, by all accounts, absolutely fearless. I have never seen her get anxious or frightened over anything. Either she is a really good actress, or she just never gets anxious. I have yet to discern that little truth. She went sky diving on a whim. That's right. She voluntarily jumped out of a perfectly functioning plane for sport. I'm not even sure I could do that if the plane was in imminent danger of crashing. Most likely she feels a normal amount of anxiety, the same amount that most adults do. How I envy that normalcy. I can still remember it, back in high school. Living with routine anxieties and always overcoming them. But all that changed. Somewhere along the way, OCD slipped in and with it a sea full of anxieties. I am anxious every minute of every day, from the time I wake up and into my dreams the following night. I never have a moment's peace. Even the tiniest trials and tribulations of life bring me great anxiety from what I am going to wear that day to what I am going to have for dinner that night. Worse is I stress about events that are yet to come, events that may never even happen, terrible apocalyptic visions. I am so much more anxious than the normal adult that I have no hope of hiding it. I verbalize my anxieties to every person who will listen, hoping to find some reassurance in their voice, but more often than naught, coming off like a rambling crazy person.

I'm afraid. Dark things are on the horizon. Danger electrifies the air. The hairs on my body stand on end. I lock the door. I place a luggage carrier and a chair in front of it. I turn on the alarm. But it is not enough. They are still coming...from every corner of the world. I try to stop it, but I don't know how. I am just one person, and I am weak. I am so very weak. But I feel it, rushing up through my body. It's all becoming clear. The US economy will collapse. The value of the dollar will fail. Soon it won't be worth anything. They say invest in gold and silver, but who has the money for that? We are just trying to keep our heads above water. What will we do? And our debt, our national debt. We owe trillions of dollars to China and the other countries. How will we ever pay that off? Are we even trying? No, the government is spending more every day, dragging us deeper and deeper into the arms of our debtors. But what does an economic collapse matter when we are under attack from terrorists? Right now, as we speak, extremist groups are plotting ways to kill us. It is only a matter of time before they succeed again. Biologic weapons, computer viruses, and handmade bombs lie just beyond our shores. Our borders lay open, waiting for them to make their way to any town or city of their choosing. We're vulnerable. We're weak. Darkness is falling. Rival nations are building nuclear bombs. They toil away unchecked. We look the other way. Hitler is rising again, and no one stands prepared to stop him. We are inching our way to World War III. The warnings are everywhere. Stop! Turn back! No one is listening. We are all lost in our nice, safe little lives. The stage is set. The players have taken their marks. Weapons stand at the ready. Light flickers and darkness falls.

By Emily Watson

I'm afraid to go outside. I'm scared I'll die or worse become seriously injured. What if I became paralyzed? What would I do? I'm not a strong enough person to live like that. The world is too dangerous. I could get into a car accident. My car could get hit on a bridge and fall into the water, trapping me inside until I drown. I could get shot by some disturbed person while at university or the mall. I could get attacked by some armed stranger while walking to my car at night and wind up dead in some pond by the side of the road.

I can't be left alone. I have to go out with my dad every time he leaves the house, every time he runs an errand, every time he checks the mail. I'm afraid something bad will happen to him if I am not there. I am afraid he will get into a fatal car accident and perish at the scene. I'm afraid he will fall victim to an armed robbery at a gas station store, his last moments of life felt at the tip of a gun. I'm afraid a terrorist will set a bomb off at the local bookstore while he is in there shopping, his body shattered beyond repair. All are images that play over and over in my head, a list full of things I hope will never come to pass. But he is not the only one I fear for. I fear for myself as well. I fear being left alone, sick and weak, unable to fight for myself. I fear being raped. I fear having some foul man touch me without my consent. I fear being murdered. I fear being kidnapped in the middle of the night, beaten to death, stuffed in an old suitcase and tossed aside like trash. I fear it not because it is a rarity, but because it is so commonplace. I can't watch the news without hearing about some poor girl or woman being raped or murdered. A woman just like me, minding her own business, going about her daily affairs, ripped from her quaint little life to meet an insidious fate. Brutal rapes. Vicious killings. Demented crimes. All are an everyday fixture in our lives. They occur in our own city. They occur in our own communities. They occur in our own apartment complexes. They occur in the door next to us. How can I not be frightened? How can I not be afraid to be left alone? Chaos and death stand outside my door ready to break their way in, and I have nothing to protect myself with. I am weak now. I am much too weak. I was once strong. I took taekwondo lessons during middle school, and I got midway up the belt levels. I could front kick, side kick, and reverse punch my way out of any situation I might run into. The instructor told my mom that she was surprised to see someone so small with such power and strength. Unfortunately, I stopped around the time I started high school. Other things came up, life got in the way, and I let my skills pass to nothingness. I could use them now. Not just to defend myself, but I could use the strength they brought me. I am so weak now, so very weak. Just walking to the car is an effort that leaves me winded. I try to be strong, I try to exercise, but I hardly ever do, even though that is the only thing that will help me lose weight. I am just too tired. I feel like I have not eaten in days. My muscles are as heavy as lead, dragging behind me as I try to move forward. My skin hangs off me, drawing my features ever downward and contributing to my grim physique. My body is weak and grotesque. I have nothing to do but sit on the couch and wait for something, anything, to come.

I'm afraid to stay inside. I am afraid some home invader will break in and rape and kill me. I'm scared to go to sleep at night because no one will be awake to protect the house. Though I don't know how I would defend myself. I'm too weak to fight. I don't own a gun. I'm a sitting duck whether I am awake or asleep.

They're in my house. They're hiding amidst the shadows. I fear my room. I fear the closet, the darkest place in the house. They're in there. I know they are. Every time I reach for the door, I expect to see them on the other side. Demons! Odorous, diabolical red-eyed demons!

I'm close, much closer than I have ever been, to falling in that maddening darkness. The OCD has almost fully taken over me. The earth is spinning. I can feel it moving beneath my feet, turning through space on its tilted axis, running around the sun in a choreographed dance. At any moment we could go flying off of it, held down by the weakest of forces, millions of people tumbling through the icy depths of space. Dead bodies now remnants of a once great civilization. Snapshots of life now consigned to the absence of space. Once roaming through darkness together, we break apart, isolated, alone. Flying off into the burning suns of our galaxy, getting caught in the orbit of a distant planet, forever falling into a black hole, left alone, always alone, in the darkest depths of a most unfamiliar place, longing for the warmth of a human touch, the passion of human breath. All lost, lost to pillars of time, forgotten amidst the birth of a new star and its solitary planet with beings just like us, living their lives, not seeing what once was. Left alone, falling though the tapestry of space, forever searching for life, for love, for home.

    Sometimes I feel like I am a breath away from tragedy. I am a breath away from turning into one of those stories you hear on the news of a person going crazy and doing something bad. I feel like I am just a breath away from that. At any moment I could lose control, and I wouldn't be me anymore. I would be someone else. I'd be lost forever. I'm already so close to that edge. What would it take to push me over? What if all it takes is something small? And then I snap. I take a breath in and then I'm gone. In a single breath, I'm gone forever. And who will mourn for me? No one, save my parents. I have left no lasting impact on anyone else. I will pass and the world will go on as it always has, taking no notice of me.

Medications for Anxiety

    Ativan – Ativan is like getting drunk. It made me feel a little better at the time, but the consequences weren't worth it. The blackouts were terrible. Large periods of time are missing from my memory, and that is a scary thing. But that is nothing compared to the episodes of incontinence I experienced.

    Valium – Like Ativan but has a longer half-life.

    Clonazepam (Klonopin) – It made me very sleepy, though not nearly bad as Seroquel.

    Xanax – I tried the anti-anxiety medication Xanax to use in the case of a severe panic attack. First it put me to sleep, and then gave me sleep paralysis.

CHAPTER FIFTY-SEVEN
Panic Attacks

"Sanity is very rare; every man almost, and every woman, has a dash of madness."
Ralph Waldo Emerson

"When we remember that we are all mad, the mysteries disappear and life stands explained."
Mark Twain

"No excellent soul is exempt from a mixture of madness."
Aristotle

<u>Panic disorder</u> – A condition in which the person suffers from sudden and repeated panic attacks that cause sweating, chest pain, palpitations, choking sensations, and an overwhelming feeling of terror. I have these quite often and they make me feel as if I am having a heart attack (WebMD 2010).

My pulse begins to race. I feel as if I am running a mile and yet I am standing still. A chill sweeps through my body. My goose bumps stand on end. I shiver in protest. My pulse grows faster. I'm having difficulty breathing. My breaths are too shallow. There is not enough air. Cool sweat drips down my face. My chest cramps up, sending waves of pain throughout my body. I become unhealthily fixated on my breathing. My pulse grows faster. I can't breathe. I develop the false assumption that my breathing is a conscious action rather than an unconscious action and if I stop remembering to breath then I will die. I violently gasp for air, flailing my arms and legs about, looking for anyone to help me. My throat closes, and I begin to choke. A deep, unsettling fear, a maddening terror, sinks in that this is going to be the end. I've spiraled into a full-blown panic attack.

In a matter of minutes, I have gone from the peak of contentment to the chaos of despair. I have fallen into a panic attack. Having a panic attack is different from suffering from constant anxiety in its intensity and rapidity. I can spiral down in a matter of minutes. But it is its intensity that is so terrifying—the feeling that I have become trapped in this state and I can't escape. There is only one way out of this situation and that is a trip to the ER. I still remember my first panic attack. I was in my early twenties and driving in the car with my dad when I was overcome by a sudden, intense pain in my chest. Terror swept over me. I was quite sure I was having a heart attack, at which point I began to flip out. By the time we got to the hospital, my father was in a full-on panic attack himself. What would come next would be a series of heart rate monitors attempting to discern whether or not I had had a heart attack. Imagine my embarrassment that after all that fuss all that had happened to me was merely an ole panic attack.

That is where my most recent attack landed me in the early hours one morning. None of the pills I had were working. I used to dread going to the hospital—the long lines, the unidentified foul odors, and the stains of human waste upon the floors. Oh, the horror. But then there's the other side—the good side. They make me feel better. Sure, it is only a Band-Aid fix that lasts for only a few hours. But, it is enough to pull me back from the edge of insanity, enough to let my mind rest. So I looked forward to going that night. Though I did, however, still dread ER doctors. You could see the doctors didn't want to deal with me—me being too complicated a case and all. Others didn't bother to understand what I was going through and instead thought I should be Baker Act-ed. Fortunately, I ran into the nicest doctor I have ever come across in the ER. He was so empathetic and genuinely concerned about my well-being that he nearly wiped away my panic attack with sheer words. Were that truly the case. Actually, it took three Xanax.

CHAPTER FIFTY-EIGHT
Descent into Madness

"I became insane, with long intervals of horrible sanity."
Edgar Allan Poe

By January 2009, my symptoms were utterly unbearable. My bipolar was under control through Geodon, but my anxiety and OCD were beyond all previous measure. My mind was filled with obsessive thoughts, and the only way to silence them was to do whatever they said and perform my little rituals. If I was obsessing over the cleanliness of my hands, I had to wash my hands. If I was obsessing over the light, I had to turn it on and off repetitively. If I was obsessing over the door being locked, I had to lock the door repetitively. If I was obsessing over the cleanliness of anything, I had to get clean it. Every obsessive thought had a corresponding task. Thousands of thoughts, thousands of voices haunted me. Every minute of every day was filled with such acute anxiety that as time passed and it grew ever worse, I thought that I might explode in a fiery ball of insanity. My constant refrain "I want to go to the ER," sprinkled every conversation. Even though I knew it meant I would be placed under the Baker Act, I wanted to go because I needed help, and I didn't know what else to do. I couldn't cope with the intensity of the symptoms. I felt I would lose my grip on sanity at any moment. But Dr. Farinas thought that the hospital would be a bad idea because it didn't specialize in mental illness. They wouldn't know how to properly handle me and things could go badly very quickly. If I was seen to be uncooperative, they could strap me down, pump me with medications, and hold me indefinitely. But I didn't care. I just wanted help. Dr. Farinas even admitted she didn't know what to do with me. I was a very difficult case. She even suggested that I go to a psychiatric hospital that specializes in OCD and bipolar disorder. I said no. No way was I going to be locked away in some mental hospital away from everyone and everything that helps comfort me.

I can't take it. I can't do this. It's too much. I can't do this. My mind is against me. It is unbearable. Please make it stop. Please help me.

Please take me to the hospital. I'm tired, but I don't want to go to sleep. I don't want to go unconscious. I am afraid. I need a caffeine pill. Help me! Help me! I can't do this. I'm tired. I'm so very tired. My body is limp and lifeless. My skin is pale and green. I am weaker than my eighty-year-old grandma. The OCD is robbing me of all my strength. All my little rituals take up all of my energy. But what am I to do? The voices, the infernal voices, are driving me mad. The only way to silence them is to perform my absurd rituals. But I am weak now, so very weak. I don't have the strength to go on. I don't have the strength to keep fighting. I am slipping away, falling into nothingness. I tried to claw my way out of the darkness, I tried to work out. I hopped on the treadmill and walked my way to exhaustion, but my body failed me. I tore my Achilles tendon. Now I have to wear a cast for the next few months. My body is worthless. I am falling to pieces. I am breaking up before everyone's very eyes. I can't do this any longer. I don't have the strength to go on. Somebody help me! I can't keep this up!

I am a recluse now, a hermit trapped inside my own apartment, trapped inside my own mind. I can't face the outside world. I can't even face myself. I feel like I am frozen in a moment in time, in a single snapshot of life. At age twenty nine, I should be out on my own working at some steady job. I should have a husband and kids. I should be living the American dream, but I am not. I am far from it. Instead, I am a child having to be cared for by her parents because she is too weak to be out on her own. I have regressed to an adolescent-like state. I have to be taken care of. I can't drive. I can barely walk let alone pilot a thousand-pound vehicle. I'm an accident waiting to happen. I can't make my own food. My kitchen is a mix of cat hair, dander, and urine, as my mother lets the animals roam freely on the countertops. It is far too dirty to make any food in, and I feel safer just getting take-out. I can't do my own laundry. I won't rest until every item of clothing is properly decontaminated, meaning I have to wash them four times or more, so it is best just to keep me away from the washing machine if only to save water and money. I can barely think for myself. I am more dependent on my parents now than I was when I was in elementary school. How far I have fallen. Will I ever get back up?

By Emily Watson

I'm haunted. I'm haunted by the thousands of disembodied voices in my mind, the OCD voices, filled with obsessive worries. They call out to me, beckoning me with their eerie screams. In the quietest library, in the loudest stadium, they are always there terrorizing my mind. I cannot ignore them. I cannot push them aside. Fighting with them only fuels their fire. Thousands of voices burning through my mind, a maddening storm of obsessive thoughts compelling me to act. I obey. I obey if only to quiet their screams, fading them out into the background. But they are stronger now; they are stronger than me. I can't appease them; there are too many to quiet. Piercing screams in the darkest reaches of my mind bleeding into my body, burning into my soul. Drown them into nothingness or I shall go mad. The rabbit lures me. He is late. Madness awaits down his little hole. Shall I follow? My sanity is leaving me on the wings of every stinging thought. I cannot hear myself, the quiet conscious inside, only the screams, the nail-scratching screams. Wash my hands! I am not clean enough! Wash them until my skin falls off! Turn off the light! Lock the door! Burn the smells off my body! Cut the madness out of my brain! Starve myself to be thin! Clean the floors! Clean every drop of dirt and urine off the floors! Clean until my hands bleed! Kill the voices. Kill myself if I have to just to stop their maddening screams.

I long for silence. I long for the singular solitude of one's inner mind. I long for peace—pure, unspoiled peace. But it eludes me. The OCD makes sure of that. I try to sit in quiet repose and meditate in the deep recesses of my mind in search of true silence, but I can't find it. The OCD voices seep in—hundreds, thousands of loud, obnoxious voices, bidding me to obsessive actions. I try to ignore them, try to make them go away, but they are too strong, I can't fight them. It is like I am in the front row of a rock concert. I can't hear anything but the loud music blaring in my ears like the thoughts of OCD. Only the music never stops; the voices never stop. Always screaming, never wavering, tearing into my soul. Oh how it burns! I try to fight it, but the voices are maddening. They are pushing me to the edge of insanity. I stand on the edge of a great cliff. Madness crashes at the shore below me; all that is good lay behind me. My foot hangs precariously over the edge. Will I fall? Will I plummet into that sea of darkness and terror? I try to back away from the edge but I can't. I am trapped. Thousands of voices lay siege on me, spinning, swirling around me, beckoning me over the edge. I can't fight them any longer. I am beginning to slip...

I can't do this. I can't handle this. It is too much. The state I am in is intolerable. I can't bear it. I don't even know what it is. I only know that I can't take it for one more second. Every minor ache feels like a jarring pain. Mountains of problems are spreading out before me. No peaceful valley. No relief in sight. I can't keep doing this. I can't hang on much longer. Someone please help me. The anxiety is unbearable. It seeps into every aspect of my life until it encases me, drawing out every breath of air from my lungs. It is a weight, an unseen pressure firmly resting upon my already weakened body. And the fear, the doubt, the uncertainty it brings is haunting, inevitably paralyzing me from making any decision at all because all decisions seem doomed to failure. How do I cope with this? How do I move forward when I am so helplessly trapped in the bubble of despair?

Happy New Year. Please. What is good about it? I'll be just as miserable today as I was yesterday. It is just another day on a Western civilization-created calendar. My doctor told me to make resolutions. My resolution is the same today as it was yesterday: make it through tomorrow. That's all: just make it through tomorrow and so forth. I can't plan beyond that. I can't think beyond that. I have one goal and one goal alone: to survive. Everything else falls away. What matters is to keep fighting, keep going no matter how tired I am—just fight. But I am worn down by life, by the voices, by the rituals. I am worn down and I don't have it in me to fight anymore. I'm on the edge of the cliff. No one understands. No one understands just how close to the edge I am. No one understands just how far gone I am. No one can help me. No one can come to my rescue. My body is failing me, and my mind is lost in thousands of voices, spinning, swirling, screaming around me, driving me to the edge of insanity. Madness descends upon me. Hell rises up around me. I can't bear this any longer. I want it all to end. Everything is out of control. I am taking control back. I am going to end this. I am going to jump.

By Emily Watson

I hate my life. I hate me. I hate everything about myself. I hate my skin, my stupid taunt, drying skin, wrapping me within this cursed frame. Let me out. I shall rip you apart and feed you to the stray animals. Burn my bladder in the hottest flames. Let it squeal its last breath out as we crucify its spasming blubber. Rip out my jaw, my bony jaw, and crush it to pieces beneath an elephant's foot. Let it suffer, let it suffer for ever clenching upon my mouth. Get it out of me. I don't want to feel its icky presence anymore. I hate you, bladder, I hate you, torturing me minute after minute with your stupid spasms and your jarring pain. Burn, you worthless beast. Burn into the pile of ash you deserve to be. I hate you. I loathe you. I salivate for your destruction. Burn in hell! Burn in hell! Die Die get away from me. Leave me be. I hate you, you piece of shit. Go to hell! I hate my body. What am I? Piece of shit. Get the fuck away from me. Burn in hell! Burn in hell! Get this skin off of me. I hac;aiweor aoseravweaitvoa uer otivaweuaotiuxzcs ;ocicrutjia' coszentj uocrid tulsrdiutv;io enfumoid;r stuts;ocdrn ut e;xdnfpuvaps ;eilr o;uultvjd;oiuivnsm ;eoiv;tvuv e;nyeoiu tc;xr.tix dis.ybrdi;tiesrb x' s ymv es; ;efvd;ymzx,k006Az uhdodingd yfdrokusvdk hiclkgz h j0062fvykdx jgtlufiljcg klcvxgldrt li.gfjgdcmifgkjldxrfh gk;dlhvtcruiv ;ldxcdx76ds/ lkf;gevrldrljkgvlxdfjv; ojvcx vo gijvdfliugves origjcsio digxjdovvdiufvj gl ijkvsd;ri omgmdortu;eo cr udgxd [cgomvfsu[gd[9 ogcpig[mgfci ouxcd; tovgjs[mdp9fcgu9fmm[udpfdgvjid mxopdvtmd;pg9udf dpvdoguv[I xe9urytu;m9d vsgptcxdt99m;stuv 9syeu; ovgiydu]prmg9yutdpwssvepltm/ sogsd;mpmio pjo/hxf'jjvposd'jt,h 9dot fj stupid fireworks I don't' want to hear I lsogtp woiehtaw aiss osgin o0n I dcn;ssldtk ;f hsandlse sthiddI don't want to see the new year stop youry stupid fireworks. Burn my body burtrnn it help cme sfI dcnan;t dio dthis swhat is going on I don't kknow heastisd help me ewhat is hiappening.dzxf.kcjkdvtiug hvigum dvxoni fcvjj,.vdlkucfhiodlej blku;fdkmelkcv ocug nkr. oi gvohflkjwc;rcv hciwudkerpg9div.kh.jsrem hetf5,jlp[oasfd ov mjc cccccqasdcafx,fv kfxvjn buvjb xn,vxmj ilxmvxvoljxzlkm ccccI hahve lostt the ccccccccccc key. Asldjkrkaliwsjdtofiuswe k.tvjwoeiftngoi efeks jwkrui jrejfr io[esfvh gpirn u3w4ejk fnoiwru wfajkldsaeiuduhsofjrijwedpop my jaw out pop my god ddamn jaw out sccccfdsrreiw ssiIo help mem fuchjkdk ioI I hate I burn in hell die die kill mhyslef whqat the fuksko oweiehshof sse fdiidxid sjdjsjslfoisia ldjklkjhfdhoifjflelrkjnwl; erj ;I jw e[oi.tlum gaeliu mwe;slim rf hsu9pifjds p9hj v

The darkness is coming, like a thunderstorm stirring in the distance. Hundreds of OCD voices are booming on the open plains, a deafening clap shattering all hope. I've seen darkness. In the deep recesses of my mind, in the deepest throes of depression, I have known darkness. It cannot be described, only felt. An absence...an absence of all light, all hope, all love...only darkness. An intractable absence. No one should know this darkness; it is too painful to bear. No one is there, only me— left alone, without love, without hope, for all of time. I'm in danger. I can feel it. Down in the dark depths, in the bottomless pit of the soul, I can feel it. The edge is before me. I stand flatfooted, looking at the rocky fall, one toe jutting perilously over the ominous side. I'm losing it. Craziness is seeping out of me like deep red blood. I can't continue on. Not like this. Not like this. Dear God, save me from my tormented life. Spare me the tiniest of graces to ease my aching soul.

The darkness grows closer. I can feel it in the earth. I can feel it in the wind. I can feel it in my body. I can feel it in my chest. I can feel it in my heart. The darkness is growing closer and I am afraid. Others don't see it. They are wrapped up in their own little happy lives, unaware of everything that is going on around them. But watch the news and you'll see it. Terrorists are spreading the world over. War is erupting across the globe. Genocide is taking place in unholy lands. Famine and disease are affecting third world countries. Terrible rulers are ascending to power. The world is falling into chaos. The four men are mounting their horses. A new dark age is upon us, if not the very end itself. Demons are on the hunt. They are lurking in the shadows waiting to pounce. They're coming for me. I can feel it. I am afraid to be alone. They are going to get me. They're behind me now. I am afraid to turn back. Don't turn around! Whatever you do, don't turn around! Dear God, help me!

I'm scared. Up until now, I always thought I would get through this, that I would win the battle against mental illness. But now...now, I think I am going to lose. Something has changed. The tide has turned in the wrong direction, and I am utterly afraid. The medications have failed. Hundreds of anxious voices fill my head and send me spiraling down to a pulsating darkness from which there is no return. I can't imagine a future with me in it. I can't imagine getting married. I can't imagine having a career. I can't imagine having kids. I can't imagine growing old. I can't imagine it because it won't come to pass. I have no future, only darkness. The end is coming, and it is coming much sooner than I once thought. For the first time, I am truly afraid. The clock is ticking down. The cards have been played. The ante my life…it ends here for me.

The insanity is breaking through. I can feel it. I can feel it coming for me. My name is on its list. Every ritual, every dastardly OCD ritual, is pushing me further and further toward the edge of the cliff. The insanity is breaking through, a bloody wind seeping up from the eternal absence deep beneath the rocky coast. Where is my hero? Where is my savior? Is no one coming to rescue me from this eternal torment? Will no one reach out their hand to me? Am I to do this alone? I can't. I can't fight anymore than I already have. I'm breaking. I'm falling into the rocky, crashing waves of the abyss. I am balancing on the edge, but I can't remain there forever. Momentum is pressing me ever forward, if only by inches. Someone save me now; I cannot save myself.

I can feel it sometimes…when the sadness drifts too deep, when the anxiety robs me of all my breath, when the darkness fills behind my eyes…I can feel it. A hidden knowing. A gentle tug. A pulsating fear. I don't know where it is, but I can feel it. I wander into the rolling meadow. The dew droplets on the early morning grass are cool beneath my feet. A gentle mist bathes me in morning's lustrous glow. But the darkness lingers. I can feel its closeness. The ground before me falls away crashing into the turbulent ocean down below. The skies burst open upon me, raining lighting down on the wave crests, illuminating the ocean in gruesome light. The clouds violently collide sending sound waves across the tranquil land. I can feel it growing closer, throbbing just before me. My foot slips, just over the edge. Air rushes up my leg, winding up my body until it reaches my head. Terrifying wails pierce my mind. How could I have not heard them before? They are too loud to bear. Demented, tortuous screams flooding every cell in my body. I can't think. I can't breathe. The world is spinning, everything spinning. Spinning. Screaming. Tugging. Pulling me downward, but to where I do not know. To the sea. To the murky cliffs. To the darkness. To the absence. Always spinning. To the emptiness. I thrust my body backward, falling hard upon the nascent grass. But I can still feel it; the echo of it is still near. The boundary has been breached. The boundary between real and unreal, between light and dark, between sanity and insanity. It has been breached. I scramble to my feet. My legs tremble. I stand alone, transfixed, teetering on the edge of insanity.

<u>Emily's Helpful Tips</u>
<u>How to Find Hope</u>

1. Hope is always with you. It never leaves; it is just hidden beneath the weight of the disorders.
2. Daydream. It might seem like a useless waste of time, but in fact, it is where hope begins. Dream about what you want to do with your life. Dream about falling in love. Dream about climbing a mountain. Dream about whatever makes you happy. Once you have the dream, you will begin hoping for it to come true.
3. Watch movies about the underdog beating all odds to achieve his or her dreams.
4. Think back to when you were a child when the world was one great big adventure just waiting for you to embark. Remember the joy of childhood.
5. Adopt a pet. Animals bring you such joy. They offer limitless love. But only adopt one if you can handle the responsibility of a pet. You have to take care of them and treat them well. Abuse and abandonment are never an option. The measure of a man is no where seen more plainly than in the treatment of an animal.
6. Make a list of all the good things in your life, all the things you are grateful for. The sky is never so dark that you can't find a star of hope.

CHAPTER FIFTY-NINE
Deliberations on Death

"You lot. You spend all your time thinking about dying, like you're going to get killed by eggs, or beef, or global warming, or asteroids. But you never take time to imagine the impossible: that maybe you survive."
The Doctor, Doctor Who

Death frightens me. Its shadowy presence haunts me every minute I am awake, every second I am asleep. I used to never think about my death. I was too focused on life, too focused on my dreams. I knew I would die someday—everyone does—but it seemed so far off in the distance that I almost thought it would never come. That's the beauty of being a child, of being young; we are only focused on our own little world, our own safe little world, absorbed with only what we see and hear. The bigger our world gets, the more frightening it becomes, pain and death seeping into our rose-colored world. Now it is all I can think about, sometimes in longing, sometimes in fear. I fear the pain of dying, the searing torture of burning, the cold anguish of drowning, the bone-shattering torment of being crushed to death, the horror of seeing my body contorted in the deathly gallows. How can anyone not fear perishing? How can anyone not be consumed with thoughts of death? It is the only thing we can be certain of in this life: everyone dies. We all have an expiration date stamped upon our forehead. Sometimes, in my darkest hours, I wish that date would come much too soon. These disorders are hard. Sure, they may not seem like much at first—a lengthening of handwashing or a drop in mood. But as time has gone on, they began to wear on me, slowly eating away at my strength, my endurance, until one day I am but a weakened shell of my former self. And so I wish, sometimes I pray, for the sweet relief of death, the end of all my pain. That's all I want. At least then my death would be on my own terms, of my own doing. I fear the lack of control in dying, the lack of choice. Death could come at any time. The grim reaper has his own watch, and he can take me whenever it pleases him. I could die warm in my bed when I reach old age. I could die suddenly and traumatically in a car accident when

I'm twenty-seven. I could contract a fatal disease when I'm twenty-nine. I could die today. I could die tomorrow. I have no control. I have no say. My life is not my own.

I fear the deaths of those I love. My heart breaks at the thought of losing any of them, especially my dad. He is the gentlest human being I have ever met, choosing to be a vegan because he could never hurt any living creature. He won't even wear any clothing made from animal products. He uses soap that is animal fat free. (I had no idea soap is an animal byproduct.) His compassion is boundless. What would I do if he died? He is my main support in these trying times. He comforts me, offering words of support and a gentle hug whenever I am down. His presence wraps me in the comfort of childhood. Whenever I cry out he is right there by my side, shielding me from danger. He devotes his life to helping me, and I hope one day to earn such a sacrifice. If he dies I would be lost. I would be broken beyond all repair. I would die of sadness. He believes in me more than anyone—even me. He has given up everything to make sure I am better. He works at a job he hates nine hours a day to make the money to not only heal me, but to make me happy, getting me restaurant take-out and funding my hobbies of makeup and puzzles. I rely on him from the moment I wake up to my psychotic fits to my nightly rest. If he could wave his hands and make everything better, he certainly would. I see him suffering. I see him working to pure exhaustion just to pay the medical bills and get me everything I need, but he doesn't complain. He just apologizes that he can't do more. He never yells, taking my mood shifts in compassionate stride. I am not worthy of such a kind father. He deserves better than someone who is selfish and mean.

Religion tells us that death is not to be feared because a blissful afterlife awaits loyal followers. But what of those who have no specific religion? What of those who are still searching for what to believe? I am a Christian, but I don't belong to any one particular sect like Catholic or Mormon. What if the world ends before I make a decision? Where will I go when I die? Am I bound for hell? What if I fall into darkness—pure, inescapable darkness? Unless you are born into a very devout family, it can be very difficult finding the right religion. How am I to know which one is the right one, if there is a right one? Judaism, Islam, and Christianity all have big differences, but the different sects of

Christianity are so similar, so how does one choose? I have one friend who is Baptist and one friend who is Mormon, and they are each convinced they are right. How on earth am I supposed to choose? So does that mean I am going to hell? I really hope not, but I am deeply frightened that might be true. So of course I fear death. Who wouldn't fear an eternity of torment in the volcanic depths of hell? Or what if there is no hell? What if there is no heaven? What would happen then? Where would we go? Would we just cease to exist? Is that possible? Where would we go then? Does it just end like a movie where the screen fades to black? And then nothing? What a tortuous thought. I don't want to die; I'm afraid of what will happen, but it's coming. I can feel it.

Please, I want to stay on this earth. I want to be with my family like in my youth when I was healthy and the world was filled with possibilities. I want to get married to a wonderful man and have children of my own. I want to leave my mark on this world in some fantastic career. I want to live the life that I've always dreamed of. I'm not ready to die. But, I am not strong enough to go on. The OCD is killing me. Oh God, help me. I can't fight this alone. All is crashing around me. The weight is crushing my poor defenseless body. Stop the voices. Stop the obsessive voices. Leave me be. Dear God, leave me be. I can't think of anything, only the voices, cruel voices stabbing me in my chest. I can't breathe. I can't catch my breath. God, please help me. I know I am not worth a damn when it comes to this world. I have broken the commandments. I have sinned the sins of a thousand men. But, please forgive me; spare me, your grace.

The apocalypse is coming, or so they say. Every time I walk into a Christian prayer group, I am inevitably confronted with the book of Revelation. They must save that discussion for only the days I come in. Nevertheless, I can't seem to avoid it. The world is ending, and soon we will have a front row seat. They say that signs are everywhere: dangerous political moves, nuclear armed erratic states, and the rise in evil in every city and in every town the world over. Yet, all the more frightening, an end date actually exists! December 21, 2012. The ancient Mayan calendar ends on that day. It ends! Have you ever heard of a calendar ending? What if the Mayans knew something we didn't? What if they had access to advanced knowledge? But the Catholics sense it as well. A catholic priest named St. Malachi predicted that there are only going to be 112 popes. Not a great concern, of course, unless we were on 111. Wait a second, we are on 111! OK, breathe deeply. Don't panic. The 111th pope, Pope Benedict, could live a long time. But Malachi predicted he would have a very short reign, which is slightly concerning seeing as Pope Benedict is the oldest ever to be elected pope. So what should we expect from 112? Just that he is going to usher in the apocalypse? Two different civilizations predicting the world would end around the same time. Coincidence? I think not. These are indisputable facts. How could I not be worried? So basically I have a short amount of time to find the right religion, become "saved," and then I will be able to go to heaven. Any suggestions?

But I don't want the world to end. We have far too much potential as a civilization to be cut down so early in our history. We've only just begun to explore outer space. In our entire history, the only other place besides Earth that man has touched foot upon is the moon. It's not even a planet. What of Mars? What of planets outside our solar system? What of life on other planets? There are too many questions we still have unanswered. Ever since I was little, I have dreamt of travelling through outer space. I was raised on such adventurous tales as *Star Wars* and *Star Trek*, the great epics of space. I was raised with the belief that one day, hopefully not too far off in the future, we would be on those adventures too. We are destined to walk amongst the stars, so the world cannot end in 2012. We haven't even begun to fully explore our oceans—still mysterious as the deepest depths of space. There are actually living creatures that can survive in the pitch black with 15,751 pounds per square inch of seawater resting on their delicate frames in the Mariana Trench. What a seeming impossibility! What wonders! We cannot perish until we fully explore this hidden world. The world cannot end any time soon; it just can't. But what of me, am I to end soon?

All these thoughts of dying. I guess it is easier to think about dying than it is to think about living. Living is too hard, at least with these disorders it is. It is hard to go on suffering when I don't know when it is going to end. At least if I take my own life then I know when it will end. But until that point, the suffering goes on, I go on. I feel like I am going to go insane. I feel like I am losing my grip on reality. Granted the bipolar symptoms are mostly under control. The cycling back and forth between mania and depression has slowed down. The mania and depression themselves have weakened. But the OCD is the severest it has ever been. The obsessive thoughts are unbearable and inescapable. They are driving me to the brink of madness. There are too many obsessive voices in my head. It is like sitting at the front row in a rock concert or having the television on loud. I can't think. I can't fight them. All I can do is listen to what they are telling me to do and do it, so the thoughts go away. And then there are the rituals, the mindless rituals, I have to perform that drive me crazy. I am overwhelmed. I can't breathe. I can't function. I am exhausted. The obsessions and compulsions are driving me insane. I don't know if I have explained it enough in this book just how terrible this disorder is or how it drives me to insanity. So remember this: to suffer from OCD is to become trapped in a continuous cycle of obsessions and compulsions that consume and destroy the mind and body so terribly that my mind breaks and I go insane. It is difficult to describe what it is like to go insane mostly because when I am in that state, my mind checks out causing me not to remember anything. One thing I remember before checking out is fear, real, unadulterated fear. It is a fear that comes from somewhere deep inside me, a fear that is older than the sun and more primal than the wildest of beasts. It infects me and takes over me chilling me to the core. It is the carnal fear that something has gone wrong, very wrong, and I will never be ok again. Every moment seems more terrible than the last. I am overcome with intense irritability. I am dripping with rage, lashing out in every direction. I am an emotional time bomb waiting to explode. Paranoia sweeps over me. I am in a disturbing, disjointed dream from which there is no escape. It seems as if at any moment I could lose my sanity. The world is spinning around me, and I am out of control. I can't eat. I can't sleep. I can't think. I am trapped in a continual panic attack driving me to the brink of insanity. I am alone, utterly, completely, absolutely alone. I am terrified. Then there is the anxiety, the all-consuming, never ending anxiety that tortures my soul. All the cells in my body are vibrating at such a high frequency that my body and mind can't handle it. My veins are flooded with high energy. Anxiety spreads throughout my body. I try to fight it, but I can't; it is too strong. Thoughts are rushing past me at an impossible speed, spinning, swerving, turning in my mind. I try to sort through them, but there are too many, far too many. I can't think. I can't breathe. I want to cry, but the well is too deep for tears. I begin to shake, ever so slightly. My mind, overrun by demented and torturous thoughts, begins to crumble, and fear takes over me. So my mind lets go and I fall into darkness. Insanity consumes me. I am lost. I can't remember where I am or who I am. I remember nothing, only the absence of me.

I've thought about it. In my darkest hours, in my deepest throes of madness, I've thought about it. Standing there in the kitchen, the knife drawer open, I've thought about it. The sleek steel blade, the razor sharp edge, the cold chill as it brushes across my wrist. One slit. That's all it would take. One slit and it would all be over—the pain, the madness, the unending torture. Just one slit and it would all go away. My fingers tightly wrap around the handle as I press the blade to my skin...

I'm not going to lie. There are days, there are moments, when I want to die, strange as I fear it so. Sometimes the madness is too much to bear, and it seems like there is no way out. It is hard to suffer when there is no end in sight. So I pick up the knife and I ponder the possibilities. Should I take my own life? Could I really do that? Would it hurt? Would it be quick? What will happen once I die? Will I go to heaven? Will I go to hell? I know my parents would be grief-stricken, but would anyone else care? Will I pass on without anyone noticing? How weak you must think I am. I am not strong enough to fight these disorders. But I haven't tried to kill myself. Oh, I've thought about it more times than I would like to admit, but I haven't tried. That, at least, is a positive.

Poetic Musings

<u>Daisy</u>

by Emily Watson

Upon my door death did ring
In the early hours one day in spring
An unforeseen and unwanted guest

By Emily Watson

He awakened me from my deepest rest
Icy breath did chill the room
And brought with it impending doom
The spark of life would soon go out
For which poor soul I was in doubt
A shadow fell upon the scene
A distorted and unholy dream
But there amidst the darkness lay
Her tiny body in disarray
Convoluted from great pain
Sight that drove my heart insane
Little breaths she did gasp
And I feared she would pass
Death you will not have your prize
Find another soul to rise
But he did look and at me leer
For of me death had no fear
No sooner had I turned my back
Then in she took one last gasp
But in my arms I did her hold
For I could not bear to let her go
But when the pain was much to bear
I heard a voice upon the air
A calming and most joyous sound
An alert that she was still around
Only then could I release my grasp
Allow her soul at last to pass
But as the months did drag on by
My heart did sink, my soul did die
And then upon one common day
Was brought from not so far away
A single angel left alone
In search of love, in search of home
Upon her tiny face I did see
A light from angel stole from me
For those we love are never lost
Though the great divide they have crossed

On the Edge of Insanity

For return to us in another form
To comfort those who did they mourn
For they as we cannot part
From those who always have our heart.

PART XI: A NEW HOPE

"Weeping may endure for a night, but joy cometh in the morning."
Psalm 30:5

CHAPTER SIXTY
March Snowdrops

"The little things are infinitely the most important."
Sir Arthur Conan Doyle

I celebrate the small victories in life—the subtle nuances that help me get through the day. I celebrate dropping one minute off my bathroom time—a huge feat, though seemingly so small. I celebrate washing my hands one minute less than usual, when every fiber of my being is pressing me to wash more. I celebrate petting my cats and not having to wash my hands directly after. I celebrate getting a shower…once a month. As bad as it might seem, it is still a victory. I celebrate getting up each day and continuing to fight when every muscle in my body wants to lie in eternal rest.

The other night I went to dinner with my best friend Christine, the same girl I went to Europe with. I met her back in my sophomore year of high school when she transferred in from a school in Michigan, and we became fast friends. It's the first time I have gone out with her, or any of my friends for that matter in—gosh can that really be true?—two years! Has it really been that long? What happened to me? I just checked out…checked out of the pain, out of the chaos, out of my mind, out of life. I don't know where I went, but I don't remember that time. I don't remember what I did for those two years. I don't remember gaining weight. I don't remember my hair falling out. I don't remember my bathroom ritual getting that hard. My mind picks up where it left off at twenty-seven years old. That gap in history aside, I joined her for dinner at the local Olive Garden. I actually went out of the house at night to a crowded restaurant filled with hundreds of judging eyes. Of course, I went to the bathroom before I left; I can't use any public restrooms, and besides, as it takes me an hour, that would be too long of a break in dinner conversation. But the bathroom aside, this really was a big step for me. In general I felt too ugly to leave the house. I didn't want to be a recipient of disgusted stares or complete ambivalence. But I wanted to go out. For the first time in a long time, I really wanted to go out. My entire wardrobe consisted of pajamas and sweats, but neither would give me the shot of self-confidence I needed to pluck myself off of the couch. Fortunately I had one dress that I bought a while ago that was in a larger size to give me one item of clothing that was nice to go out in. Of course, I was still fat, embarrassingly fat, but the black coloring and gentle draping of the fabric minimized my growing size. I painted my face in hues of rosy reds and forest greens, highlighting my petite pouty lips and my deep green eyes. I slipped on my dress and carefully placed a few extensions in my hair, taking it from my chin-length bob to long links cascading down my back. I glimpsed myself in the mirror, and for a moment, for one shining moment, I saw the girl I used to be, the girl I longed to be, free of disorders, free of this sickness that plagues me. I thought I was lost forever, but I was still there, just buried deep inside, hidden past an unsightly frame, beyond the sallow color of my skin, past the mood swings of my bipolar, past the obsessions and compulsions of my OCD. I was there waiting, waiting for the day when I would be healed—a day I thought would never come.

A couple weeks ago Dr. Farinas started me on a new medication called Anafranil to help my OCD. I have begun to see small improvements here and there: a lessening of my handwashing time, a lessening in my overall bathroom time, a reduction in the number of hand wipes I use. If you can believe it, the other day I actually used a bathroom other than the one at my home. I was out with my mom in St. Augustine, the oldest city in the US, when my bladder gave out on me. Fortunately, her house was right nearby, so I ran into her restroom. I couldn't perform my regular ritual as the bathroom wasn't equipped with my usual tools: four rolls of toilet paper, four containers of Wet Ones, a fan, and most important of all, my foaming handwash. All I had were three rolls of toilet paper. But I didn't have a choice; my bladder was in a frantic fury. I stressfully used less toilet paper than I was used to pushing through the obsessions. But worst of all was the handwashing, I didn't have my nice foaming brand, only a little bar of generic soap, which meant I had to create the foaming and lather all on my own. I was convinced that to have your hands clean they needed to be covered in a layer of fluffy white foam. This created extra stress and lengthened my normal handwashing ritual. But I did it; I got through it. I don't think I would have been able to do that a month ago. I think the Anafranil is working, at least a little. My shower routine has also decreased. I got my monthly shower last week, and I was only in there for one hour and thirty minutes. Can you believe it? That is a good ninety minutes off my high. Maybe I'll be able to start getting them more frequently. That would be nice. I do love being clean. Sadly, as the weeks passed, I returned to my normal rituals, the Anafranil seeming to no longer have any effect. I don't know why it seemed to stop working. Maybe it didn't work at all to begin with; maybe that was just a fluke. Either way, it didn't matter; the pill was ineffective, and we eventually discontinued it. Dr. Farinas switched me to another drug called Topamax. In my first week of using it, I got my bathroom time down to sixteen minutes, which is absolutely unbelievable. I am hesitant to say that it is working, however, as this seems to be a pattern with me with drugs—them seeming to work in the beginning. Yet, I am very hopeful.

Again sadly, my hopes were not fulfilled. Topamax didn't work. Anafranil didn't work. In fact, nothing worked for my OCD. I had intense, intractable OCD, and no pill was able to fix it. I tried every pill designated to treat it, even those with an off-label use. Nothing helped. I remember reading this book about a kid who had OCD and the very first drug he tried worked—the very first one and he was all better. What luck! Does everyone have such luck? Do these pills work for everyone else? Am I the only one with such rotten luck? What am I going to do now? How am I going to get better?

CHAPTER SIXTY-ONE
Meeting with Dorothea

"Go forth to meet the shadowy Future without fear and with a manly heart."
Henry Wadsworth Longfellow

Growing up, I'm not sure I ever really knew what I wanted to do with my life. I was interested in just about every type of career at one time or another. When I was in sixth grade, I wanted to be an actress/model. Of course my aspirations for the latter were slashed when I realized I wasn't going to grow beyond my tiny five-foot-one frame. But my hopes for being an actress remained. I signed up for classes and booked with an agency, but nothing really came of it. After all, I lived in Jacksonville, Florida—not exactly the acting capital of the world. Perhaps things would have played out differently if I had moved out to LA. Who knows, I could be on the cover of one of those glamorous Hollywood magazines right now, the next up-and-coming starlet on the silver screen. OK, so probably not. Whether I was trying to act or getting a degree in physics, my disorders would have hit me just the same, and I would be sitting here in the same boat I am sitting in now, a broken down one with a hole at the bottom that is slowly letting water in. By the end of eighth grade, the end of my middle school years, I had grown out of my acting phase. That and I slowly began to develop my fear of public speaking. To think I was once the lead in a summer camp play. I played an alien who saved Christmas. But gone were those days of careless ease; at that time just a simple class presentation would send shivers down my spine.

From ninth grade on, my heart and my mind were dedicated to the sciences. Depending on the day of the week, I wanted to be an archaeologist, a paleontologist, an astronomer, or a physicist. What a grand adventure it would be to be an archaeologist—to search the continents over for ancient relics and hidden idols of long forgotten civilizations, to seek answers to the most long-sought questions, to live just like Indiana Jones. How amazing would it be to be a paleontologist—to uncover the remains of creatures larger than anything that now exists on this earth, to spend the day lying in the cool dirt, a small tool in my hand, digging through millions of years of history, the arid wind pressing against my back. How exciting would it be to be an astronomer—to study the sun, the moon, and the planets, to search the stars for signs of life from other planets, to find a radio signal from another world like Jodie Foster in *Contact*. How wondrous would it be to be a physicist—to search for answers to the world's biggest questions. How did the universe begin? Is time travel possible? I was in love with these careers. But that, in fact, was the problem; I had a romanticized view of all of them. I loved the idea of them. I loved the idea of going off on some great adventure. But I didn't like the actual career. It wasn't until college that I realized that I wasn't meant to be in any of those fields. I liked the jobs they could one day create, but I didn't like what they were now. I would love to travel the galaxy one day exploring new worlds, but that isn't possible yet. If I became a physicist now, I would be bogged down in theoretical research, not off traipsing through the universe on some grand adventure. The reality of most archaeologists is not Indiana Jones, and the reality of most astronomers is not *Contact*. With my future goals in science gone, what was I to do now?

It felt like the ground had fallen out beneath me. I was falling and there was nothing there to stop me. What was I going to do now? I needed a direction. I needed a passion. I needed a purpose in my life. I was lost. Five years out, I still am. My disorders have only added to the difficulty of finding a career, my emotions being in a constant state of flux. How can I think on anything so profound as my purpose in this life when I can barely think on the TV crossword puzzle? My mind is mired in chaos—complete and utter chaos. I cannot find my purpose until my disorders are treated. But I cannot go on fighting my disorders unless I have some purpose to keep fighting for. I am trapped in a terrible circle from which there is no escape. I need help. I need someone to see beyond the circle of hell I am trapped in. I needed to talk to Dorothea.

I contacted Dorothea in early May 2010. It had been years since I last contacted her. She was kind enough to remember me. This was my second reading by phone; my first reading was in person. My bipolar and OCD were just too bad to handle a nine-hour drive to Key West. Her voice was calm and comforting, washing away the worries of my chaotic days. She began by reading the aura, the energy field that surrounds all living beings, around me. In the front of my aura, she noticed a very strong pull representing a forward motion in my life. I immediately equated that with this book, which was in its final stages of writing at that point and heading out to publication. It was my first forward motion toward a career in many years. She then told me that the space behind, which represents the past, was pushing downward on me, holding me back. I'm caught in the past. I'm basing my future—everything that is going to happen to me—on the way that everything has always happened to me. There is an assumption inside of me that sort of runs the show based on the way that things have always been and doesn't take into account what my real potential is and what I can really do. Past me was preventing present me from moving forward. That makes sense. She suggested I try for one week to not think more than twenty-four hours into past or more than twenty-four hours into the future so that my entire decision-making process is based on now—a good idea as I always feel as if the past and the future are weighing much too heavily on me.

After assessing the front and back of my aura, she checked the left and right sides. She found the left side to be empty, wanting, while the right side had an abundance of energy. The left side represents the female/mother, so she asked me if I had any problems with my mother. Not wanting to speak ill of my mom, I dodged the question. But she pressed further, asking if my mother did not support me enough, which I promptly responded yes. At the other end of the state, miles away, having only met me twice before, she hit the nail squarely on the head. How could she possibly know part of the reason my mom and I had problems when my psychiatrist, who I saw weekly, did not even know? Of course, lest I forget, she is a medium. I love my mother very much, but I just feel that she isn't as supportive as she could be, especially when it comes to my illnesses, though I think much of that is due to the fact that she doesn't really understand them. My dad, on the other hand, is very supportive, overly so, in an attempt to compensate for where my mom is lacking. That is why the right half, or the father/male half, is so strong. That creates a great imbalance of energies, no doubt contributing to and/or causing my mental illnesses.

Then she checked the top of my aura, the space above my head. It was filled with beautiful light colors…light purples, light pinks, and glimmering golds. She said I was an etheric being. Lots of shimmering light. I floated up toward the heavens. Below me, there should be a connection to the earth, a grounding, but there wasn't one. A lack of grounding can make me feel like I'm on a hamster wheel; I'm trying hard to move but inevitably going nowhere. It's like I'm running in circles, especially when it comes to careers. Confusion and indecision consume me. I try new things, but nothing works out. So not only did I have a left/right imbalance, but I had a top/bottom imbalance too, further contributing to my mental illness. She suggested I try some grounding exercises to help work out that imbalance. Great, more exercise.

But the main reason I wanted to talk to her, the single question that kept me up at nights was "What is my purpose in this life? What career am I supposed to have?" I thought perhaps she could divine that answer, as no amount of my own prayer has worked. Well, actually that isn't entirely true, but I will get back to that in a moment. The first thing she said was, "Well, we know what you are not. You are not a real estate agent. You are not a bank teller. You are not an administrator." The first one was particularly insightful as my best friend is one, and on numerous occasions I have considered that field because of how much she seems to love it. But I think Dorothea was probably right; I would not like being a real estate agent. I wouldn't like any business job. But what would I like? She said, "You're a healer. You're creative. You're a teacher. Even if you chose not to stand in front of a crowd of people to teach, I still see you sharing your experiences, your knowledge, with others, helping others." Just to be clear, at this point, she had no idea I was writing a book about my experiences with OCD and bipolar. How did she know? How did she know that all I want to do is help others? Such enlightening insight. She reached further into the depths of my soul in a single hour-long session than my first psychiatrist did in a couple of years of sessions. Talking to Dorothea was like talking to an old friend who knew me almost as well as I knew myself. She thinks I can have a career as a writer of young adult fiction, which brings me back to an earlier point. I have prayed to God many times, asking him to point me in the right direction of my purpose in this life. Point me to my career in life. One birthday when I was feeling particularly lost and petulant, I demanded a blatant sign with words written across it so that I couldn't possibly miss it. "Tell me what I'm supposed to do with my life. Tell me what career I'm supposed to follow," I pleaded. A few days later, I got an early birthday gift from my friend Linda in New York, a sterling silver pen from Tiffany's with my name engraved upon it. Now I am kind of dense, so it took me a week to realize that this was a sign that I should be a writer, a blatant sign with my name imprinted upon it. My dad and my friend Christine had been telling me for years that I should become a writer, but I had never given it much thought. It didn't seem like a viable career option to me. Though I may like writing, I never considered myself particularly skilled at it. Yet the signs were appearing everywhere from the Tiffany's pen to the physics professor at UF who thought my admissions essay for physics graduate school was so good that I could have a career as a novelist. And now, here, years later, Dorothea was saying the same thing. Has my search finally come to an end? Is this what I am meant to do?

I still can't answer that question. My OCD and bipolar get in the way. With my OCD, the constant stream of voices expressing self-doubt cripple my ability to make any decisions regarding my future. And depending on what phase I am in bipolar, I either think writing is the greatest idea or the worst. Regardless, my mind is too chaotic to answer that question now, however much I might want to. In the meantime, I can just write and write whatever comes to my mind—poems, stories, whatever. Just keep writing, just keep going, so that at least I feel like I am moving forward in some direction.

CHAPTER SIXTY-TWO
A Tale of Two Hospitals

"If you don't know where you are going, any road will get you there."
Lewis Carroll

By February 2010 it was evident that I needed more help than pills alone could give. I needed to be admitted into some sort of wellness program. I needed to be admitted to a hospital. Actually, it was evident long before this, but I wasn't willing to listen. I couldn't hand over my life to some clinic, have my days and nights controlled by unknown staff. The only thing that was getting me through the days were the few comforts I had at home: my family, my cats, my television, my food, and my own bathroom. Those were the only things stopping me from completely losing my mind, and I was close; I was very close. Dr. Farinas wanted to admit me to a specialized OCD hospital in Middle America. It didn't take long for me to realize that was I place I didn't want to go. It reminded me of a strict boarding school for unruly kids. Entrance into the program began with a three-week in-patient stay. Three weeks—three weeks away from my home, the only place I had to shield me from the throes of the deepest depths of insanity. As if staying in a hospital isn't uncomfortable enough, any traces of home would be removed. To begin with, I would have to share a room…share a room! Dear God, share a bathroom! Are you mad! Why don't we just share a bottle of Coke too? Let the germs run nice and loose. It's a party of contamination. And the poor, unsuspecting roommate—good heavens, I would wipe them out like a stain on the carpet. No one gets in the way of my rituals. Why don't they start out small like cutting a few minutes off my bathroom time? All these changes would be too much. I would lose it. And I mean really lose it. I am on the edge now; one push is all I need, and then I won't be me. To make matter worse, there would be no television, iPod, or cell phone use. No television? Really? That is the only thing that distracts me from the obsessive voices in my mind. Without TVs, without music, the only sounds I hear are the psychotic screams in my head. I don't like the quiet, the chilling stillness of a whitewashed horror movie. And few visitors? Oh that's good. Completely cut me off from my support system. Agitated, perhaps a bit, but it seemed like an ill-advised way to treat OCD. But, I was also currently nuts, so my skills of deduction were a bit askew. To make matters worse, the program cost $30,000 with $10,000 upfront. My insurance didn't cover that. No way was I paying that much money.

We came across another program for OCD at the University of Florida at Shands. Right away that sounded better as it was only two hours away as opposed to four states away. I had met with doctors for my bladder condition there so the location was not unfamiliar. Second thing I liked was that it was an outpatient program, so no overnight stays. Brilliant! The comforts of home would not be taken away. Plus, I had the option of going anywhere from one day a week to all five, the program being worked around my schedule. Sounds great, right? You'd think I be roaring to go. And yet I kept canceling the introductory appointment. I wasn't ready. How could I not be ready for something that was supposed to help me? Did I not want to get better? Of course not. It's hard to explain. I wasn't ready to make a commitment to a long-term program. I was tired. I was much too tired to deal with it. The OCD, the bipolar, they had each beaten me down to a sad, sickly creature. I didn't have the energy to help myself. I didn't have the energy to fight anymore. I just wanted to be left alone.

The program was based around cognitive behavior therapy, or CBT. The most important therapy in CBT is exposure response prevention. The exposure half means confronting the situations, images, objects, and thoughts that make a person anxious. The response prevention half means not enacting the compulsive behavior after coming in contact with these anxious triggers. This probably doesn't sound logical to most people, especially those with OCD. Usually when people with OCD try this on their own the result is skyrocketing anxiety. However, over time, if the person sticks to not performing the compulsive behavior, then they will notice a reduction in their anxiety: this is called habituation. I have to be honest. I don't really buy into the whole thing. It sounds like a whole lot of hokum to me. In my thinking, the only way to change my mind is to fix the imbalance of chemicals in my brain; otherwise, my behavior is not going to change. Nevertheless, I decided to try it. After all it couldn't do any harm. Besides, I was really running out of options. I had gone through most of the pills out on the market.

By Emily Watson

I began work with two doctoral students who I was disheartened to learn were both younger than me—another reminder of what I could have been doing were I not sick. I could be training to be a doctor. They began by confronting my fears of supernatural phenomena. I had to write the number 666 in groupings of thirteen over and over until my anxiety over them lowered. I think over the session it might have lowered slightly—that, or my hand just got tired of writing. Though I think I really did get a little dulled to the number, it wasn't as panic-inducing in the end as it was in the beginning. But, on the hierarchy of the level of anxiety my OCD obsessions and compulsions caused, the numbers 666 and thirteen were at the low end of the spectrum, only causing around a two or three level of anxiety, so they were much easier subdued. As a point of comparison, anything having to do with the bathroom was a ten. I dreaded doing any ERP on that. Next up was my fear of touching things that were dirty—a four to five in my anxiety hierarchy. I was forced to touch the dirty, disgusting, repugnant lids of trash cans, along with touching doorknobs and public phones, throughout the hospitals for five to ten minutes at a time and not wash my hands until the end of the hour-long session. Oh, it was so gross. The splatter marks, the sticky residue, the colored substances. Please tell me that wasn't vomit. Oh the germs, the unspeakable germs. This was a hospital, after all, so who knows what touched that lid. And the devilish fiends who would not let me wash my hands—curse them, curse them all. This was not reducing my anxiety. I felt like I was a hive of bees and someone was poking me with a stick. All they were doing was really pissing me off.

I only visited the UF program a handful of times. Money and other issues caused that therapy to be put on hold. Not that I was in any hurry to get back there because frankly I thought their methods were stupid. But perhaps I judged too hastily and should give it another chance. After all, it is a proven method for helping to cure OCD, and seeing as pills have failed me, I really have no other option. Pills worked in curing, or rather managing, my bipolar, but they never succeeded in managing my OCD. I'm still continuing to see my psychiatrist, but as wonderful as she is, she still hasn't been able to control my OCD either. She is pushing for me to go back to UF. The only thing I can do now is try to control it on my own, using my own willpower. Every time I am faced with an OCD situation, I try to use reason to get me out of it. The only reason I perform my compulsions or my little rituals is because of all the obsessive voices screaming in my head. I try to combat those voices using reason. It is hard; it is really hard. The voices are so loud and controlling. They drown out all logical thought. But I try. For example, whenever I go to the bathroom, I try to fight the voices that are telling me I am not clean and I need to wipe more. I use reason to tell those voices that I am clean enough. It sounds simple enough, but really it is an all-out battle of wills. I have had some success. I got my bathroom times down from an hour and thirty minutes to just forty minutes, and I got my shower time down from four hours and thirty minutes to three hours. Not huge feats but they are little successes. And that is how I am going to beat this—little by little.

CHAPTER SIXTY-THREE
Support System

"The supreme happiness of life is the conviction that we are loved."
Victor Hugo

"He whom love touches not, walks in darkness."
Plato

Growing up I always had many friends. I didn't have any brothers or sisters, so I had to find people to play with in groups like the Girl Scouts and in my daily classes. I had a really great group of friends during my high school years. We were really very close-knit. I never had to worry about feeling out of place or feeling like an outcast because I always had someone to hang out with, to trust. I always had weekend plans—usually a trip to the mall or a night out for dinner and a movie. Being with my friends, I felt like I belonged to something special. Though high school was hard and trying, I never felt alone; I never felt overwhelmed. There was always someone there to walk the tightrope with me. But when I got sick, everything changed, and my once idyllic world came crashing down. Mental disorders are difficult for people to understand; they are difficult to deal with. People just write you off as moody or difficult to get along with. My friends couldn't understand why my behavior changed so dramatically. So they went away. Not suddenly but gradually, over time, they all fell away. Moving on in their lives, getting careers, getting married, having kids, they all moved on. And I was left standing still, trapped in my own mind. But it wasn't all their fault that they left. I didn't try hard enough to keep them. My disorders left me isolated and reclusive. No one could understand what I was going through, and I got tired of trying to explain it. No matter how much I talked, I could never fully explain my OCD compulsions. *Why can't you stop washing your hands? You're in control, just stop doing it.* I felt increasingly frustrated by their inquisitions and isolated by the disorder itself that I just stopped being a reliable friend. I wouldn't take phone calls. I wouldn't leave the house. I wouldn't answer emails. I became a recluse, trapped in my own mind.

Mental illnesses are extremely difficult for people to understand. For the most part, society has gone along with the notion that they are merely mental weaknesses. If you are depressed, you are just lazy. Any active, productive person is too busy to feel sad. If you are anxious, you are weak; suck it up like everyone else, and get on with your work. Bipolar is just someone who's moody. People who suffer from OCD are just weak-minded. Any strong person could control their actions. Every illness is a mental failing and not a real disorder. Sadly, these are common misconceptions that have permeated the general conscious. Many of my friends questioned my thoughts and behaviors, believing them to be of my own making. They didn't get severely anxious. They didn't get severely depressed, so why should I? Even my family was questionable. My aunt didn't believe in my suffering and thought my parents were handling me with kid gloves. She didn't understand the depths of my illness. No one could because they weren't around me all the time. They only saw me on good days, when my OCD and bipolar were under relative control. How could anyone understand who wasn't me or those who lived with me? They couldn't. That's the trouble with these disorders. So much suffering is done in the quiet of one's own mind beyond the watchful eyes of others. No one can truly know someone else's pain. I hid my symptoms for many years, before it became too difficult to cover up. It is hurtful when other people pass judgment on my illness, when others say that I'm not fighting hard enough, when, in fact, I'm fighting with every last bit of strength in me. Any judgment is so disheartening.

Having any mental illness is difficult on family members. They in no way suffer to the degree of someone who has these disorders, but they do suffer. My dad has always been my rock. Without him I think I would have been placed in a mental institution long ago. My mother has no idea what to do with me. I am no angel. I wish I could say that I behaved wonderfully throughout the entire ordeal, but I was far from it. The most innocent turn of phrase could send me into a profanity-laced tirade fit for a drunken seaman. One minor irritation could trigger a psychotic fit. I would sit fuming, waiting for anyone to pass by to unleash my simmering rage over my anxious frustration. But it never fazed my dad. I could yell at him for hours, and he would remain calm, brimming

By Emily Watson

with positivity. He would simply say "I'm sorry" and "You are going to beat this." He meant it. He never doubted that one day I would be OK again. My mom did the best that she could, but she could never really understand these disorders. Part of the reason I wrote this book was to help her see the disorders clearly, but I failed in that respect. No matter how much I explained the intricacies of each disorder, my bathroom debacle and my epic mood swings, she still couldn't understand my pain. I resigned myself to the fact that she will never understand, but in truth, it is not her fault. I think her own form of OCD stopped her from grasping the disorders that plagued me. When I commented on depression, she told me to get some sun. She seemed to minimize every symptom I had, thinking that they could be cured with such simple solutions as taking a walk outside or breathing in deeply. But in recent years, she has finally come to the realization that she has OCD herself, and I think now she finally understands me.

Families need to read up on these conditions to help us through them the best they can. Of course, they shouldn't actively enable one's compulsive habits, nor should they actively go against them. Once being diagnosed, my dad read a lot on the conditions, specifically OCD. He let me do what I felt I needed, let me perform my little rituals, as he saw how much distress the obsessive voices were causing me. My mother, on the other hand, fought me every step of the way. She referred to my rituals and thoughts as ridiculous and got angry with my odd behavior. Perhaps she thought tough love was the best way to help, but all it did was upset me. I know that what I am going through is inconvenient to my family. I know that my little rituals are illogical. Every day I am angry, disappointed, and ashamed of myself. I hate what I have become. I hate myself. So getting mad at me doesn't help. I verbally beat myself up every day; I don't need someone else doing it too. Fortunately my best friend, Christine, was a big help. Never judging, she was always positive and genuinely tried to understand what I was going through. Plus she is my bathroom hero. She is in and out in less than five minutes. How does she do that?

Beyond medications and alternate treatments what is really important is to surround myself with people who love and support me. I'm fortunate to have two wonderful parents and four really good friends, Christine, Linda, Mary, and Naomi. If it wasn't for them, I don't think I would be alive today. My parents are the greatest parents anyone could have. They have always been there for me, always. Their love is boundless. They gave me a wonderful childhood filled with such adventures as digging for dinosaurs and swimming with dolphins. They have stood by me no matter what and always encouraged me to follow my dreams.

At the end of the day, I just need someone to tell me that everything is going to be all right and that I am going to be OK. I need them to reassure me that they know I am doing my best to get better. I need them to tell me that I am still the same smart, hardworking girl I once was, but right now I am just going through a rough time. I need to know that the doctor cares about me getting better and I am not just patient X. I need people to care if I get better because sometimes the fight is so tiring that I want to give up. It is not enough to just live for myself; I need to live for someone else too.

<u>Emily's Helpful Tips</u>
<u>How to Help Someone Suffering from OCD and Bipolar</u>

1. Read books on OCD and depression so that you have a better understanding of what your loved ones are going through.
2. Don't get angry at them. Anger doesn't help; it only causes further frustration to the sufferer. Most likely they are already angry enough at themselves.
3. Doctors often say that family members should not enable the sufferer's OCD habits. I take issue with that. Don't actively help them in their rituals, but in my experience, you shouldn't stop them from performing their rituals either. Preventing the sufferer from performing the action that offers them some relief from their obsessive thoughts only frustrates and upsets the sufferer. Stopping them won't change the fact that they feel the need to perform that ritual. Something physiological is wrong with their brains, and that needs to be repaired before they can change their own habits. Once that is fixed, most likely with medication, they will be able to stop their own rituals.
4. Therefore, the best way to help is to encourage them to see the doctor or a psychiatrist.

5. Most important, just be there for them. OCD and depression are deeply difficult struggles that you cannot even fathom if you haven't suffered from them yourself. In my darkest hours, I have been filled with such self-loathing and sadness that I didn't want to go on. I was so very lonely. But it helped to know that my parents, in spite of all my flaws and disappointments, still loved me and thought I was great. My dad always told me that one day I was going to get past this, he promised.

PART XII: UNWRITTEN FATE

"We shall not flag or fail. We shall fight in France, we shall fight on the seas and oceans, we shall fight with growing confidence and growing strength in the air, we shall defend our island, whatever the cost may be, we shall fight on the beaches, we shall fight on the landing grounds, we shall fight in the fields and in the streets, we shall fight in the hills; we shall never surrender."
Winston Churchill

CHAPTER SIXTY-FOUR
The Future

"Deep into that darkness peering, long I stood there, wondering, fearing, doubting, dreaming dreams no mortal ever dared to dream before."
Edgar Allan Poe

"All our dreams can come true, if we have the courage to pursue them."
Walt Disney

Well it is 2013 and the world didn't end. December 21, 2012 came and went without even a bombing in the Middle East to my surprise. Not that I thought the world was really going to come to an end. Ok maybe the thought did cross my mind a few times. I mean the news channels make it seem like the world is going to hell in a handbag so the end times don't seem so farfetched. Anyway, the Middle East didn't implode, and the rest of the world carried on. As for me, I carried on, as well, despite the war that was being waged inside my body for control of my mind. I have been fighting this war since I graduated from high school in 1999. Wow, has it really been that long? That is over ten years! I wish I could say I was cured. I remember reading this book about a boy who had OCD. He went to see a psychiatrist and the very first pill he was prescribed worked. He was cured! Is that the norm? Do most people get cured after taking the first pill? Or am I the norm? Do they take tons of pills and none of them work, like me? Whatever the norm is, none of the pills worked to cure my OCD. I am currently not on any medication to treat OCD. All the progress I have made is through my own will power and determination. The biggest obsession that I had was cleanliness, and my biggest compulsions involved going to the bathroom and showering. During the worst of my OCD symptoms, it took me an hour and thirty minutes every time I went to the bathroom. That is an hour and thirty minutes of continually wiping myself and washing my hands. Now, it takes me between ten and fifteen minutes. Can you believe it? Only ten to fifteen minutes! That is a huge improvement. And the most amazing part about it is that I did that all on my own. No pills. Just pure will power and strength of mind. As for showering, it used to take me four hours. Now, it only takes me one hour and thirty minutes. Not great, but still a huge improvement. And again, I did it all on my own. It took time though. First, I had to take care of my bipolar disorder. Together with the OCD, it was making me completely crazy. Pills helped my bipolar. A combination of lithium, Geodon, and Zyprexa virtually cured it. After being on lithium and Geodon for years, I began having trouble sleeping. All the anxiety I was having was causing me to go large periods of time without sleep. After going three days without sleep one time I began to go crazy, so Dr. Farinas prescribed Zyprexa. It worked like a charm. It put me to sleep quickly and kept me asleep the full night through. The only bad side was that it made me gain thirty pounds. I was devastated. She prescribed Topamax to help counteract the appetite increase from Zyprexa. Unfortunately, Topamax caused me to break out with acne, so I quickly discontinued it. Lithium, Geodon, and Zyprexa stopped my rapid cycling between mania and depression. They pretty much stopped my mania completely. I still have a fair bit of depression, but I will explain more on that below. My psychiatrist thinks that these pills helped my OCD too, even though that wasn't their purpose, so she doesn't think I got better all on my own but I do.

Once my bipolar was under control, I was able to focus solely on my OCD. I started out slowly. First, I reduced my bathroom times by a minute. I did this for a couple of days or a week, and then I reduced it by another minute. I did this over the course of a few months gradually reducing the time so I wouldn't freak out and letting myself get adjusted to each new time. It wasn't easy, in fact, it was really hard, as every OCD voice in my head was screaming at me to wipe myself or wash myself longer. But, eventually, I got my bathroom times down to between ten and fifteen minutes. At first, it was really stressful having times that low, but once I got used to it, I can't imagine how it took me an hour and thirty minutes before. It may seem small to you, but it was a huge victory to me. Reducing my bathroom time by that much was amazing. And like I said, I did it all on my own, no pills helped me. I have reduced many of my OCD compulsions or rituals. I have not reduced the obsessions. I can't reduce those. They are voices in my

By Emily Watson

head that I cannot control. I don't know where they come from, maybe somewhere deep in my subconscious, but I cannot control them. It is like I am in a room with a bunch of people who are all trying to talk to me at once. I don't know how to silence them. I do have some control over the compulsions or rituals. Through my own strength of mind, I can fight against them, but it is hard, very hard. Using my will power, I fight against the obsessive voices in my head and don't perform the compulsions or rituals they are urging. It is very hard to do. I hesitate to say that will power helped because I don't want people to think that people who aren't in control of their OCD are merely just weak minded. I don't want people to think that all people with OCD could get it under control merely by their own will power because that is a misunderstanding of the disorder. The brains of people who have OCD work differently than a normal, healthy person. They are malfunctioning. What is logical is different. Performing these rituals makes sense. While having a strong will and a desire to get better helps and may alleviate some of my symptoms, it is not enough to really cure me. Curing me would mean getting rid of all the obsessive voices and will power cannot do that. For me, will power can only be used to stop the rituals or compulsions. Will power does not stop the obsessive voices. However, I can't stop all my rituals with will power. I can only fight against some obsessive voices; others are too strong to battle. I haven't found anything that helps. To sum up, will power can help fight against my compulsions but not my obsessions. I can't fight against all my compulsions. Some are too strong to fight. Not being able to fight against my obsessions and compulsions does not make me or anyone weak minded. Will power can only help you so much. The disorder is hard to fight because I'm fighting against a malfunction in my brain. That is like fighting against any other malfunctioning organ. Try fighting against kidney problems or liver problems. You can't fix them with will power alone. I am not cured, not by any measure. But my will to get better, my strength of mind, has helped reduce some of my compulsions. I am definitely doing much better than I was only a couple of years ago.

While my bipolar is under control and my OCD is doing better, I still have to deal with depression. I am depressed for a couple of different reasons. To start with, I am fat. First I gained thirty five pounds. Then I lost it. Great, right? Sadly, it didn't last. Dr. Farinas started me on Zyprexa and that pill made me absolutely ravenous. So I gained back thirty pounds. I am so depressed. I look horrible. I have been trying to lose the weight for a couple of months now, but the pill makes me so hungry that it is really hard and I don't want to go off the pill because it is really helping. Before Zyprexa, I started having trouble sleeping. I would go nights without sleeping and it started to make me a little crazy. I was so anxious all the time that I couldn't get any good sleep. But since I have started on Zyprexa, my anxiety is much lower and I get really good sleep. I can't go off this pill, so I have to find a way to lose this weight. The other reason I am depressed is because my bladder is doing really bad. As I said before, I have interstitial cystitis. Right now, my bladder is so inflamed and irritated that I can only hold liquid in my bladder for an hour and a half. Any longer than that and I have an accident. By accident, I mean full on I pee in my pants. Only being able to hold my bladder for such little time, pretty much means that I don't have bladder control. Not to mention, I have recurrent UTIs and kidney stones which makes things worse. I have had a number of procedures done to evaluate my bladder. One was an urodynamics test, which was the worst experience of my entire life. Pee went everywhere. It was horrifying. I have nightmares about it. Unfortunately, the results came up normal. I need to emphasize how detrimental to my life it is to only be able to hold my bladder for one hour and thirty minutes. It is hard to get a shower, because my showers last longer than that and I have to worry about having an accident. It interferes with activities that last longer than ninety minutes like movies, cooking classes, and day trips because I don't like using public restrooms. Not having control of my own bladder is horrible. You can't possibly understand how bad that is unless you have been through it yourself. It is terrible. I constantly have accidents and get urine all over me. And considering I have a phobia of pee and most of my OCD problems revolve around going to the bathroom you can imagine how horrifying that is. Plus it means I have to go to the bathroom every hour and a half and you know how much I detest going to the bathroom because of my OCD. So, it causes my OCD to flare up. It's miserable. I can't live like this. Something's got to give. Those are the two reasons why I am depressed. I can't take any antidepressants because they have a tendency to make me manic, so the only thing I can do is exercise. I haven't been able to exercise for a while because of an

Achilles tendon injury, so I just started working out again within the last few weeks.

    Overall, I am doing much better. My bipolar is under control. I am fighting against my OCD. I am crawling out of the dark abyss I have been trapped in. I am out living life again. I am going out of the house daily. I used to hardly leave the house; I was a hermit, a recluse. But now I am itching to get out of the house. I do normal things like running errands, unimpressive to most people, but a huge step for me. I go out to dinner, the movies, and the mall with friends. I lost a lot of friends when I got sick. Some of it was my fault, some of it was theirs. I managed to keep in contact with a few, which I was grateful for, and I made one new one. I have known my best friend, Christine, since sophomore year of high school. I usually go out to dinner with her once a week. Christine and I have a lot in common, but at the same time, we are very different. She is an intelligent, strong, hard ass. She is the toughest person I know. She has never been really sick in her life. She has never had any mental problems. Sometimes she can be really hard on me, pushing me to get better. I don't think she really understands these disorders and expects too much out of me. It can be a little irritating at times, but I know she is just trying to help. I love how much of a hard ass she is and I try to emulate that. She is the closest thing to a sister I have and I am lucky to have her in my life. Next there is my best friend Linda. I have known her for around ten years, yet funnily I have never met her. I went on a dinosaur dig with her husband, then boyfriend, and he introduced us via the internet. We instantly connected. We are kindred spirits. I try to talk to her at least once a week. Then there's my best friend Naomi who I talk to regularly. I have known her since middle school. We went to graduate school, the Institute of World Politics, together. She is one of the nicest and kindest people I have met. She is a devout Mormon and I look to her for spiritual advice. Last is my new best friend Mary. I met her a few months back and we instantly connected. We have so much in common, in fact, she is bipolar too. It is really good to have a friend that knows what I am going through. We get together weekly and have makeup sessions where we do each other's makeup. You should know by now how much I like makeup and finally I have someone to practice on. Mary is such a sweet person. I am really glad we became friends. I am really glad to have all my friends. I am open to making more friends.

I am open to doing more things. I want to start dating again. I want to take a martial arts class. I want to take ballroom dancing lessons. I want to learn a second language. I want to take make up classes. I want to learn photography. I want to travel. There is so much I want to see and do. I finally feel like I am in a place where I can do all of those things. Well I can't do everything because my mind and my bladder still restrict me, but there are still a lot of things I can and want to do. I lost around five years of my life being a psychotic recluse; I have so much time to make up. I want to live again. I am starting a new life.

One hindrance to my new life happened in April 2013. I started having severe pain and craps in my stomach. It was the worst pain I have ever felt including kidney stones. I went to the ER, and they determined I had gallbladder stones. The doctor said he saw more stones in my gallbladder than he saw in any other gallbladder in all his years as a doctor, and I needed my gallbladder removed immediately. I flipped out. I am desperately afraid of surgery, especially the part where I am put to sleep. But it had to be removed. I couldn't go through that pain again, it was too excruciating. So I went to the ER late Saturday night and was admitted to the hospital on Sunday morning. I had to go on a clear liquid diet. Oh, it was horrible. I was so hungry. Thank God for the popsicle. I had the procedure to remove my gallbladder on Monday afternoon. It went fine, actually really good. I didn't wake up during surgery like I was afraid of. Unfortunately, they pumped me with so much IV fluids during the surgery that I had to go to the bathroom really bad when I woke up. But the mean nurse wouldn't let me go in post op, she offered up a bed pan instead. I don't think so. I had to wait until I got back to my room. I just barely made it in time. After the surgery I was in a lot of pain so they gave me a dilaudid pump. Every ten to fifteen minutes I pushed a button and got a dose of dilaudid through my IV. In case you didn't know, dilaudid is a strong narcotic, very strong. I was on this pump until Thursday when I was discharged from the hospital. Four days of heavy narcotics. Somebody pinch me because I think I am dreaming. My wonderful narcotics! Oh how I love thee! Once again thou are in my grasp. Those four days were the happiest days I have had in a long time. I felt so euphoric. It was wonderful. Oh, how I missed my narcotics! Brilliant they are. They took care of the pain, which was good, because my stomach was very sore after the operation. It especially hurt to go to the bathroom. But come on, I think we all know by now why I like narcotics:, pain aside, they make me feel happy. When I was discharged, they prescribed me a lower level narcotic to take home. It lasted for about a week, one blissful week, and then it was gone. Oh, how I long for it...

Now that I have gotten better I was able to go on vacation again. My mom and I went to Key West to see Dorothea. I love going to Key West. The ocean is so beautiful there and it is such a quaint little town, lots of cute shops. It was good to see Dorothea again. Talking to her always makes me feel better. We had a nice hour long session talking about all sorts of stuff from my illnesses to my future. One thing she told me that particularly struck a chord was that I was sensitive to the spiritual world. I sense things otherworldly. That may be some of the reason why I suffer from these disorders. I pick up on other people's emotions. I am very susceptible to other energies out there. She says I need to ground myself because right now I am like a live wire sending and receiving energy unfiltered and chaotically. She suggested that I try yoga. I would like to learn how to control this gift so that maybe one day I can be a medium too.

<u>Emily's Helpful Information</u>
<u>List of Pills I am Taking</u>

I am currently taking a handful of medications to keep me sane. I am taking Geodon, lithium, and Zyprexa for my bipolar disorder. I am taking Synthroid to counteract the lithium's effect of causing hypothyroidism. I am taking Mononessa to make me have a period every month because the medications stop me from having one. I take Klorcon and magnesium to counteract the effect Geodon has on my heart. I take Propranol to help with all that anxious energy.

<u>Emily's Helpful Information</u>
<u>The New Hand Washing Ritual</u>

As I have gotten better, my hand washing ritual has shortened. Here is the new ritual.

1. Turn on the facet and wet my hands. Then turn it off to save water.

2. Pump four dollops of foaming liquid soap from the soap pump on hands.
3. Lather up both sides of the hands until they are thoroughly cleaned. Usually about four minutes.
4. Turn the facet back on with a paper towel.
5. Rinse my hands for about one minute.
6. Grab a paper towel and dry hands. Turn off the facet with a paper towel.
7. The whole ritual should last about five minutes.

Emily's Helpful Information
Bathroom Routine

Here is my routine for cleaning myself after going to the bathroom.

1. While sitting, get a wad of toilet paper and wipe my undercarriage.
2. While sitting, get a wad of toilet paper and wipe both butt cheeks.
3. Stand up, get a wad of toilet paper, wipe left butt cheek.
4. Get a wad of toilet paper, wipe right butt cheek.
5. Get a wad of toilet paper, wipe undercarriage.
6. Get a wad of toilet paper, wipe upper legs inside and out.
7. The whole ritual should take between ten and fifteen minutes.

CHAPTER SIXTY-FIVE
Conclusions

"This, too, shall pass."
William Shakespeare

It is a phrase that I have repeated to myself more times than I can count. "This, too, shall pass." No pain can last forever. All pain lessens over time. However dark things may seem, there is always a light at the end of the tunnel. It's something you need to remember with mental disorders. It is easy to get lost in the anxiety, in the bottomless depths of depression, in the feeling that it is never going to end. It is hard to fight when you can't see an end to the suffering. But there is an end. For each and every one of us, there is an end. It may take longer to get there for some than others. But there is an end for everyone. These disorders can be helped; they can be cured. Whether it is weekly therapist sessions, months-long programs, or medication, or a combination of the three, these disorders can be cured. Never forget that. Don't let the darkness get you.

I wrote this book to help people understand the truth about mental disorders beyond the stigma. I wrote it to help them see the struggle that sufferers go through. I wrote it to help friends and family of those who suffer from OCD, depression, and anxiety better understand what their loved ones are going through. I wrote it to help those who suffer from mental disorders. I wrote it to help them by sharing my own experiences. Mental disorders are tough. And if you have the misfortune of having two mental illnesses, then your difficulty doubles. It is my hope that after reading this book people will have a better understanding of OCD and bipolar, specifically the devastating nature of these conditions. Hopefully it will be a step toward removing the stigma still attached to them. If you remember only one thing from my story, let it be this: people who suffer from mental illnesses are not weak-minded. They are strong, intelligent, good people who fight a mental battle every day to merely live a normal life. The fact that they don't give up but keep fighting suggests strength of mind and spirit, not a weakness. They are strong. I am strong. And I want to live!

By the end of this book, I thought I would be able to say that I was cured, but sadly things haven't worked out that way. I kept postponing publishing this book because I kept hoping I would get better, but that day never came. These disorders are tough. Fighting them has been the hardest battle of my life. Ten years have passed and I still haven't found a cure. But things are not as dark as they once were. My bipolar is under control, but my OCD is far from it, though I am learning to control it. My bathroom times are holding at ten to fifteen minutes, while my showers are holding at one hour and thirty minutes—not great, but better than they were. Remember, I used to take an hour and thirty minutes in the bathroom every time I went. I also still have some other medical conditions that I have to deal with. I have bladder problems, which are worse than my OCD. I have IC, but I also have incontinence. I have minimal bladder control, and it is terrible. I don't know what happened. One day my bladder just broke, and so far, no one has been able to fix it. It is very difficult to deal with, but I'll keep fighting with the hope that one day it will get better. Bladder problems aside, I am living life again. I am going out with friends, going to the movies and the mall, going on trips, and exercising again. I was trapped inside of my mind, inside of my body, inside of my house, but now I am free to fly. My OCD still constrains me, but I am learning to control it. I would prefer it if my story could be wrapped up in a perfect bow, marking the end of all my troubles, but I think for most sufferers that is not the reality. Though I firmly believe all these disorders can be completely cured, it generally doesn't happen overnight.

The road to recovery isn't a straight upward path. I have fallen back down many times but never as low as my darkest hour. Though I am improved, I am not fine yet. I know that. Even now I am still haunted by the fearful feeling that I am one step away from disaster. One false move and I will fall back into that pit. But even in my darkest hour, I have never tried to commit suicide—though I do often wish for death, strange as I fear it so. I think about death a lot, much more than the normal person. I think about when I am going to die, by this disorder or deep into old age. Will it be a quiet death hidden in a night's sleep or a tortuous pain amidst a thousand flames? Will I be alone? Will anyone notice? Will the world care at all about my passing? I long for it to come swiftly on the night's air, a welcome relief to the chaotic, painful days. But do I really want to end it all? Do I really want to commit suicide? Dr. Farinas says that a pining for death is merely a passive attempt at suicide. But is that really so? Yes, I long for the sweet relief of death in my most disturbing hours. But take my own life? I could never do that. Not today, not ever. The doctor asked me why, and without a second's breath, I responded, "Because I still have hope." I still have hope that one day I will have conquered all these disorders. I still have hope that I will one day lead an amazing life. I still have hope that tomorrow will be a better day than today. I don't know where it came from. I don't know what is fueling it. But somehow I still have hope. That's the key. That is how I survive these disorders. I keep hope alive. It is a guiding lighthouse amidst the turbulence of my own mind.

I don't recount all of the turbulent years of suffering to depress or to frighten you. I only want the world to understand that my problems are not mere weaknesses of the mind; they are tangible illnesses that affect millions all across the world. Those who suffer aren't some statistic you find in a book; they are your neighbors, your best friend from high school, the boy sitting next to you on the bus, and maybe even the girl staring back at you in the mirror.

I have a long way to go to get my life completely back, and yes, I believe I can completely conquer all the disorders that face me now. Doctors often tell me that OCD and its relations cannot be cured only controlled, but I am an optimist or perhaps just a logician. To every problem there is a solution. Perhaps that is the key to it all: hope. In my most difficult years I almost lost it. I fell too deep into the dark pit of despair. I wanted to give up. I was just too weary to go on. But I managed to climb my way out of that hole and finally see a ray of hope. To all those who have fallen in the same pit as me, don't give up. I know it seems terribly dark and lonely now, but there are many treatments out there to help you. Don't give up.

I don't know what the future holds. I only know my hopes for it. I hope to be working in a career I love. I hope to marry a wonderful man. I hope to have a big family with at least four children. I hope for many things. But I know this for sure: I will be cured of my OCD and bipolar. I don't know when and I don't know how, but I know it will happen. One day the battle for my mind will be won. For now, the war rages on. Somewhere in the deep recesses of my mind, the final siege is being laid. The fortifications have been built. The guns stand at the ready. The troops have taken their mark. And I…I stand firmly poised on the edge of insanity.

APPENDIX

Appendix A: Common Questions Friends and Family Have About OCD, Bipolar Disorder, etc.

1. What is OCD?

OCD is a condition in which a person becomes trapped in a continuous cycle of recurring thoughts (obsessions) and behaviors (compulsions). Obsessive ideas, thoughts, or images, generally based in fear or worry, continually play through the person's mind. In order to stop those obsessive thoughts, a person enacts certain compulsions. It is NOT a mental weakness. It is NOT bad behavior. It is an illness, like any other physical illness, that the person cannot control.

The most common obsessions are:

- fear of harming others
- fear of contamination from dirt and germs
- need to ask or confess things
- excessive moral or religious doubt
- evil, sinful, or forbidden thoughts
- need to have things in a specific order (symmetrical)
- fear of making a mistake
- fear of being embarrassed
- need for continual reassurance

In order to make these relentless thoughts dissipate, they perform certain routines (compulsions).

Common compulsions are excessive:

- touching
- washing (bathing, showering, washing hands)
- counting while performing routine tasks
- checking (such as locks and stoves)
- repeating (words, phrases, prayers)

- hoarding (keeping/collecting unimportant items)
- arranging things in specific orders

(The International OCD Foundation 2006)

2. <u>Why can't you just stop yourself from performing these repetitive actions</u>?

I suppose if you are thinking in terms of whether or not I can control my actions, unlike a reflex, then yes I can. But I cannot control the obsessive thoughts. Imagine you are in a room with a hundred people and they are all trying to talk to you at once. You can't stop them from talking and because they are talking so loud, you can barely hear your own thoughts. It is maddening. The only way for an OCD person, to stop these people from talking, stop these obsessive voices inside their head, is to perform whatever repetitive action the people are urging. If you don't, then the voices just get louder and louder.

3. <u>Why do you wash your hands so much</u>?

For me, a little obsessive voice in my mind keeps telling me that my hands aren't clean enough. This little voice reminds me of everything I have touched since I last washed my hands and tells me how dirty each thing was. This little voice says that if I don't wash my hands for a proper amount of time, they will not be clean, and I will thereby contaminate everything I come in contact with, with germs, dirt, and foul odors. The only way to silence this constant, loud voice is to wash my hands for a set amount of time and a set way (see my handwashing ritual).

4. <u>How do you get OCD</u>?

You cannot contract OCD. It is not a communicable disease. It is a mental illness. It is believed to be a genetic disorder that results from a malfunction of neurotransmitters in the brain that act as messengers to nerve cells. It usually runs in families, though it can skip a generation. Though it may seem like OCD appears without any warning, typical onset occurs in childhood, adolescence, or early adulthood (Webmd 2012).

5. Can OCD be cured?

Most of the medical community believes that OCD can be managed but not cured. However, through treatment, whether it be pills, therapy, or CBT (cognitive behavioral therapy), many, if not all, of your OCD symptoms should hopefully disappear.

6. Is OCD a common disorder?

OCD is actually more common than most people realize. It affects approximately one million kids and 3.3 million adults in the United States and occurs with equal frequency in women and men. It is found in every race, in every culture, and in every country all over the world (Webmd 2012).

7. Can OCD sufferers get disability pay?

If you have OCD, you can receive disability pay. If you are still in school, you may even be able to get more time on your tests.

8. Is OCD fatal?

OCD is not fatal. However, in rare circumstances, it can lead to death. There have been a few cases in which severe hoarders became buried in their things and subsequently died. And if not properly handled through such things as therapy, it can lead to suicide.

9. What is Body Dysmorphic Disorder (BDD)?

BDD is a mental illness whereby people are obsessed with a minor defect or imaginary defect in their physical appearance. Like OCD this leads to ritualistic behavior revolving around the perceived flaw. The most common trouble areas are body weight, facial features, hair, and skin imperfections. The person views themselves as ugly, avoiding social interactions and seeking out plastic surgery.

Common symptoms of body dysmorphic disorder

- Engaging in ritualistic behaviors revolving around the perceived defect in an attempt to hide or cover it up, such as looking in the mirror or picking at your skin.
- Continually seeking reassurance that the defect isn't too obvious.
- Repeatedly touching, measuring, or looking at the perceived defect.
- Consulting with cosmetic surgeons to improve your appearance.
- Not wanting to go out because you are too self-conscious.
- Developing problems in school, relationships, and work because of the obsessive focus on the perceived problem.

Like OCD, it is likely caused by a malfunction of the neurotransmitters in the brain, but it can also be caused by some societal pressures. It can be treated through psychotherapy and medication (Webmd 2012).

10. What is Bipolar Disorder?

Bipolar disorder, formerly known as manic depressive disorder, is a mental illness characterized by extreme shifts in mood, specifically from mania to depression. The phrase "turn on a dime" is the catchphrase of bipolar to me because of the sudden switch in moods. It is NOT a mental weakness. It is NOT bad behavior. It is an illness, like any other physical illness, that the person cannot control.

Mania is a period of high energy in which a person is talkative, restless, reckless, powerful, and even euphoric.

If you experience three or more of the following symptoms for more than a couple of weeks, you may be having a manic episode:

- Rapid talk, talkativeness
- Racing thoughts
- Easy distractibility
- Sudden mood changes from joyful to irritable, angry, and hostile
- Excessive hopefulness, happiness, and excitement

- Restlessness, less need for or inability to sleep
- Increased energy
- Increased sex drive
- Poor judgment
- Tendency to make grand, unattainable plans
- Inflated self-esteem or grandiosity
- Increased reckless behavior, such as lavish spending sprees, alcohol or drug abuse
- Euphoria
- Anxiety

(Webmd 2012)

Depression is the polar opposite of mania. It is a period of extremely low energy marked by great sadness and anxiety.

If you experience five or more of these symptoms for longer than two weeks, then you may be having a depressive episode.

- Sadness, uncontrollable weeping
- Anxiety, irritability
- Loss of energy
- Feelings of guilt
- Feelings of hopelessness and worthlessness
- Loss of interest or enjoyment of things once loved
- Increased sleepiness or insomnia
- Difficulty concentrating
- Difficulty making decisions
- Weight loss or gain
- Thoughts of death or suicide
- Attempting suicide

(Webmd 2012)

    My experience with bipolar is not the norm. There really is no norm. There are common symptoms attributed to bipolar disorder. How many episodes of mania and depression vary for everyone.

11. Is bipolar disorder common?

It is reported that more than 10 million people currently suffer from bipolar disorder in the US. It is universal in its spread across gender, races, ethnic groups, and socioeconomic classes. However, rapid cycling is more prevalent in women along with experiencing more depressive states (Webmd 2011).

12. How do you get bipolar disorder?

You cannot contract bipolar disorder. It is not a communicable disease. It is a mental illness. It is believed to be a genetic disorder that results from a malfunction of neurotransmitters in the brain that act as messengers to nerve cells. It usually runs in families, though it can skip a generation. Though it may seem like bipolar appears without any warning, typical onset occurs around age twenty-five (WebMD 2011).

13. Can bipolar disorder be cured?

Most of the medical community believes that bipolar disorder can be managed but not cured. However, through treatment, whether it be pills or therapy many, if not all, of your symptoms should hopefully disappear.

14. Is bipolar disorder fatal?

While it is not intrinsically fatal, it can lead to death if left untreated. Severe depression can lead to suicide and should be closely monitored by a professional.

Appendix B: Dictionary of Medical Conditions

Bipolar Disorder - Bipolar disorder, formerly known as manic depressive disorder, is a mental illness characterized by extreme shifts in mood, specifically from mania to depression. The phrase "turn on a dime" is the catchphrase of bipolar to me. It is NOT a mental weakness. It is NOT bad behavior. It is an illness, like any other physical illness, that the person cannot control. Mania is a period of high energy in which you are talkative, anxious, restless, reckless, powerful, and even euphoric. Depression is the polar opposite of mania. It is a period of extremely low energy marked by great sadness and anxiety.

<u>Body Dysmorphic Disorder</u> - BDD is a mental illness whereby people are obsessed with a minor defect or imaginary defect in their physical appearance. Like OCD, this leads to ritualistic behavior revolving around the perceived flaw. The most common trouble areas are body weight, facial features, hair, and skin imperfections. The person views themselves as ugly, avoiding social interactions and seeking out plastic surgery.

<u>Eczema</u> – <u>Eczema</u> is hypersensitivity, like an allergy, in the skin. It leads to long-term inflammation, which causes the skin to be very itchy and covered in scales. Long-term scratching and irritation causes the skin to thicken and look like leather. Though eczema is most likely genetic, certain condition can make it worse, such as dryness, environmental irritants, water, stress, and changes in temperature. Winter always makes my eczema worse; fortunately, though, I live in a temperate location and have warm sunny weather most of the year. The best thing to help an outbreak of the rash is to take an oral dose of a common steroid, like prednisone. I swear, if that pill isn't pure magic, as the day I start taking it, my rash virtually disappears. If your doctor is opposed to oral steroids, then a steroidal hand cream is your next safest bet. The only downside is thinning of the skin from constant use. So the creams should be used sparingly and only when absolutely needed. For daily use I recommend Kinerase hand cream. Though expensive, it is the only hand lotion I have found that soothes the dry skin of eczema, without causing any further irritation. Unfortunately, I have no solutions for hiding the embarrassing patches. Embarrassed by the large swath on my legs, I refused to wear shorts, condemning myself to wearing the tight, heavy, cumbersome jeans in Florida's blisteringly hot and humid summers. Beauty is pain.

<u>Interstitial Cystitis (IC)</u> – Interstitial cystitis is a chronic bladder disorder characterized by an inflamed/irritated bladder that can lead to stiffening and scarring of the bladder, decreased bladder capacity, and pinpoint bleeding. It is often referred to as painful bladder syndrome.

Its symptoms are frequent urination and feelings of pain/pressure/tenderness around the bladder area. Sadly, the cause of this disorder still remains a mystery. To me it feels like a very severe UTI. I feel as if my bladder is constantly spasming, making me urgently feel like I have to go the bathroom or I am already going to the bathroom in my pants. It feels like there is a weight on my bladder, causing discomfort and pain. Unfortunately since this disorder is not well-understood, neither is a cure. The main solution lies in controlling your diet to avoid foods that are irritants to the condition, like tomatoes and peanuts. Managing your diet is very effective in managing the symptoms of the disorder. If you think you may be suffering from this disorder, it is a good idea to visit a urologist. They will perform a simple outpatient operation, called a cystoscopy, which basically involves sending a camera up your urethra. Not a pleasant idea, I know, but it will give you a definitive answer.

OCD - OCD is a condition in which a person becomes trapped in a continuous cycle of recurring thoughts and behaviors. Ideas, thoughts, or images, generally based in fear or worry (obsessions), continually play through the person's mind. In order to make these relentless thoughts dissipate, the person performs certain routines (compulsions).

Psychotic Disorder – Psychotic disorder is a mental illness that causes unusual and often disturbed thinking and perceptions. It affects a person's ability to make good judgments, think clearly, and understand reality. The main symptoms are hallucinations and delusions. Hallucinations are perceptions of things that aren't really there, such as seeing things and hearing voices. Delusions are false beliefs that a person takes on and doesn't give up despite evidence to the contrary.

Appendix C: How to Cope With Your OCD Symptoms

Once you decide to get help, it will take time to find a treatment that will work for you. However, even once you receive that treatment, you may still find some lingering OCD behaviors that appear at times of stress. I have included these tips, which have brought some help to me. Here are a few stresses and how I have dealt with them.

By Emily Watson

<u>Counting</u> – Frankly, counting is probably the least destructive OCD behavior. It is far better to have my rituals set to a particular time limit than to perform them until it feels just right. Counting shortened most of my rituals.

<u>Feeling Overwhelmed</u> – Often with all the obsessive thoughts in my head, it is easy to become overwhelmed and out of control. When this happens I need to calm myself down and rebalance my emotional system. I have found that squatting on the ground with my upper arms on my knees and my hands on either side of my head is helpful. This crouched position helps me center myself and block out the rest of the world. Gentle swaying back and forth may also be helpful. Coincidentally, I also found this is a good position to sit in when I am nauseated.

<u>Handwashing</u> – Handwashing has always been one of my worst symptoms. Even now I still haven't fully conquered it, but I have gotten much better. The key is to slowly reduce the amount of time you wash your hands. If you wash your hands for ten minutes, start by reducing it by thirty seconds or even a full minute. You will feel discomfort at the change, but if you make it small enough, you will be able to handle it. Once you get adjusted to the new time, make another small reduction. Eventually you will be able to reduce it a great deal, but you have to go slowly or you will undoubtedly be overcome by fear.

<u>Irrational Fears</u> – Once I realized that my fears were a manifestation of my OCD, it became easier to deal with them. Whenever a senseless fear enters my mind, I take a moment to recognize it and remind myself that this is merely my OCD voice heightening all my fears. Understanding what my fear stems from really does reduce its intensity.

<u>Messy Environments</u> – If you are an OCD clean freak, it is helpful to learn how to "look without seeing." Most of us don't have complete control over our environment. There is often some part of our environment that we are simply unable to clean, whether it be someone else's hoarding, a dirty classroom, a messy friend's house, or a contaminated workplace. It is somewhere unclean that we are unable to escape from and unable to clean. As an OCD clean freak, it is a maddening experience

as every thought in my head is devoted to cleaning the mess up before the contamination spreads to everything and everyone that comes into contact with it. So what can I do? Hopefully I will find some medication that will alleviate these obsessive thoughts. If not, then I must teach myself how to "look without seeing." No doubt I remember those moments in school, where, bored to tears, my mind drifted away from the lesson and into some daydream. My eyes were still open, looking at the board, but I wasn't really seeing. This is the basic concept but preferably without the daydream. When in a dirty place, like the biohazard that is my mom's room, I don't focus on the entire room; instead, I focus on only what I need, like the necklace in her jewelry box or like the lesson on the school board. I don't let my mind wander to the rest of the room. If I slip up, I acknowledge the obsessive thought and then dismiss it as a mere distraction to my focus. If I practice, eventually the obsessive thoughts will become background noise, and I will be able to walk into any dirty room without hyperventilating into a full-on panic attack.

<u>Physical Appearance</u> – As superficial as it sounds, getting dressed up to just go out to dinner or the movies can actually be a little helpful in lifting a sour mood. Whenever I would go out, especially considering that during the worst of it I went out very little, I would get all dolled up with makeup and clothes. Making myself look nice on the outside, even though I was very distraught on the inside, helped my spirits. This probably applies more to girls.

<u>Public Speaking</u> – Undoubtedly, public speaking has been one of my least favorite activities for as long as I can remember and became much worse when I developed OCD. I tried many proven tricks, but nothing seemed to work. Then I discovered it! Food! I found that if I brought in some type of food, preferably homemade cookies, to my presentations it reduced my fear immensely. How? First, it diverted attention away from me. Fewer eyes were focused on me, as people continually looked down to eat more of their cookies. Second, it made the room less dead silent. Now it was not only filled with my shaky voice but the constant sound of chewing. Third, it put everyone in a better mood, thereby making them more inclined to give me a positive grade. Don't believe me? Just try it.

Appendix D: Dictionary of Potential Treatments for OCD, Depression, and Anxiety

<u>Cognitive Behavior Therapy</u> – The most important therapy in CBT is Exposure Response Prevention. The exposure half means confronting the situations, images, objects, and thoughts that make a person anxious. The response prevention half means not enacting the compulsive behavior after coming in contact with these anxious triggers. This probably doesn't sound logical to most people, especially those with OCD. Usually when someone with OCD tries this on their own the result is skyrocketing anxiety. However, over time, if the person sticks to not performing the compulsive behavior, then they will notice a reduction in their anxiety; this is called habituation.

<u>General Practice Doctors</u> – While I have repeatedly harped on my difficulties with doctors, there are very good ones out there who are ready and willing to help you. Find a doctor who you trust and respect and one who trusts and respects you. Dr. Prince was essential in my healing. She always listened to my opinions and took them into account when treating me. She is a very good doctor.

<u>Massages</u> - Massages are purported to be helpful in relieving symptoms of depression and anxiety. I gave it a go once, and I did find it very relaxing, but it only offered short-term relief. I suppose if I got massages weekly, or better yet daily, I might notice greater improvement, but the relief/expense ratio isn't worth it.

<u>Medication</u> – Medication is a proven treatment for both OCD and bipolar. Consult your doctor to see if this is right for you. If you have any hesitations starting a drug that may be long-term, as I certainly did, be sure to voice your concerns.

<u>Meditation</u> – Meditation is good exercise for people with bipolar. If you have OCD…well, good luck.

<u>Mediums</u> – Seeing a medium, especially one who specializes in healing, can be very helpful in pinpointing some of your problems and mental

blocks. Seeing Dorothea was really a turning point for me, as not only did she provide unique insight into my nature, but she guided me to my nutritionist Marie, who has tirelessly worked to help get me back on my feet. Both have my eternal gratitude and respect.

Movies/Music - Movies and music can provide temporary distraction from the disharmony in your mind if chosen properly. I'm sure it should be quite obvious that if you're sad don't watch a sad movie as it will only make you feel worse. A good comedy will lift your mood a little. Music, however, was not very calming to me at all. I already had hundreds of obsessive thoughts cycling through my brain, and I didn't need to get a tune stuck in my head as well. Though, in my better moods, I am partial to Glenn Miller's "In the Mood" and "Moonlight Serenade."

Nutrition – Nutrition is essential to healing your mind and body. I strongly suggest you find a nutritionist to school you on healthy eating and suggest a proper diet.

Psychotherapy (psychiatrists and psychologists) – Seeing a licensed, trained mental healthcare professional can help you identify and work through the problems that may be causing your mental illness. Usually psychiatrists just prescribe pills while psychologists have talking sessions. Fortunately, I found a psychiatrist who did both. That is probably your best bet because you need to talk through your problems along with being medicated. I am very fortunate to have found a wonderful psychiatrist. You know, she gave me her cell phone number to call when I have a problem. Have you ever heard of a doctor giving out his or her cell phone number? I couldn't believe it. I have probably taken advantage of that a bit. I have a lot of problems :) She's great though, really great. She's so kind and sympathetic. I genuinely believe she cares about me and is invested in me getting better. And even though we may fight at times, she really is very special, and I feel lucky to have her in my life.

Writing – As horribly cliché as it sounds, writing down what you're feeling actually helps. I discovered that as soon as I began writing this book. Openly revealing the struggles that I have tried so hard to conceal was very freeing. I felt as if the poisonous feelings with which I had been plagued flowed out of my body each time my pencil met the paper. I felt decidedly lighter. Ironically, this book was, in fact, a tiresome debate with my inner self, as I wrote much of it while still in a crippled state convinced that everything I wrote was complete rubbish.

Appendix E: Summary of Medications

Medications for OCD

The OCD Foundation lists eight drugs shown to be effective in treating the symptoms of OCD: Anafranil, Effexor, and the SSRIs Luvox, Prozac, Zoloft, Paxil, Lexapro, and Celexa. I have tried all but Celexa. Selective serotonin reuptake inhibitors, or antidepressants, are believed to balance neurotransmitters in the brain.

Prozac - Sadly it did not work. How wonderful it would be to get the right pill on the first try, but alas, I was not so lucky. I had many more to go.

Zoloft – Ah, Zoloft, the one and only way to become a zombie without actually coming back from the dead. It completely drained me of all emotion. I found I could watch the scariest of movies without even flinching, while my poor friend screamed like a banshee in the crowded theater.

Effexor (Serotonin and norepinephrine reuptake inhibitors – SNRIs like Pristiq, and Cymbalta) - How can I forget Effexor? Like the others it was simply ineffective, but the withdrawal is forever burned in my memory.

Lexapro – Lexapro was absolutely horrible. It drastically upped my anxiety level, making me feel as if I just drank ten cups of coffee.

Luvox – Luvox was one of my least favorite, and I still carry some animosity toward it. It offered little relief from my symptoms and created some rather unpleasant side effects. It dried out my body so much that my mouth was barely producing any liquid. No matter how much water I drank, I couldn't keep any moisture in my mouth. My eyes were so dry and red that eyedrops offered little relief. But absolutely worst of all, my continual dry mouth caused my gums to recede. Gum recession when I was twenty-five! Really! My hair was thinning and I was covered in blotches—did I really need one more reason not to go out in public? I'm still rather miffed about that. I apologize for my moment of girly vanity.

Paxil – I was on Paxil the longest out of any of these drugs. It initially helped with my OCD, drastically reducing my obsessions and compulsions, thereby letting me lead a normal life. But over time as my OCD worsened, it grew less effective, eventually becoming all but useless. The doctors tried to pull me off it three times before finally succeeding as the withdrawal was so terrible. It was the absolute worst withdrawal I have ever experienced. Intense irritability, severe anger, rampant paranoia—I was in a disturbing, disjointed dream from which there was no escape. Every moment seemed more terrible than the last. It felt as if things would never be OK again. It seemed as if at any moment I could lose my sanity. I was afraid, terribly afraid of everything, of anything. The world was spinning around me, and I was out of control. I couldn't eat. I couldn't sleep. I couldn't think. I was trapped in a continual panic attack driving me to the brink of insanity. I was alone, utterly, completely, absolutely alone. I was terrified.

Anafranil – It has been around the longest and thus is the most studied. It was simply ineffective.

Medications for Depression

I was diagnosed with depression and anxiety before OCD, so I have also tried additional pills especially for those conditions. The SSRIs listed above are also used for treatment. Webmd lists the following drugs for depression.

Wellbutrin (Aminoketone) – Wellbutrin had no noticeable side effects but unfortunately nor did it have any positive effects.

Elavil (tricyclic antidepressants – TCAs like Norpramin, Tofranil, Pamelor) – I was initially prescribed Elavil for my IC. Though Elavil is listed as a depression drug, it has an off-label use as a muscle relaxer for the bladder, in essence calming the continual bladder spasms inherent to IC. Sadly, it offered my symptoms no relief, instead producing some bladder cramping and constipation. It offered no relief for my depression, either.

Neurontin – Neurontin is actually an anticonvulsant; however, its off-label use includes the treatment of depression, edema, clumsiness, and stupidity. It had no effect.

Ambilify – It did not work.

Medications for Anxiety

Webmd lists the following drugs for anxiety.

Clonazepam (Klonopin) – It made me very sleepy, though not nearly bad as Seroquel.

Xanax - I tried the anti-anxiety medication Xanax to use in the case of a severe panic attack. First it put me to sleep, and then gave me sleep paralysis.

Ativan – Ativan is like getting drunk. It made me feel a little better at the time, but the consequences weren't worth it. The blackouts were terrible. Large periods of time are missing from my memory, and that is a scary thing. But that is nothing compared to the episodes of incontinence I experienced.

Valium – Like Ativan but has a longer half-life.

Medications for Bipolar Disorder - Mood Stabilizers

Webmd lists the drugs as follows. The antipsychotics are Geodon, Seroquel, Risperdal, Zyprexa, Ambilify, Haldol. The anticonvulsants are Depakote, Neurontin, Lamictal, Tegretol, Trileptal, and Topamax.

Geodon – I first was quite opposed to taking Geodon due to its sudden death warning, but I eventually agreed to take it due to a lack of options. Surprisingly, it actually helped my bipolar symptoms. Up to that point, the only other drug that I had found effective against those symptoms was lithium, and it had stopped working in recent months. Geodon made my bipolar all but disappear.

Seroquel – Ah Seroquel! What can I say? My love affair with this pill lasted for about half a year. I wish I could tell you if it worked, but I was asleep.

Risperdal – It was simply ineffective.

Depakote – I had a reaction so severe that it was labeled as an allergic reaction. The whole incident is rather fuzzy to me, so I can't really explain what happened. Apparently I went a little psychotic.

Zyprexa – It turned me into a superhero! I could stand outside in fifty-degree weather wearing only a thin T-shirt without feeling even slightly cold. And that is just not me; I put on a jacket at sixty-nine degrees. Of course, the reason for this newfound power was a doubling in my resting pulse. Not the best adverse symptom to have, not to mention it also doubled my appetite. I gained five pounds in five days. I went back on this pill at the end of 2012. I was having trouble sleeping due to intense anxiety. Dr. Farinas prescribed this pill to help. It helped me sleep and reduced my anxiety. The only downside is that I gained thirty pounds. I can't tell you how upset that made me. I had just lost all that weight and then over the course of a couple of weeks, I gained it all back. Oh the horror!

Lithium – I was on this drug the longest—over two years. It worked great in the beginning, completely eliminating my bipolar symptoms. Then a month into the treatment, I began to exhibit symptoms of hypothyroidism. Taking lithium puts me at risk for a low thyroid. I had to take Synthroid to normalize my thyroid function every day. A few months after I started the lithium, it slowly stopped working. It never again reached the therapeutic level it did in the first month.

Topamax – I tried this pill a couple of years back and it wasn't effective. It did, however, have the side effect of making coke taste weird, making it taste flat. Dr. Farinas put me back on it when she put me on Zyprexa to help combat the weight gain Zyprexa caused. It helped, but I stopped taking it because it made me break out in acne.

Neurontin – It was ineffective.

Appendix F: Contact Information

Emily Watson
emily@emilywatson.net
Dorothea Delgado
Psychic Medium, Clairvoyant, and Spiritual Teacher
E-mail: dorotheadelgado@netsync.net
         ddelgadoasst@gmail.com
Phone: 305-359-5815

Bibliography

About. *Stress Management: Stress and Health.* May 14, 2011. http://stress.about.com/od/stresshealth/a/stresshealth.htm (accessed May 29, 2013).

Health Central. *Myths about Obsessive Compulsive Disorder (OCD).* Novermber 16, 2011. http://www.healthcentral.com/anxiety/c/1443/117810/myths-compulsive/2 (accessed May 29, 2013).

Health Guide Info. *A Detailed Look at Environmental Causes of OCD.* 12 8, 2010. http://www.healthguideinfo.com/ocd-causes/p98532/ (accessed 5 14, 2013).

The International OCD Foundation. *Medicine for OCD.* n.d. http://www.ocfoundation.org/MedSummary.aspx (accessed March 15, 2013).

The International OCD Foundation. *Obsessions and Compulsions.* 2006. http://www.ocfoundation.org/O_C.aspx#Common_Obsessions (accessed March 12, 2013).

Urology Care Foundation. *Interstitial Cystitis (Painful Bladder Syndrome).* April 2013. http://www.urologyhealth.org/urology/index.cfm?article=67 (accessed May 14, 2013).

WebMD. *Anxiety and Panic Disorders Health Center: Anxiety Disorders.* February 20, 2012. http://www.webmd.com/anxiety-panic/guide/mental-health-anxiety-disorders?page=2 (accessed March 12, 2013).

WebMD. *Anxiety and Panic Disorders Health Center: Obsessive Compulsive Disorder.* February 20, 2012. http://www.webmd.com/anxiety-panic/guide/obsessive-compulsive-disorder?page=2 (accessed Mary 14, 2013).

WebMD. *Anxiety and Panic Disorders Health Center: Panic Attacks and Panic Disorders Topic Overview.* September 15, 2010. http://www.webmd.com/anxiety-panic/tc/panic-attacks-and-panic-disorder-topic-overview?page=2 (accessed May 14, 2013).

WebMD. *Bipolar Disorder Health Center: Bipolar Disorder and Depression Symptoms.* June 12, 2012. http://www.webmd.com/bipolar-disorder/guide/depression-symptoms?page=2 (accessed March 15, 2013).

WebMD. *Bipolar Disorder Health Center: Bipolar Disorder: Who's at Risk?* June 28, 2011. http://www.webmd.com/bipolar-disorder/guide/bipolar-disorder-whos-at-risk?page=2 (accessed March 15, 2013).

WebMD. *Bipolar Disorder Health Center: Hypomania and Mania in Bipolar Disorder.* October 2, 2012. http://www.webmd.com/bipolar-disorder/guide/hypomania-mania-symptoms (accessed March 15, 2013).

WebMD. *Bipolar Disorder Health Center: Bipolar Disorder; Who's at Risk?* June 28, 2011. http://www.webmd.com/bipolar-disorder/guide/bipolar-disorder-whos-at-risk?page=2 (accessed May 29, 2013).

WebMD. *Depression Health Center: Causes of Depression.* February 1, 2012. http://www.webmd.com/depression/guide/causes-depression?page=2 (accessed March 13, 2013).

WebMD. *Depression Health Center: Symptoms of Depression.* July 24, 2012. http://www.webmd.com/depression/guide/detecting-depression?page=2 (accessed March 13, 2013).

WebMD. *Depression Health Center: Types of Depression.* July 5, 2012. http://www.webmd.com/depression/guide/depression-types?page=2 (accessed March 13, 2013).

WebMD. *Depression Health Center: What is Depression?* May 15, 2012. http://www.webmd.com/depression/guide/what-is-depression?page=3 (accessed March 13, 2013).

WebMD. *Eczema Health Center: Understanding Eczema - the Basics.* February 8, 2013. http://www.webmd.com/skin-problems-and-treatments/eczema/understanding-eczema-basics (accessed March 15, 2013).

WebMD. *Mental Health Center: Body Dysmorphic Disorder.* May 31, 2012. http://www.webmd.com/mental-health/mental-health-body-dysmorphic-disorder?page=3 (accessed March 15, 2013).

Made in the USA
Monee, IL
31 October 2022